The Realignment of the Priestly Literature

Princeton Theological Monograph Series

K. C. Hanson, Charles M. Collier, and Christopher Spinks,
Series Editors

Recent volumes in the series:

Richard Valantasis et al., editors
The Subjective Eye: Essays in Honor of Margaret Miles

Anette Ejsing
A Theology of Anticipation: A Constructive Study of C. S. Peirce

Caryn Riswold
Coram Deo: Human Life in the Vision of God

Paul O. Ingram, editor
Constructing a Relational Cosmology

Michael G. Cartwright
Practices, Politics, and Performance: Toward a Communal Hermeneutic for Christian Ethics

David A. Ackerman
Lo, I Tell You a Mystery: Cross, Resurrection, and Paraenesis in the Rhetoric of 1 Corinthians

Lloyd Kim
Polemic in the Book of Hebrews: Anti-Judaism, Anti-Semitism, Supersessionism?

The Realignment of the Priestly Literature

The Priestly Narrative in Genesis and Its Relation to Priestly Legislation and the Holiness School

THOMAS J. KING

◦PICKWICK *Publications* · Eugene, Oregon

THE REALIGNMENT OF THE PRIESTLY LITERATURE
The Priestly Narrative in Genesis and Its Relation to Priestly Legislation and the Holiness School

Princeton Theological Monograph Series 102

Copyright © 2009 Thomas J. King. All rights reserved. Except for brief quotations in critical publications or reviews, no part of this book may be reproduced in any manner without prior written permission from the publisher. Write: Permissions, Wipf & Stock, 199 W. 8th Ave., Suite 3, Eugene, OR 97401.

Pickwick Publications
A Division of Wipf and Stock Publishers
199 W. 8th Ave., Suite 3
Eugene, OR 97401

www.wipfandstock.com

ISBN 13: 978-1-55635-612-4

Cataloging-in-Publication data:

King, Thomas J.

    The realignment of the priestly literature : the priestly narrative in Genesis and its relation to priestly legislation and the Holiness School / Thomas J. King.

    xx + 180 p. ; cm. Includes bibliographical references.

    Princeton Theological Monograph Series 102

    ISBN 13: 978-1-55635-612-4

    1. Bible. O.T. Pentateuch—Criticism, interpretation, etc. 2. Bible. O.T. Genesis—Criticism, interpretation, etc. 3. Bible. O.T. Leviticus—Criticism, interpretation, etc. 4. P document (Biblical criticism). I. Title. II. Series.

BS1181.6 K55 2009

Manufactured in the U.S.A.

For my teachers:
David Root and Song Nai Rhee,
who first awakened a love for Scripture;
Toni Craven and William Baird,
who inspired a love for scholarship;
John Endres and Jeffrey Kuan,
who opened doors of opportunity;
and Jacob Milgrom,
who enlivened all things Priestly.

Contents

Abbreviations and Sigla / ix

Introduction / xi

PART ONE: P: A Priestly Legal Manual

1. The Composition of P / 3
2. The Provenience and Intent of P / 28

PART TWO: P^N: A Northern Priestly Component

3. The Composition of P^N / 77
4. The Provenience and Intent of P^N / 109

PART THREE: The H Redaction of the Priestly Literature

5. The Composition of H / 125
6. The Provenience and Intent of H / 152

Bibliography / 175

Abbreviations and Sigla

AB	Anchor Bible
ABD	*The Anchor Bible Dictionary.* 6 vols. Edited by David Noel Freedman
AnBib	Analecta Biblica
ANET	*Ancient Near Eastern Texts Relating to the Old Testament.* 3rd ed. Edited by James B. Pritchard
CBH	Classical Biblical Hebrew
CBQ	*Catholic Biblical Quarterly*
D	Deuteronomic source
E	Elohist source
H	Holiness School
HSM	Harvard Semitic Monographs
HUCA	*Hebrew Union College Annual*
IDB	*The Interpreter's Dictionary of the Bible.* 4 vols. Edited by George Arthur Buttrick
J	Yahwist source
JBL	*Journal of Biblical Literature*
JSOT	*Journal for the Study of the Old Testament*
JSOTSup	Journal for the Study of the Old Testament Supplements
LBH	Late Biblical Hebrew

MT	Masoretic text
OTL	Old Testament Library
P	Priestly writings
P^g	Priestly source *Grundschrift*
P^N	Northern Israelite material in Genesis traditionally attributed to P
P^s	Supplements to P
VT	*Vetus Testamentum*
ZAW	*Zeitschrift für die alttestamentliche Wissenschaft*

Introduction

The Documentary Hypothesis and P

CONTEMPORARY STUDIES IN THE PENTATEUCH CANNOT ESCAPE THE IMPACT of the classic theory attributed to Julius Wellhausen (1844–1918).[1] The basic outline of the Documentary Hypothesis has consistently dominated pentateuchal discussions since its inception. Within this theory, the priestly literature has its particular place in relation to the other sources of the Pentateuch. Wellhausen's theory signified a shift in the position that the priestly material occupied, in comparison to previously held views.

Abraham Kuenen (1828–1891) described the dominant theory among the critical scholars of his day as one in which the priestly material was viewed as being among the earliest of the pentateuchal components. The Yahwist was dated to around the eighth century B.C.E., and the priestly material (identified as the *Grundschrift*) was identified as even earlier. "To this Yahwist we owe the first four books of the Pentateuch and the earlier (præ-deuteronomic) recension of *Joshua*. His work was in its turn based upon a still earlier composition—the 'Grundschrift' or 'Book of Origins'—which came from the pen of a priest or Levite and might be referred to the century of Solomon. Embedded in this 'Grundschrift' were still more ancient fragments, some of them Mosaic."[2] The shift from this view of P to that represented by the Documentary Hypothesis (as synthesized by Wellhausen) was not brought about by Wellhausen alone. Wellhausen himself pointed to Martin Leberecht de Wette (1780–1849) as the first to clearly perceive the historical disjunction which suggested a later date for the priestly literature.[3]

---

1. Developed especially from his *Prolegomena*.
2. Kuenen, *Hexateuch*, xi.
3. Wellhausen, *Prolegomena*, 3–5.

This historical disjunction is based on the observation that the elaborate cult system described in the priestly material of the Pentateuch is not evident in the early period of the history of Israel. De Wette described this disjunction in reference to the picture of public worship in the book of Kings. He reasoned that the presence of idolatry and other abuses, as well as the absence of Mosaic ceremonies, indicated that the actual worship practices in the time of the kings of Israel did not correspond to those portrayed in the Mosaic legislation. This judgment included the suspicion that the Chronicler embellished the situation of public worship in comparison to that described in Kings. For example, in relation to Josiah's celebration of the Passover, Kings implies that a Passover, "as written in this book of the covenant," had not been celebrated "all the days of the kings of Israel and of the kings of Judah" (2 Kgs 23:21–22). The parallel passage in Chronicles, however, appears to emphasize that previous Passovers had only lacked the particular splendor or attendance which was evident for the Passover celebrated by Josiah (2 Chr 35:16–18). This is illustrated by the Chronicler's account of Hezekiah's Passover (prior to Josiah), which is described as being carried out "according to the law of Moses" (2 Chr 30:16). It is suspicious that Kings makes no mention of Hezekiah's Passover, though the Kings account does give a report of his reforms and praises his piety (2 Kgs 18:3–6). Accordingly, it appears as though Chronicles reflects a retrojection of cultic practice common during the period of its own composition, into the earlier time of the monarchy. De Wette concluded that the actual state of public worship during the period of the monarchy and earlier was characterized by freedom, with a lack of priestly hierarchy and control. This situation is illustrated by accounts of sacrifices offered at high places, on hills, and under trees, as well as by the continuing struggle with idolatry. Such practices were maintained religiously without being abolished by the official court priesthood. De Wette maintained that this state of anarchy in regard to public worship only came to an end with the finding of the book of the Law under Josiah. Furthermore, he determined that the picture of the hierarchical priesthood as described in the Mosaic legislation could not have belonged to the Mosaic age or the following age of the monarchy. This was because such an established priesthood would never have allowed the state of freedom and anarchy which was apparent in the worship cult as just described.⁴ De Wette continued this line of thought in the second volume of his book and concluded that at least part of the Mosaic legislation was the product of later priests. He also argued that some of the Mosaic laws implied a more sophisticated culture which reflected a higher degree of moral decay. For example, simple prohibitions such as that against murder were sufficient for Israel in its emergence; however, additional detailed laws, such as prohibitions against the mating of dissimilar animals, the mixing of dissimilar seeds and dissimilar threads to a fabric, or against the shaving of the hair of one's head and of the beard (Lev 19:19, 27), could only have been produced by later Judaism. Such observations led de Wette to the conclusion that much of the Mosaic legislation (including sacrificial and ritual laws) must have developed gradually. He suggested that such legislation was refined over time by the priests, and was later recorded in writing.⁵ Clearly, de Wette opened the door which led to the shift of understanding the priestly material as late rather than early.

Wellhausen pointed to Eduard Reuss (1804–1891) as among the disciples of de Wette.⁶ As de Wette discussed the historical disjunction between the picture of the cult in P and the description of public worship in Kings, Reuss observed a similar absence of priestly influence in the prophetic books. In relation to the question of which period in Israel's history reflected most the impact of the priestly legislation, the discussion was directed to the post-exilic period of Ezra. With Ezra, the promulgation of the law of God marked a turning point in the history of Israel. At that point, God's law prompted the community to align itself into a new order, based on a revelation that proved as mighty as the Spirit of the old days in the sermons of the prophets. The impact of the Mosaic legislation in that period prompted the question of whether or not Ezra may have authored some of the priestly material himself.⁷ Thus, Reuss pushed the date of some of the priestly material to possibly the latest component of the Pentateuch rather than the earliest.

Wellhausen acknowledged that he was ready to accept the hypothesis that the Law might be placed later than the Prophets when

4. De Wette, *Kritischer Versuch*, 102, 115–16, 255–58, 263–64.
5. De Wette, *Kritik der Israelitischen Geschichte*, 279–81, 288–89.
6. Wellhausen, *Prolegomena*, 4.
7. Reuss, *Die Geschichte*, 86, 485, 487.

he heard that Karl Heinrich Graf (1815–1869), a student of Reuss, had advocated such a thought.[8] Graf further detailed the arguments for a late date for the priestly legislation. He echoed de Wette's observation that the legislation of the Pentateuch did not appear valid or applicable to the period described in the Historical Books, and shared Reuss's suggestion that the legislation was intended for conditions that took place after the exile. Graf contributed heavily to the discussion by providing a detailed argument defending the idea that the legislation of Leviticus and related laws in Exodus and Numbers comprised the latest part of the Pentateuch. Graf concluded that the writing of the Yahwist was still based on the oldest portion of the *Grundschrift*, but the Yahwist's document had been reworked and extended much later through the addition of the priestly laws in the period associated with Ezra.[9]

Kuenen recognized that Graf had split the *Grundschrift* into two components. He summarized the result of Graf's work on the *Grundschrift* as follows: "The smaller, or historical portion retains its place as the earliest element of the Hexateuch, the basis on which the Yahwist built in the eighth century B.C., and itself therefore still more ancient. The greater, or legislative section of the supposed 'Grundschrift,' on the other hand, is the latest of all the great strata of the Hexateuch."[10] Kuenen disagreed with this separation of the "Grundschrift." He argued that both sections resembled each other too closely to be separated by so much time. In light of Graf's work, Kuenen was more fully convinced than before that the priestly material was post-exilic, and added the argument that it should be considered a unity.[11]

On the foundation of such works as those of de Wette, Reuss, Graf, and Kuenen, Wellhausen produced a synthesis and refinement of source investigation which has come to be known as the Documentary Hypothesis. Within this theory, P is considered the latest strata of the sources of the Pentateuch. R. N. Whybray provides a helpful summary outline of the theory:

---

8. Wellhausen, *Prolegomena*, 3.

9. Graf, *Die Geschichtlichen Bücher*, 2, 4–95, 112.

10. Kuenen, *Hexateuch*, xxi.

11. Ibid., xxii–xxiii. Kuenen mentions that he had already been mostly convinced that the priestly material should be assigned a late date. Graf's presentation only confirmed his previous investigations.

1. J is considered the earliest work. It begins with Gen 2:4b, and is found in Genesis, Exodus, Numbers, and a few passages in Deuteronomy.
2. E begins with the story of Abraham (Gen 15), and follows the same general course as J.
3. JE is formed by a redactor through the combination of J and E. This process involved the omission of parts of each, but mostly omission of parts of E.
4. D consists mainly of the book of Deuteronomy.
5. JED is formed by a second redactor who basically appended D to JE. This process included, however, the insertion of a few passages into JE by the redactor, and the incorporation of a few JE passages into D.
6. P is the final work. It begins with Gen 1:1, and follows the same chronological scheme as J. P material predominates in Exodus and Numbers. P is the sole source of Exod 25–31, 35–40, and of Leviticus.
7. JEDP constitutes the combination of JED and P by a third redactor, to form the Pentateuch.
8. A few passages are considered as independent fragments which do not derive from any of the four main sources.[12]

Various scholars since Wellhausen have modified and refined the Documentary Hypothesis, and subsequent research has produced various perceptions of the sources. Specifically with regard to the priestly literature, arguments include the understanding of P as: an independent document, a redaction of the sources which make up the Pentateuch, both earlier compositions and a later redaction, and a limited redactional strand within a portion of the Pentateuch.

Legal versus Narrative Material in P

Such a range of views regarding the priestly literature demonstrates that the question of the composition of the Pentateuch continues to generate stimulating discussions with a variety of conclusions.[13] One

---

12. Whybray, *Making of the Pentateuch*, 20–21. Helpful reviews of the criteria used for distinguishing the sources can be found in the works of Campbell and O'Brien, and Whybray. Campbell and O'Brien, *Sources*, 6; and Whybray, *Making of the Pentateuch*, 23–24.

13. Gordon Wenham illustrates this multiplicity of views in his essay highlighting

might be tempted to despair over the lack of scholarly consensus, and conclude that pentateuchal studies have stalled progression in the midst of numerous indefinite directions. However, it is also possible to look upon the "lively and sometimes heated" discussion, not as scholarship that is stalled, but as an opportunity for stimulating new and enriching discoveries in relation to the text of the Pentateuch.[14]

Within source-critical circles, the conversation has advanced to the point at which reasonably standard and accepted indexes of the contents of the sources of the Pentateuch (J, E, P, D) have been produced.[15] Divisions evident within the Pentateuch continue to drive pentateuchal discussions to the extent that scholarship will not soon abandon the categories or language we have inherited from Wellhausen and those who influenced his work. Despite the significant revisions, challenges, and in some cases outright rejection of the Documentary Hypothesis, source-critical dialogue remains the dominant base on which pentateuchal discussions take place. In a book which surveys the varied history of arguments following Wellhausen, including more recent developments and suggestions, Ernest Nicholson rightly affirms the proper foundation for further investigation. He writes at the close of the twentieth century that, "the Documentary Hypothesis should remain our primary point of reference, and it alone provides the true perspective from which to approach this most difficult of areas in the study of the Old Testament."[16]

With the recognition of source criticism as a significant point of departure, this book will focus on the issues related to the priestly strand

---

recent key developments in pentateuchal studies. Wenham, "Pondering the Pentateuch," 116–44; also, idem, "Pentateuchal Studies," 3–13.

14. See Wenham's conclusion in "Pentateuchal Studies," 11.

15. A good illustration of this is evident in the work of Campbell and O'Brien (this work deals solely with J, E, and P) who present a helpful synthesis, with slight refinement, of Martin Noth's source critical analysis. Campbell and O'Brien, *Sources*, 259–63.

16. Nicholson, *The Pentateuch in the Twentieth Century*, vi. Nicholson's statement is true, in part, simply because purely synchronic approaches to the Pentateuch cannot fully account for the complexities found in the biblical text. This is not intended to deny the importance of synchronic investigations, which are needed to demonstrate unity within identified sources and to affirm or challenge proper divisions between sources. Clearly, there is a need for dialogue between diachronic and synchronic approaches. For a helpful discussion of the benefits of the interplay between diachronic and synchronic approaches, see Campbell and O'Brien, *Sources*, 17–18.

of the Pentateuch.[17] The P source is often considered the most identifiable of the sources of the Pentateuch, with its narrative considered reasonably coherent, and its content considered the most easily discernible of the pentateuchal sources.[18] Despite this observation, the P source continues to generate debate regarding its composition, date and intent. Of particular concern regarding the composition of the priestly writings is the relationship between the legal and narrative material within P. Clarifying the connection between the narrative and legal components of P has consistently disrupted scholarly discussion regarding the priestly literature. It can be readily observed that arguments regarding the character of P have often been based on either the narrative or the legal material, but rarely both. For instance, the *composition* of P might be determined by one scholar based on the narratives, while the *date* of P is determined by another scholar based on distinct legal material.[19] This results in various conclusions regarding the Priestly source that do not seriously take into account all of the P corpus, and how its components are related. Consequently, a scholar may build a convincing argument regarding some aspect of P based on the legal material, only to be accused of neglecting the narrative material, or vice versa. This has created somewhat of an impasse within the source-critical debate regarding P. In his brief review of the history of the arguments for dating the Priestly source, Blenkinsopp highlights this impasse in the following summary statement:

---

17. For an index of the priestly texts alone, see Campbell, *Study Companion*, 87–91 (this appendix lists the P texts as identified by Noth, Elliger, and Lohfink); McEvenue, *Interpreting the Pentateuch*, 173–74 (this appendix lists the priestly narrative); and Friedman, *Exile and Biblical Narrative*, 141–47 (this appendix lists Friedman's analysis of P texts).

18. Brueggemann and Wolff, *Vitality*, 101; McEvenue, *Interpreting the Pentateuch*, 116–17; Blenkinsopp, *The Pentateuch*, 119.

19. Arguments for the date of P are often built upon the foundation of Wellhausen's synthesis of the development of Israel's religion from simple primitive worship to a complex ritual system (Wellhausen, *Prolegomena*, 1–170). This analysis clearly focuses on the cultic texts in P that comprise much of the legal material of P. In contrast, Noth's analysis of the composition of the P document seeks to exclude the legal material altogether, while focusing predominantly on the narrative (Noth, *Pentateuchal Traditions*, 8–10). Other scholars have followed Noth's example by labeling the legal material in P as later additions to the text, and have proceeded to analyze the composition of P based solely on the narrative portions of P. McEvenue, *Narrative Style*, 19; idem, *Interpreting the Pentateuch*, 116; Whybray, *Making of the Pentateuch*, 10.

It is important to note that throughout this entire discussion the focus was on the narrative content of the Pentateuch, especially on the narrative in Genesis and the early chapters of Exodus up to the point where the Tetragrammaton is revealed. Some early documentarians did nevertheless assign equal antiquity, even Mosaic antiquity, to at least part of the cultic and ritual legislation in Leviticus and sections of Exodus and Numbers though no one, to my knowledge, argued the case in any detail. In the most recent phase, on the other hand, arguments tend to be drawn from the legal material to the relative neglect of the P narrative. In any case, one of the problems most resistant to argument was, and to this day remains, not least for the Kaufmann school, the relation between narrative and legislation in the P source.[20]

An informative illustration of this impasse is presented in a written dialogue between Rolf Rendtorff and Jacob Milgrom on the occasion of the publication of the first volume of Milgrom's masterful commentary on Leviticus. In an initial article, Rendtorff reflects upon sharing a panel discussion with Milgrom in which Rendtorff came to the realization that they were discussing two different concepts of P. One view saw P in relation to its narrative elements, beginning with creation and continuing to the point of reaching the promised land. The other view of P saw it in relation to cultic and legal material, including the building of the tabernacle and the installation of cultic institutions. Rendtorff reviews for the reader that this distinction was already recognized by Wellhausen who distinguished an original narrative source from later legal materials which were appended to the narrative nucleus. These portions of P were eventually labeled by scholars with the designations P^g (*Grundschrift*, basic document) and P^s (supplements). While scholars like Martin Noth focus on P as purely a narrative work, Milgrom holds to the second concept of P as a document composed of cultic and legal material. Rendtorff reacted to Milgrom's failure to address the narrative concerns of P and pressed the question regarding how Leviticus relates to the rest of P.[21]

In response, Milgrom wrote that he could no longer evade the issue of dealing with the narrative of P and stated that it would be addressed in volume 2 of his Leviticus commentary. In preliminary remarks,

20. Blenkinsopp, "Alleged Pre-Exilic Date," 495–96.
21. Rendtorff, "Two Kinds of P," 75–78.

Milgrom discussed the significant role of H as the redactor of P (and possibly the entire Tetrateuch), thereby introducing an added complexity to the issue.[22] In the second volume of his Leviticus commentary, which focuses on H, Milgrom explains his ongoing hesitancy to "be drawn into the quagmire of the priestly narrative."[23] Due to the lack of terminological controls in the narrative, absence of clearly distinctive traits in the narrative, at least three recent works which contribute turmoil to the identification and dating of the priestly narrative, and the added complexity of attempts to distinguish between P and H in the narrative, Milgrom determined to "concentrate exclusively on the *legal* passages attributable to H."[24] Thus, the impasse within source-critical discussions of the priestly writings appears further entrenched.

I contend that the dilemma created by the lack of continuity between the narrative and legal material of P can be resolved by recognizing the independent character of the narratives traditionally associated with P, particularly those in Genesis. The understanding of the priestly corpus, with respect to the *legal* material and the redactional work of H, has already been significantly advanced by the work of Jacob Milgrom and Israel Knohl.[25] I embrace much of their work, and set forth a new understanding of the role of the *narrative* material identified with P in the book of Genesis, thereby presenting a more complete picture of the priestly writings in the Pentateuch.[26]

22. Milgrom, "Response to Rendtorff," 83–84.
23. Milgrom, *Leviticus 17–22*, 1334.
24. Ibid. The three works which Milgrom cites in relation to adding turmoil to the identification and dating of P narrative are: Frankel, "The Stories of Murmuring in the Desert in the Priestly School" (Ph.D. diss., Hebrew University, 1994 [Hebrew]); King, "The Priestly Literature and Its Northern Component" (Ph.D. diss., The Graduate Theological Union, 1996), the dissertation underlying this book; and Wenham, "The Priority of P," 240–58.
25. Especially represented in Milgrom's distinguished three-volume commentary on Leviticus, and Knohl's publication regarding the Priestly Torah and the Holiness School. Milgrom, *Leviticus*, 3 vols.; Knohl, *Sanctuary*.
26. As stated earlier, this work embraces a *source-critical* approach to the Pentateuch and seeks to extend source-critical dialogue in relation to the priestly literature. For examples of more recent *literary* and *rhetorical* investigations that seek to explain the relationship between law and narrative in the Pentateuch, see Watts, *Reading Law*; and Carmichael, *Illuminating Leviticus*. Watts argues that P shaped the Pentateuch in accordance with an old rhetorical pattern based on public readings of the law, while Carmichael contends that ancient Israel's lawgiver created laws in response to the history recounted in Genesis—2 Kings.

PART ONE

P: A Priestly Legal Manual

1

The Composition of P

The Character of Priestly Writings

To a great extent, the discussion of the composition of P has focused on narrative material, to the exclusion of the legislation in P. Scholars often begin their work by pointing to the two types of material in P (narrative and legal). Then, they make a brief statement regarding the antiquity of the legal material, label the legal material as later additions to P, and ultimately proceed to discuss the significance of P based on investigation of the narrative material alone.[1]

Noth's reasoning for this procedure is that the legal sections are additions to P, which originally had no direct relation to the narrative in P. The legal material was inserted into what he considers an originally independent P source. For example, the instructions on sacrifice found in Lev 1–7 were inserted appropriately before the narrative about the first sacrifices. This insertion interrupts the continuity of the narrative between Exod 25–31; 35–40; and Lev 8–9. The same can be said of the laws in Lev 11–15, the Holiness Code (H), and Num 5–6. These sections of Law may have been added to P, or even to the already assembled Pentateuch. Accordingly, Noth contends that it is misleading to label the legal material as P or P^s (supplements, additions to P). Noth concludes that this material should rather be given a neutral sign as simply additional legal material which should be disregarded in the consideration of P narrative.[2]

---

1. For example: Noth, *Pentateuchal Traditions*, 8; McEvenue, *Narrative Style*, 19; idem, *Interpreting the Pentateuch*, 116; Whybray, *Making of the Pentateuch*, 10.

2. Noth, *Pentateuchal Traditions*, 8–10. See also, Campbell, *Study Companion*, 67. Campbell elaborates on how the laws on ritual purity (Lev 11–15) were appropriately

P narrative is normally identified with certain passages in Genesis, Exodus, a small portion of Leviticus, Numbers, and a small portion of Deuteronomy. The characteristic style of P is defined predominantly by these narratives, and mostly those in Genesis (i.e., much is based on the investigation of the creation account, genealogies in Genesis, the flood account, Abrahamic covenant, the purchase of the cave, etc.). The narratives are seen as the definitive portion of P, while the legal material is pushed aside as mere additions and supplements. In contrast to this approach, Milgrom's work characterizes P almost exclusively in terms of the legal material. These diverse approaches reflect an impasse among scholars in regard to the primary identification of the priestly literature. The resolution to this dilemma calls for a re-evaluation of the divisions and relationships evident within the composition of the priestly writings.

P as an Independent Document

Recognizing the independent character of the priestly literature is foundational to understanding its own composition as well as its association with other sources of the Pentateuch. Arguments defending P as an independent document are based on isolating P in the midst of other pentateuchal sources, and identifying unique characteristics within the priestly material.

Noth's work provides a simple illustration of tracing P within the Pentateuch. He saw P as the work of one person who integrated received materials and fixed texts into his own work. The resultant P narrative was then used as the foundation for the entire Pentateuch.[3] Campbell and O'Brien help to clarify this view of P through the analogy of a necklace. The thread of the P narrative consists of genealogies, itineraries, and a terse story line; while the pearls on this necklace consist of major stories placed at strategic points on the thread. These major stories include: creation, flood, Abrahamic covenant, burial of Sarah, promise

---

inserted between Lev 10 and 16 (which are connected by the link in 16:1); and how the Holiness Code (Lev 17–26) was appropriately inserted after the Day of Atonement in Lev 16.

3. Noth, *Pentateuchal Traditions*, 10–12. Campbell and O'Brien explain that, according to Noth, the Pentateuch was formed by simply filling out the text of P with additions from JE. Noth felt that P was preserved almost entirely intact in the Pentateuch. Campbell and O'Brien, *Sources*, 9; Noth, *Pentateuchal Traditions*, 17.

to Jacob at Bethel, revelation of God to Moses, the plagues, Passover, deliverance at sea, the manna, the spy story, and the Sinai story.[4] This complete necklace was then used as a framework for the Pentateuch. P has few major stories in comparison to JE which emphasizes dramatic storytelling. As a result, "P could be enriched by stories from JE, with only a minimum of adjustment required."[5]

Accordingly, the norm for compiling the sources of the Pentateuch was to choose one source as a base and enrich it with any unique or important material from another source.[6] In some instances, however, two complete stories from different sources may be preserved side by side, such as the two creation accounts (Gen 1 and 2). Such passages provide the best opportunity for distinguishing the separate sources.

Another departure from the norm for the compilation of sources is evident when two complete accounts are interwoven. An example of this occurs with the flood story, in which the J and P accounts both appear to be preserved intact and interwoven together.[7] Campbell and O'Brien explain why the flood account was compiled in this exceptional way. First, the two accounts are not narrated back to back because the flood story cannot be told twice. This is because both the J and P accounts end with a statement of God's determination never to destroy the earth again. "Were these versions juxtaposed, as the creation accounts are, the first would end with a guarantee never again to destroy the world only to be followed immediately by the second version of divine destruction. The two stories would subvert each other."[8] Secondly, the dual composition of the story serves to reinforce the decisions of God. The decision to flood the world and the promise never to destroy it again are both narrated twice, once in heaven (Gen 6:7; 8:21) and once on earth (Gen 6:13; 9:11). Thus, "confronted with the massive theological and human

---

4. Campbell and O'Brien, *Sources*, 9, 21.

5. Ibid., 9.

6. Noth, *Pentateuchal Traditions*, 12; Campbell and O'Brien, *Sources*, 210.

7. Campbell and O'Brien, *Sources*, 210. Noth does not describe the compilation of the flood story exactly the way that Campbell and O'Brien imply here. Noth still describes P material as the "basis of the flood story," and states that "the other narrative has been cut." Noth, *Pentateuchal Traditions*, 12.

8. Campbell and O'Brien, *Sources*, 220.

significance of these decisions, any inconvenient duality in the remaining texts pales into insignificance."⁹

In conjunction with the work of isolating P from the midst of other pentateuchal sources, its status as an independent document is verified by identifying characteristics unique to P. Seán McEvenue provides three major characteristics of the priestly style: various forms of symmetry and repetition, the repeated structure of command and fulfillment, and an emphasis on fine distinctions with a love of detail. An example of the first characteristic can be seen in the carefully constructed panels of Gen 5. These panels repeat the following pattern for each member of the descendants of Adam indicated.

ויחי X‏ Y שנה ויולד את־Z

ויחי X אחרי הולידו את־Z‏ W שנה ויולד בנים ובנות

ויהיו כל־ימי X‏ V שנה וימת

> "And X lived Y years and became the father of Z;
> And X lived, after becoming the father of Z, W years, and became the father of (other) sons and daughters;
> And all the days of X were V years and he died."

The command-fulfillment structure is simply illustrated in Gen 1. In this creation account, the imperatives spoken by God, which summon various elements of the creation into existence, are followed by the phrase ויהי־כן ("and it was so"), indicating the fulfillment of each of God's commands (see vv. 6–7, 9, 11, 14–15, 24). The third characteristic is illustrated by the fine distinctions and detail evident in such texts as the Abrahamic covenant in Gen 17.¹⁰

McEvenue further elaborates specific characteristics of P through the examination of two composite accounts. In relation to the flood story, he concludes that the hand of P is evident in that "he changed a

---

9. Ibid.
10. McEvenue, *Narrative Style*, 14–18.

free-running narrative into a relatively mannered account marked by symmetry and repetition; he eliminated the psychological aspects, the interiority of both Noah and God, and so turned a dramatic interaction into a simple act of divine power; he replaced a story-teller art of writing with the arts of rhetoric."[11]

The spy story of Num 13–14 serves as a second composite account revealing the character of P. In addition to the expected repetition and symmetry in the P account, a "fairytale" type of psychology in the P spy story is revealed: "the concept of desiring death because the promised land is a man-eater, and that such a desire should be taken literally, is at home in fairy-tale literature, with its black-and-white, unperturbed, unsentimental acceptance of death or cruelty as an outward fact."[12]

McEvenue attempts to confirm these findings by analyzing a third, specifically priestly, unit (not a composite account) in Gen 17. He found that the P characteristics of repetition, symmetrical structures, attention to detail, and a concern for names are all evident in this text. Based on the investigation of the above three accounts, the characteristics of P can be summarized as: 1) faithfulness to the detail and order of the JE sources used; 2) a tendency to reduce storytelling qualities to an extreme minimum; and 3) a tendency to order and systematize.[13]

Norman Gottwald provides a similar summation of P characteristics by reviewing a number of features unique to the P document, including: 1) distinctive vocabulary, 2) a measured style illustrated by fixed formulas, 3) the command-fulfillment scheme, 4) a methodical and precise style evident in numerous regulations and lists, and 5) symmetry and structure.[14] Such features serve to distinguish P and depict the priestly material as a unit. Blenkinsopp affirms this distinction by

---

11. Ibid., 78.

12. Ibid., 139. McEvenue notes that the P account describes a death sentence on the people with the immediate death of the scouts (Num 14:37), while the JE account is not so severe. The fairy-tale like mentality is similar to that of Gretel pushing the witch into the oven to cook, and happily telling Hans the good news (ibid., 140).

13. Ibid., 145–77, 179–83. In regard to P's use of sources, McEvenue states that "action is replaced by idea, dialogue by discourse, suspense by symmetry, aspects of personal interiority and psychological interchange are simply eliminated, dramatic values give way to rhetorical ones" (ibid., 182).

14. Gottwald, *Hebrew Bible*, 469–71.

stating that "P has stood up best to scrutiny, because of its more distinctive vocabulary, style, and ideology."[15]

Dual accounts in the Pentateuch and unique characteristics reflected in the priestly strata suggest the independence of the composition of P. The additional view, however, that P served as the skeletal foundation upon which the entire Pentateuch was framed appears inadequate as an explanation for P's relation to other sources. The observation that P has too many omissions in comparison to JE tends to refute such a view. That is, P's narrative is not extensive enough to provide a complete framework for the entire Pentateuch. It may be more appropriate to argue that JE was the foundation of the Pentateuch, and elements of P were integrated into it.[16]

The concern over numerous omissions in P reflects an underlying assumption that JE and P must have originally represented complete and parallel narratives. Such an assumption has misconstrued the understanding of P. P may never have appeared as a complete narrative reflecting events from creation to reaching the promised land, but rather may have followed its own much more limited story line. Recall, much of the investigation concerning unique characteristics in P has been based on narratives in Genesis because relatively little P narrative is found beyond the accounts in Genesis. Thus, P fails to serve as the framework for the entire Pentateuch; not because of supposed omissions in the text (when compared to JE), but rather because P is made up of compositions (complete in themselves) which extend over only a limited section of the Pentateuch. This becomes more evident as the dynamics of the priestly literature are examined further.

The Redactional Character of P

Despite the recognition of P as an independent document, the priestly strata appears to reflect characteristics of a redactional layer as well.

---

15. Blenkinsopp, *Pentateuch*, 26.

16. Since my initial consideration of this suggestion (in my 1996 dissertation), Wenham's article appeared contending that, at least in Genesis, J supplements and expands P material. He reverses the more common view by concluding that P was prior to J and served as a source for J's narrative. Wenham, "Priority of P," 240–58. Wenham does not go so far as to claim that J served as the framework for the Pentateuch. Yet, his argument raises the notion that P material in Genesis is earlier and less extensive than commonly considered.

Frank Moore Cross represents those who see P purely in the form of a redaction, with the statement that, "priestly tradition seems never to have taken the form of an independent 'Code.' It is most easily described as a ... systematizing expansion of the normative JE tradition in the Tetrateuch."[17]

The two major features in P which suggest its redactional character are the use of framing formulas and, once again, the perceived omissions in P. Cross points to two sets of framing formulas employed within the priestly material. The first is the formula, אלה תולדות ("these are the generations of ..."). This priestly formula is used to frame the major sections of Genesis. It appears ten times in Genesis: five times before Terah (Gen 1–11), and five times in the patriarchal history (Gen 12–50).[18] The formula is placed before a genealogy or a section containing stories about the descendants of whomever the genealogical formula designates. Cross argues that the sections following these framing elements derive from older sources (e.g., a genealogy), or contain JE narrative, or are made up of J narrative which has been reworked by P (e.g., the flood story). Material stemming directly from the P redactor includes very little narrative. The only material which comes close to being literary narrative is the account of the purchase of the cave in Machpelah (Gen 23). The rest of the independent P material is made up mostly of blessing and covenant pericopes, and are not proper narrative.[19]

The second framing device appears in Exodus through Numbers. In this section of the tradition, P uses the formula, ויסעו ... ויחנו ("they set out from ... and encamped at ..."). This formula serves to divide the tradition according to stations in the wilderness sojourn. The divisions following the formula are short until the wilderness of Sinai is

---

17. Cross, *Canaanite Myth*, 294. With this quote, Cross cites his own previous work (idem, "The Tabernacle," 57–58).

18. See Fohrer, *Old Testament*, 183. Fohrer lists the following eleven appearances of the formula: Gen 2:4a; 6:9; 10:1; 11:10, 27; 25.12, 19; 36:1, 9; 37:2; Num 3:1. He notes a twelfth related occurrence at Gen 5:1 (זה ספר תולדת ["this is the book of the generations ..."]). Of these twelve, Cross notes that two are secondary (Gen 36:9 which is redundant to 36:1; and Num 3:1 which is conflated with the following genealogy headed by אלה שמות). Cross, *Canaanite Myth*, 302 n. 33, 308 n. 47.

19. Ibid., 301–5. In 305 n. 40, Cross lists the blessing and covenant pericopes as follows: Gen 9:1–17, Noachic covenant; Gen 17:1–22, Abrahamic covenant & blessing of Sarah; Gen 28:1–9, Isaac's blessing of Jacob; Gen 35:9–13, Jacob's blessing on return to Bethel; Gen 48:3–7, blessing of Joseph's sons.

reached. At that point the priestly legislation runs from Exod 19:1 to Num 10:10. This framing formula occurs twelve times: six times up to the last station before Sinai, and six times from Sinai to the Plains of Moab.[20] Cross summarizes the priestly writer's material by contending that, "his primary work was imposing the framing elements, and supplementing JE with his theological formulae and an occasional discrete document, until reaching the Sinai sojourn when his supplementation became massive."[21]

Perceived omissions contribute to the view that P represents a redactional layer, due to accounts in JE which have no apparent parallel in P, yet seem to be vital to P's presentation. For example, it appears that P presumes the stories of sin and rebellion found in JE. The elaborate cultus of P serves for the atonement of such sin, yet P material alone has no story of the origin of human sin. Thus, Cross has concluded that P must presume the J narrative. Similarly, P alone has no account of the birth of Moses, his years in Egypt, his flight to the wilderness, or his return to Egypt. Such omissions seem impossible for a P document, given P's interest in Moses as a central figure, and in the reconstruction of the institutions of the Mosaic period. Even more stunning is the omission of the covenant ceremony at Sinai in P. The Sinai material is the heart of P's presentation, yet the covenant ceremony is missing in P. This has led Cross to the conclusion that either a later redactor mutilated and suppressed much of the supposed P source, or that P was never an independent document. Cross affirms the latter, and states that P was a redactor who shaped and supplemented the received JE tradition.[22]

At this stage of the investigation, it is natural to consider that the priestly material may include elements of both independent composition and redaction. This is supported by the contention that it is unlikely that a redactor would combine newly composed alternative accounts with earlier sources which contradict those new accounts. Richard Friedman presents this insight as part of an argument proposing that

---

20. Ibid., 308, 310–16. The formula appears at Exod 12:37a; 13:20; 14:1–2; 15:22a; 16:1; 17:1a; 19:2; Num 10:12; 20:1a; 20:22; 21:10–11; 22:1. Cf. Noth, *Pentateuchal Traditions*, 224–26.

21. Cross, *Canaanite Myth*, 305.

22. Ibid., 306–7, 317–18.

The Composition of P 11

the priestly literature should be considered in two stages: 1) as earlier priestly compositions, and 2) as a later redaction.[23]

Friedman reasons that priestly accounts which appear as alternatives to (conflicting or recasting) JE or D accounts must stem from a pre-exilic P composer. He states, "the Priestly retelling of JE tales, removing all appearances of angels and dreams, seems likewise an impossible enterprise for the tradent who is combining the Priestly products with the very JE versions which they retell."[24] It is conceivable that historical circumstances would cause an exilic redactor to be willing or bound to combine conflicting traditions (out of concern for the integrity of each). It is difficult, however, to explain why such a redactor would compose conflicting materials himself, as elaboration of the received traditions that they contradict. Friedman therefore contends that a late priestly redactor combined earlier P compositions with other source materials in the Pentateuch.[25]

Disjunction between Narrative and Legal Material

We will return to the question of the character and extent of a redactional layer within the priestly literature later in this work. At this stage, however, in contrast to the views described above, I submit that the framing formulas and supposed omissions in P, by themselves, do not conclusively demonstrate that P either represents a redactional layer, or that P reveals a distinction between early priestly compositions and a later redaction.[26] The two framing formulas attributed to P as a redactor (genealogical formula, and wilderness stations), not only frame other sources of the Pentateuch, but they also serve to frame the priestly materials. Thus, these devices may reflect, not the redaction of the

---

23. Friedman, *Exile and Biblical Narrative*, 76–118. Marc Vervenne comes to a similar conclusion regarding the dual character of P compositions after his examination of the "Sea Narrative" in Exod 13:17—14:31. He suggests that the P redactors may have made use of existing priestly material, which paralleled JE traditions. Vervenne, "The 'P' Tradition," 76–88.

24. Ibid., 78.

25. Ibid., 78.

26. At this point, the argument still centers mostly on narrative materials. The redactional layer of the priestly literature will not be clearly evident until the discussion reaches the question of how the legal and narrative components of P were brought together.

Pentateuch, but rather the organization of the priestly writings themselves. Furthermore, it must be recognized that the connection between the two framing devices (genealogical formula and wilderness stations) has not been established.

The perceived omissions in P are based on comparison to the narrative in JE. Admittedly, when held beside the more "historical," story-telling flavor of JE, P falls short as a parallel. Yet, grounding the evaluation of P in relation to how it matches up with JE presumes that P was intended to function in a manner similar to JE. It is evident, however, that the tendency to minimize storytelling, along with an emphasis on blessing and covenant pericopes, genealogies, and birth and death notices, suggests a different focus for P. Accordingly, I contend that the priestly material reflects a unique concern of its own, and was never meant to be the same kind of work as JE.[27]

The disjunction between the elaborate cultus of P (legal material) and the narrative of the origin of sin, and the disjunction between the focus on the institutions of the Mosaic period (further legislation) and the narratives concerning the life of Moses, do not require dependence on JE, as if the priestly audience would be otherwise ignorant of sin or the authority of Moses. Rather, sin is presumed in P simply because it is recognized as intrinsic to the community of Israel. As with sin, there is likewise in P no narrative explaining the origin of impurities, such as skin diseases or sexual emissions. Nevertheless, P addresses these concerns, as it does sin. The legislation in P is aimed at dealing with sin and impurities, and codifying the sacrificial rites which are intended to address their consequences. The existence of these problems was not questioned by P, but rather taken for granted.

The absence of the stories of the birth and some of the early life of Moses in the priestly narratives can be understood in the same way. The legal material in P is not concerned with presenting historical background for the character of Moses. The presence or authority of Moses is not a question for the priestly work. The traditions regarding the centrality of Moses are assumed for the priestly context. The same holds for the absence of the Sinai covenant ceremony. The independent presentation of the events surrounding Sinai focus on the giving of the Law. As Cross himself recognized, P's supplementation at

---

27. See Emerton, "Priestly Writer," 392–93.

Sinai becomes massive.[28] This large portion of P's work suggests that the priestly concern is upon the legislation itself, while the traditions regarding the covenant ceremony are simply understood. Accordingly, I suggest that the original character of the legal material in P should be understood as a priestly manual conveying instructions regarding the tabernacle and its related cult, in the context of a community that already acknowledged the problem of sin and the traditions concerning Moses. Recognizing the original independence of this priestly manual establishes the foundation for sorting out the relationship between the narrative and legal material in P.

Clarifying the nature of P begins with the simple observation that P material in Genesis is predominantly narrative in form, while P material in Exodus–Numbers is overwhelmingly in the form of legislation. The limited priestly narrative in Exodus–Numbers, when employed, serves to establish the framework out of which certain legislation emerges, as well as to communicate the priestly concern for demonstrating the fulfillment of God's commands. Much of the struggle to clarify the character of the priestly literature stems from the assumption that the P narrative in Genesis and P materials (narrative and legal) in Exodus–Numbers all derive from the same strata of the Pentateuch. Yet, clearly there is a history of recognizing elements of division between these materials. Noth rejected the legal portions of Exodus–Numbers in affiliation with P, while Milgrom has isolated the same material as if it is the only significant focus of P. The problem lies in accurately identifying the dividing line within the traditional demarcation of P materials. The division should not be made between the limited P narrative in Exodus–Numbers and the corresponding legal material in Exodus–Numbers. Rather, the dividing line needs to be recognized between the P narrative in Genesis and P materials in Exodus–Numbers (which are predominantly legal in form). Rolf Rendtorff's discussion of P initiates this insight; though, due to his lack of recognition of P as an independent document, he does not derive the same conclusion as that described below.

Following a tradition history approach, Rendtorff focuses on the large units of text within the Pentateuch which share a common theme, such as: the primeval story, the patriarchal story, Moses and

---

28. Cross, *Canaanite Myth*, 305.

the Exodus, Sinai, the sojourn in the desert, and the occupation of the land. He views each of these as a self-contained unit.[29] Rendtorff argues that these larger units of tradition are virtually unchanged, except for a seemingly unobtrusive reworking layer that gives an intentional sense of composition and interpretation to the Pentateuch as a whole. This layer is identified as Deuteronomistic, and besides it, there is no immediate evidence of a comprehensive reworking that shapes the whole Pentateuch or a source within it.[30]

In relation to P, Rendtorff sees no continuous narrative, but notes that a small group of theological texts attributed to P stand out in the story, along with several chronological notes from P. The theological texts attributable to P are not restricted to the patriarchal story. Links or cross-references between these texts are found in the primeval story (Gen 1–11), the patriarchal story (Gen 12–50), and as far as Exod 6. However, no evidence of these priestly theological texts appears beyond Exod 6. Similarly, some connections appear between the chronological notes attributed to P within the different larger units of tradition in the Pentateuch. These notes appear to make connections between the primeval story, the patriarchal story, and the Moses story. Again, however, the chronological notes, like the theological texts, do not reach beyond the Moses account. Rendtorff concludes that the priestly texts are a layer of reworking, which places emphasis on specific key themes, such as covenant, and a unique concept of creation with its significant pronouncements.[31] This priestly layer of reworking does not extend beyond the Moses account: "After this there is no further sign of the priestly layer in the Pentateuch."[32] Rendtorff sees P as a post-exilic priestly editorial strand that only goes as far as Exod 6.[33]

Rendtorff's argument limits the identification of P material to that in Genesis (up to Exod 6). Like Noth, Rendtorff implies that P legislation should not be counted among P material. However, he adds the

---

29. Rendtorff, *Problem of the Process*, 41. See Campbell and O'Brien, *Sources*, 12–13.

30. Rendtorff, *Problem of the Process*, 84–99. Rendtorff specifies that the ideology associated with this layer of reworking is also called "early deuteronomic" or "protodeuteronomic" (ibid., 99).

31. Ibid., 136–70, 192–94.

32. Ibid., 194.

33. See Blenkinsopp, *Pentateuch*, 24.

argument that the pentateuchal strata associated with P does not appear in any form beyond Exod 6. This affirms the proposition that a significant line of division appears between materials associated with the P narrative in Genesis (up to Exod 6) and materials normally attributed to P in Exodus–Numbers. To further clarify the distinction between P narrative in Genesis (up to Exod 6) and P material in Exodus–Numbers, it is necessary to evaluate some of the arguments that claim that these materials reflect an original unity.

Gottwald points to three covenants that serve to divide the sacred history in P: the covenant with Noah (Gen 9:1–17), the covenant with Abraham (Gen 17), and the covenant with the people of Israel (Exod 31:12–18). He also discusses a completion formula that marks three other important moments in the priestly history: creation (Gen 2:1–2), completion of the tabernacle (Exod 39:32; 40:33), and the division of the land (Josh 18:1; 19:51). All three cases conclude with a formulaic remark regarding the completion of the corresponding work.[34]

In regard to the three covenants that periodize the priestly history, two of them appear within the Genesis narratives of P. As for the third, Gottwald himself notes that the Mosaic covenant of Exod 31:12–18 lacks the development of the other two covenants, and therefore he considers it a secondary insertion.[35] Interestingly, Robert Coote and David Ord list the third covenant as the "Covenant of Moses" taken from Exod 6.[36] As suggested already in relation to Rendtorff's views, Exod 6 appears to be the boundary between the priestly narratives in Genesis, and the predominately legal material in Exodus–Numbers. Thus, the unity implied by the three covenants does not necessarily cross the Exod 6 border line.

The references that mark three important "completion" moments in P (Gen 2:1–2; Exod 39:32; 40:33; Josh 19:51) appear questionable as examples of formulaic usage. The only common term making up the supposed formula that ties all three moments together is the appearance of the verb כלה ("to complete"). The common appearance of a single word in only three instances seems weak as evidence for formulaic identification. In addition, the word does not appear to be a priestly

---

34. Gottwald, *Hebrew Bible*, 471–72. See also, Blenkinsopp, "Structure of P," 275–76.

35. Gottwald, *Hebrew Bible*, 472.

36. Coote and Ord, *In the Beginning*, 43.

technical term. Thus, these three moments may appear as indicators of the successful completion of a work, but they are not necessarily moments intrinsic to the structure of P. Similar moments related to the completion of a work, making use of the same verb, appear in texts that are clearly outside of P.[37] Thus, "completion" moments are not necessarily part of a unified structure in P, nor are they necessarily characteristic of the P source.

Another alleged unifying element appears to tie the P narrative of Gen 1 to the dietary restrictions found in the legal material of P, by means of a supposed concept of order reflected in the priestly material. Gottwald explains that, in accordance with the creation account, P presumes three orders of living creatures. These are generally recognized as land creatures, creatures of the air, and creatures of the water. The dietary restrictions in P are supposedly based on these proper categories of distinction derived from creation.[38]

This concept of order is based on the work of Mary Douglas who explains the dietary laws of Lev 11 on the basis of studies in anthropology.[39] Accordingly, "culture" provides basic categories in which ideas and values are ordered. Such a given system of classification will give rise to anomalies that must be addressed. The dietary laws of Lev 11 provide an example of cultural provisions for dealing with anomalous events.[40] That is, those creatures that do not fit the basic categories set forth in the creation account constitute anomalies that defy the created order. These anomalies are dealt with by being labeled unclean, and therefore unfit for consumption.

Coote and Ord follow Douglas' approach, and recognize that the conditions that make an animal acceptable (clean) for food are tied to the characteristics that define what is normative for a creature in its particular realm; that is, land, air, or water.[41] Thus, in order for something to be considered clean, it must abide by the original created order. The

---

37. 1 Kgs 6:9, 14—Solomon's completion of the temple; 1 Kgs 7:1—Solomon's completion of his own house; 1 Kgs 7:40—Hiram's completion of his work in the temple; Ezra 10:17—Ezra's completion of investigating marriages to foreign wives.

38. Gottwald, *Hebrew Bible*, 477.

39. Douglas, *Purity and Danger*, 38–57; see also, Soler, "Dietary Prohibitions," 24–30.

40. Douglas, *Purity and Danger*, 38–39.

41. Coote and Ord, *In the Beginning*, 63.

priestly principle is that every creature was intended to be attached to a single realm. Any creature that deviated from its intended realm was to be considered unclean. Attachment to a particular realm was defined by the mode of locomotion that the creature exhibited. Thus, land animals have hoofs to walk, sea creatures have fins to swim, and animals of the sky have wings to fly. A second principle taken from the creation account is that the ideal (clean) creature must eat plants, and not other creatures. Thus, for the realm of land, clean animals include those that have hoofs to move about on land and chew the cud (eat plants) as instructed in Lev 11:3. For the realm of air, Lev 11 only lists certain flying creatures that are unclean. From this list, however, it can be deduced that the clean birds are those that do not eat meat, and do not walk on land or water. For the realm of water, clean fish include those that have fins to swim. It is presumed that the priests could not distinguish what fish eat, so the requirement of eating plants was replaced by the requirement that the fish be covered with scales (Lev 11:9). Simple examples of creatures that do not abide by these regulations include: the crab, which does not swim through the water with fins, and the ostrich, which is a feathered bird that walks on the ground but does not fly. Thus, these creatures do not abide faithfully by the characteristics associated with their given realm, and are therefore unclean.[42]

The idea that the priestly dietary restrictions are based on a concept of orderliness reflected in the creation account appears suspect. If the dietary laws of Lev 11 were intended to reflect a priestly principle regarding ideal creatures representing the distinct realms of land, air, and water, then why is such a principle not simply stated as the defining factor for clean and unclean animals? That is, why not simply state that clean animals are those that walk on the land and do not eat meat? The obvious response is that the restrictions in Lev 11 do not actually correspond to such a principle. The restrictions of Lev 11 define clean land animals as those with a split hoof and that chew the cud. Clearly this does not correspond to all animals who walk on land and eat plants. For example, the camel is explicitly excluded from allowable diet, though it certainly walks on land and is not a meat eater (the two principles of order supposedly derived from the creation account). Instead, it is excluded by reason of lacking a split hoof. This particular reason is not

42. Ibid., 62–65.

reflected in any principle of order in the creation account.⁴³ Similarly, the creation account does not reflect any principle of order that distinguishes sea creatures based on the presence, or lack of presence, of fins and scales.

Michael Carroll provides further critique of Douglas' work. He refers back to Douglas' original contention that the dietary restrictions of Lev 11 point to anomalies in regard to the classification system of the culture as reflected in the created order. He points out that many land animals defined as unclean in Lev 11 would easily fit into the category of "beasts of the earth," which is specifically identified in the creation account (Gen 1:24, 25, 30). Therefore such animals are not anomalous to the created order. Similarly, some flying creatures, and "swarming things," which are identified as unclean in Lev 11, are not anomalies to the classification system represented in the creation account.⁴⁴ Carroll also points to Douglas' argument regarding the perverse locomotion of those quadrupeds that use "hands" for walking, and are thus unclean.⁴⁵ He corrects her rendering of the Hebrew word כף (Lev 11:27) to mean "the palm of a hand or the sole of a foot."⁴⁶ Thus, it is incorrect to state that animals with paws are unclean because they walk on their

---

43. Douglas treats the named exceptions to the dietary law (camel, rock badger, rabbit, pig; Lev 11:4–7) as borderline cases that fit one ruling but not both (i.e., they have split hoof, but do not chew cud, or vice versa). The main principle here is that allowable animals must correspond to both distinctive characteristics of *domestic* animals (cud chewing and split hoof). However, the creation account does not reflect such a principle. Accordingly, Douglas does not explicitly tie this principle to the creation account. Douglas only ties the distinctions based on the categories of land, air, and water to the creation account. Douglas, *Purity and Danger*, 54–55. However, Soler does attempt to tie the criteria for domestic animals to the creation account. Soler argues that the plan of creation originally included only herbivores (Gen 1:30), and that cud chewing and a split hoof was recognized as a way to define true herbivores. However, the ruling of "a split hoof" eliminates some purely herbivorous animals (such as the camel, rock badger, and rabbit). Thus, being herbivorous is not enough to make an animal clean. In addition, the animal must conform to the norm of domestic animals by virtue of having a split hoof. Soler, "Dietary Prohibitions," 26–27. The argument has come full circle. The bottom line is that clean animals must reflect the characteristics of domestic animals. But the creation account reflects no such principle: it does not emphasize domestic animals over wild, nor does it make any explicit distinctions based on split hoofs or cud chewing.

44. Carroll, "Leviticus Revisited," 118–20.

45. Douglas, *Purity and Danger*, 55–56.

46. Carroll, "Leviticus Revisited," 119.

"hands."⁴⁷ The point of Lev 11:27 seems to be that animals who walk on flat paws, as opposed to split hooves, are excluded from allowable diet. Accordingly, the distinction is not based on any supposed "perverse locomotion" (i.e., walking on "hands" as opposed to feet).

Therefore, it does not appear that the rationale behind the dietary restrictions of Lev 11 is based on a principle of abiding by that which is normative according to a created order set forth in the creation account of Gen 1. Consequently, an explicit unity is not evident between material normally attributed to P in Genesis, and the legal material in Exodus–Numbers.⁴⁸

P as Defined by Legal Material

The unity and distinctiveness evident within each component (exclusively) of the priestly literature further verifies the disjunction between P material in Genesis (up to Exod 6) and P material in Exodus–Numbers. It seems most appropriate to label the predominantly legal component (in Exodus–Numbers) as "P" due to its focus on specifically priestly concerns, such as the tabernacle and its related cult. The narrative material in Genesis may be assigned a related, though independent, label. That material (P in Genesis up to Exod 6) will be further addressed later in this work, along with a suggested designation.

I define P legal material following the listing of Brueggemann and Wolff, which includes: Exod 25–31; 35–40; Leviticus; and Num 1–10.⁴⁹ This is in contrast to Noth who categorizes Exod 25–31; 35–40 and Lev 8–9 as part of the P narrative.⁵⁰ I maintain that the core of P should be

---

47. Jacob Milgrom points out the same mistake in Douglas' argument, *Leviticus 1–16*, 726.

48. In a later work, Mary Douglas changed her argument regarding the rationale behind the dietary restrictions in Lev 11. Her new explanation, based on covenant and a respectful approach to life, strongly echoes Milgrom's understanding of the purity laws as grounded in a theology of reverence for life (Milgrom's argument will be discussed later in this work in relation to the intent of P). See, Douglas, *Leviticus as Literature*, esp. chs. 7–8.

49. Brueggemann and Wolff, *Vitality*, 102.

50. I define the legal material as priestly legislation (including the description of its execution) characterized by its relation to the temple and the sacrificial cult (including purity regulations). Noth restricts legal material to legislation that interrupts the flow of the narrative as he identifies it. Consequently, he designates what he identifies as legal material using the label "Additions to P" (Noth, *Pentateuchal Traditions*, 8–9; cf.

identified as legal material which specifically focuses on the sanctuary and its surrounding cult.

The Core of P: Sinai Legislation

The priestly literature is often defined in terms of its interest in cultic concerns, which are expressed most definitively in P through the legal material. For example, the foundation of identifying and dating P, according to the source hypothesis, was the development of the religious cult in ancient Israel (i.e., P represents a developed picture of the cult which reflects that of exilic or post-exilic literature and times). The description of these cultic matters appears in the legal material of Exodus, Leviticus, and Numbers.

In contrast, the P narrative in Genesis rarely deals with cultic matters. The only possible exceptions might be the mention of the Sabbath and the concept of covenant. P material in Genesis, however, contains no reflections of the elaborate sacrificial system or concerns related to the sanctuary. In fact, brief references in Genesis to purity concerns (Gen 7:2, 8) and references to matters of offering and sacrifice (Gen 4:3–5; 8:20; 22:13) are normally not attributed to P at all.

Consequently, I submit that the definitive element of P is the legislation in Exodus, Leviticus, and Numbers, with some brief surrounding narrative providing the appropriate frame and historical backdrop. The major line of demarcation for P consists of divine legislation and its execution, focused especially on the subject matter of the sanctuary and the surrounding cult. The core of P is comprised of the legal material which is set within the Sinai account. More explicitly, this core consists of:

271–75). Some of what Noth has identified as narrative, however, is actually legislation (commanded by God through Moses) and its execution; for example, the *instructions* regarding the building of the tabernacle (Exod 25–31) and the execution of those instructions (Exod 35–40).

The brief narrative that does appear in P serves to frame the legislation within its wilderness setting. As will become evident later in this work, I attribute much of the priestly narrative, beyond this brief framework, to the redactionary work of H. Thus, P itself includes little narrative.

Exodus 25–31	instructions concerning the tabernacle, the tabernacle furniture, priestly garments, and priestly consecration
Exodus 35–40	execution of the instructions regarding the tabernacle, the tabernacle furniture, and priestly garments
Leviticus 1–7	sacrificial laws
Leviticus 8–10	execution of the instructions regarding priestly consecration, and the first sacrifices
Leviticus 11–15	purity laws
Leviticus 16	The Day of Atonement
Numbers 1–10	instructions, including the roles of priests and Levites, and the ordering of the camp around the tabernacle

It can be seen that the priestly characteristic of command-fulfillment is illustrated in much of this material. As identified in the list above, the instructions in Exod 25–31 are carried out in Exod 35–40.[51] Similarly, the instructions regarding sacrificial laws (Lev 1–7) are initially carried out in the description of the first sacrifices (Lev 8–10). The remaining P material from Exod 6 through Num 36 consists mostly of brief narratives which serve to frame the legal material and give it the appropriate historical setting, namely, that of the wilderness period, and specifically, the giving of the Law at Sinai.

Wilderness itineraries found in Exodus and Numbers serve to frame the P material, and add flow to the limited narrative. As mentioned previously, twelve wilderness itinerary notices appear in P as a framing device and are identified by the formula ויסעו . . . ויחנו ("they set out from . . . and encamped at . . .").[52] The argument that P incorporated these twelve wilderness itineraries to frame other source materials appears to be an oversimplification. The precise wording of the formula (with both verbs, ויסעו . . . ויחנו), outside of the stations list in Num 33, appears only in five of the twelve occurrences which Cross identifies

---

51. The instructions regarding the consecration of the priests are carried out in Lev 8 in conjunction with the first sacrifices.

52. Cross, *Canaanite Myth*, 308. Cross lists the wilderness itineraries as follows: Exod 12:37a; 13:20; 14:1–2; 15:22a; 16:1; 17:1a; 19:2; Num 10:12; 20:1a; 20:22; 21:10–11; 22:1 (ibid., 310–16).

as wilderness itineraries.⁵³ G. I. Davies points out a number of significant complications in relation to assigning the wilderness itineraries to various sources, including P. He notes a much longer list of wilderness notices than simply twelve and argues that few should be ascribed to P.⁵⁴ Distinct series within the itineraries can be identified based on linking terms. For example, Exod 15:27; 16:1; 17:1, and 19:2a form the series: Elim—wilderness of Sin—Rephidim—wilderness of Sinai. Doublets and at least one overlap among the itineraries prompt the recognition that multiple itinerary lists have been combined by some redactor. This is illustrated by the redundancy in Exod 19:1–2a, and the doublet between Num 10:12 and 12:16 in conjunction with 11:35.⁵⁵

This raises an awareness that the list of twelve wilderness notices attributed to P fails to account for a number of additional itinerary statements, and the explicit links between some and redundancy among others. Jerome Walsh brings some clarification to the issue by identifying chains of linked notices within the wilderness itineraries.⁵⁶ By means of a careful analysis of the itinerary texts, he isolates three chains of itinerary notices, each of which form a consistent series of linked movements through the wilderness. The chain which Walsh identifies as "chain-I" includes all five of the notices which contain the full formula, ויסעו . . . ויחנו ("they set out from . . . and encamped at . . ."). Due to inconsistencies in the series, however, chain-I does not include all twelve of the wilderness stations which Cross attributed to a P redactor, though it does include other itinerary notices which are consistent with the series. Thus, chain-I consists of the following itinerary notices: Exod 12:37; 13:20; 17:1; 19:2a;

---

53. Exod 13:20; 17:1a; 19:2; Num 21:10–11; 22:1. The following station notices include only the first verb of the formula pair: Exod 12:37a; 15:22a; 16:1; Num 10:12; 20:22. The text of Exod 14:1–2 contains only the second verb of the pair. The wording of Num 20:1a does not include either of the formula verbs.

54. Davies, "Wilderness Itineraries," 1–2, 1 n. 2. For fuller listings of wilderness itinerary notices, see also Coats, "Wilderness Itinerary," 135; and Walsh, "From Egypt to Moab," 21.

55. Davies, "Wilderness Itineraries," 2–4. Numbers 10:12 and 12:16 both designate the "wilderness of Paran" as the next encampment. Numbers 11:35 is linked to 12:16 by the term "Hazeroth" (ibid., 4).

56. Walsh, "From Egypt to Moab," 20–33. Davies' article notes his desire to produce a fuller discussion by taking into account this previously produced study by Walsh. Davies, "Wilderness Itineraries," 1 n. 1.

Num 10:12; 12:16b; 21:10–11; 22:1.[57] Walsh does not attempt to assign any of the itinerary chains to particular source documents. Nevertheless, it seems reasonable to suggest that his chain-I be associated with P, based initially on the inclusion of every instance of the formula ויסעו . . . ויחנו ("they set out from . . . and encamped at . . ."), outside of Num 33, within this chain.[58]

The list of wilderness stations in Walsh's chain-I forms a structure of eight itinerary notices that encompass the central portion of P legislation. This structure highlights the Sinai account as the heart of the priestly concern, with four notices appearing on the way to Sinai and four notices appearing following the stay at Sinai. The vast majority of priestly legislation is placed within the setting of the Sinai station (the Israelites arrive at Sinai at Exod 19:2a and depart Sinai at Num 10:12). This corresponds to the core of P as delineated above, all of which is set within the Sinai wilderness station. Thus, the core of the priestly legislation (Exod 25 through Num 10), set within the Sinai station, is enveloped in the center of this priestly framework (defined by chain-I of the wilderness stations as identified by Walsh).

The Parameter of P

The parameter of P is clearly identified through the placement of the phrase, וידבר יהוה אל־משה ("And the Lord spoke to Moses"), which occurs 91 times in the Hebrew Bible, all within the priestly literature. This characteristic formula of P can be considered P's "command formula." The formula first appears at Exod 6:10, and recurs throughout the P material until its next to last occurrence at Num 35:9.[59] Thus, the main parameter of P extends from the deliverance from Egypt through the final instructions on the Plains of Moab.

This formula which introduces God's instruction to Moses is complemented by the "execution-formulae" in P. Blenkinsopp identi-

---

57. Walsh, "From Egypt to Moab," 20–29.

58. In affirmation of the inclusion of those notices in the chain which are not commonly attributed to P, it is interesting to note that Lohfink includes all of the itinerary notices in Walsh's chain-I among his listing of wilderness stations attributable to P's narrative. Lohfink, *Theology of the Pentateuch*, 151–53, 151 n. 39.

59. The final occurrence of this formula is at Deut 32:48. This occurrence identifies the notice of Moses' death, and will be discussed later in relation to the H redaction of the priestly literature.

fies the most usual form of this formula as: "X did according to all that YHWH (God) commanded him" (ויעש [ ] כאשר צוה יהוה/אלהים אתו).[60] Blenkinsopp then lists 68 verses where this formula, along with its variants, appears.[61]

The difficulty with Blenkinsopp's presentation is evident in the variations in which he allows the formula to appear. For example, among the references which he lists for the formula are Exod 16:34 and Num 3:42 which do not contain the formula verb ויעש ("he did"). Instead, these references contain two different verbs, that is, ויניחהו ("he placed it") and ויפקד ("he appointed") respectively. In addition, Blenkinsopp includes Exod 7:10, 20; 39:43, and Num 20:27 in his list of formula occurrences.[62] Each of these references does not include the formula direct object אתו ("him"), but rather contains no direct object at all. My point is that the character of a formula should suggest some consistency. Any variations should not only be minor, but should remain consistent with the content and grammatical pattern of the formula. That is, the variations should be practically interchangeable with the content of the original formula without disrupting its grammatical pattern. In the case of Blenkinsopp's suggested formula, if the verb and the direct object can be altered as just illustrated, then 2 Sam 24:19 and Jer 13:5 could be included in the list of occurrences for this formulaic phrase. These two verses also contain the executionary formula characteristic of P as Blenkinsopp would allow it to appear. Another illustration of this problem is evident in Gen 7:5, which also appears on Blenkinsopp's list of formula variations. This reference breaks the pattern of the original formula by not including a direct object at the end of the phrase, and instead indicates the object by means of a suffix pronoun on the verb "command" in the center of the phrase (ויעש נח ככל אשר־צוהו יהוה). This variation of the formula appears in other texts, including some which are clearly outside of P, and thus brings into question whether

---

60. Blenkinsopp, "Structure of P," 276–77. Blenkinsopp's translation of the usual form of the formula should actually read "X did according as YHWH commanded him." The inclusion of the word "all" is actually among the variations which Blenkinsopp lists.

61. Ibid., 276–77.

62. Ibid., 277. Numbers 20:27 does not appear in Blenkinsopp's list, although Num 20:9 appears twice. I assume that the second listing of 20:9 is a misprint because the description which Blenkinsopp includes for this second listing of 20:9 actually fits the content of 20:27.

this variation of the formula is characteristic of, or unique to, P (cf. Exod 19:7, 2 Sam 5:25; 1 Chr 24:19).

Another inconsistency with Blenkinsopp's rendition of the execution formula in P is the variant use of אלהים ("God") in place of יהוה ("the Lord"). It appears that יהוה is the preferred referent for God in the P source. This is evident in the command formula (וידבר יהוה אל־משה), which in all of its 91 occurrences never includes אלהים.[63] Thus, it seems unlikely that P would use אלהים in its execution formula. As it turns out אלהים only appears in Gen 6:22; 17:23; 21:4 within Blenkinsopp's list of execution formula occurrences. These are clearly outside of the parameter of P as defined above.

Such inconsistencies in the forms of the execution formula constitute an overly flexible rendering of the formula and confuse the parameter of P. Such renditions of the formula call into question exactly which phrases should be included as acceptable variations, and therefore, which occurrences should be included in the parameter and structure of P. A more consistent execution formula that is characteristic of P is simply the phrase, כאשר צוה יהוה את־משה ("according as the Lord commanded Moses"). This formula appears consistently 41 times in P without variation.[64] It is significant that this executionary formula does not change the basic parameter of P as defined by its complement described above, that is, the command formula וידבר יהוה אל־משה ("And the Lord spoke to Moses"). Thus, the parameter of P ranges from Exod 6 to Num 36.[65] The two formulas clearly reflect the priestly characteristic of command and fulfillment throughout P. The formula introducing the Lord's instructions to Moses reflects God's command (וידבר יהוה אל־משה), and the execution formula points to how Moses carried out the Lord's instructions "according as the Lord commanded Moses"

---

63. The one and only exception in which אלהים appears in place of יהוה in the command formula is at Exod 6:2, which will be discussed later in relation to the redactional link between P and the narrative in Genesis normally attributed to P.

64. Exod 12:28, 50; 39:1, 5, 7, 21, 26, 29, 31; 40:19, 21, 23, 25, 27, 29, 32; Lev 8:9, 13, 17, 21, 29; 9:10; 16:34; 24:23; Num 1:19; 2:33; 3:51; 8:3, 22; 15:36; 26:4; 27:11; 31:7, 31, 41, 47; 36:10 Deut 34:9; Josh 11:15, 20; 14:5. It is significant, that Gottwald also indicates that the executionary formula appears "at forty-one places in P," despite indicating so in the midst of referring to Blenkinsopp's article. Gottwald, *Hebrew Bible*, 472.

65. As noted with the command formula, occurrences of the execution formula beyond the book of Numbers will be discussed in relation to H's redaction of the priestly literature.

(כאשר צוה יהוה את־משה). Beyond Num 36, these two P formulas appear in only seven more instances which report four events: 1) the death of Moses, 2) the conquest of the land, 3) the division of the land, and 4) the assignment of Levitical cities. These final notices all show signs of the priestly redactor H, and will be discussed later in this work.

The Priestly Source

Following is a list of passages that have been identified as P in the course of this investigation. This list is not intended to be a comprehensive index of every verse attributed to P. Rather, it reflects the core of P and defines its parameters as described above.

Exodus:

6:9–27
7:7–13
9:8–12
12:28, 37, 50
13:1, 20
17:1
19:2a
24:12–18
25–31 [H = 25:1–9; 27:21; 29:42, 45–46; 31:1–17]
32:7
33:1a
35–40 [H = 35:1–19]

Leviticus:

1–16 [H = 1:1–2; 3:17; 6:7–18a (Eng. vv. 14–25a); 7:20–29a, 34–36; 10:9; 11:1–24, 26–29, 31, 33, 35, 38–39, 42–45; 14:33–34; 15:31; 16:29]
27:1, 30

Numbers:

1–10 [H = 3:1, 11–13, 40–51; 5:1–4; 6:22–27; 9:1–14; 10:1–10]
12:16b
13:3–16, 17, 21
14:6–7, 38

17:1, 9 (Eng. 16:36, 44)
19:1
20: 7
21:10–11
22:1
25:16
26:4, 52
27:12–23
28–29 [H = 28:2b, 3a, 11a, 18b, 19a, 20b, 22b, 23b, 24a, 25, 26, 27a, 30b, 31; 29:1, 2a, 5b, 7, 8a, 12, 13a, 35, 36a, 39]
31:1, 7, 31, 41, 47
36:13

2

The Provenience and Intent of P

The Preexilic Provenience of P

IT IS STRIKING THAT THE BULK OF THE DEBATE REGARDING THE DATE and historical setting of P centers on the legislation in P, which is otherwise considered supplementary and even rejected in relation to determining the character of P. However, recognizing that the legal material in P constitutes the central component of the priestly composition affirms that the discussion rightly focuses on the legislation in P. The foundations for the modern debate regarding the date of composition for P lie in the works of Wellhausen and Kaufmann. Wellhausen claimed a late date for P (exilic, postexilic), while Kaufmann initiated rebuttal in favor of an early date for P (preexilic).

Wellhausen grounded his position with the observation that the sacred cult and the Mosaic law are not evident in the accounts of the settlement period or the period of the judges, and are only rarely evident in the accounts of the monarchic period. This is in contrast to the observation that in postexilic Judaism, Mosaic law suddenly emerges into prominence everywhere. This led to the conclusion that the author of P imitated the Mosaic period and concealed the true date of P's composition by keeping the historical setting of the writing strictly within the limitations of the wilderness period.[1] Wellhausen's understanding has been summarized as a progression of religious development, with P at its latest stage. In the literature, the acceptable place of sacrifice moved from multiple locations in Samuel's time, to exclusively at the Jerusalem temple in Josiah's day, and then exclusively to the tabernacle in Leviticus (which was understood as a retrojection of the Jerusalem

---

1. Wellhausen, *Prolegomena*, 5, 9.

temple back into the Mosaic period). Sacrifices evolved from a joyous fellowship meal to a complicated priestly ceremony. The festivals were originally held as agricultural celebrations which took place at varying times in accordance with the harvest in a particular area, while later, worship became centralized and the festivals were put on a fixed timetable. In earlier times priests were not required for offering sacrifices, while later, priests were required for sacrificial acts, and divisions of rank emerged among the priesthood (high priest, priest, Levite). Finally, it was perceived that in the early stages of Israel's religion, gifts to the priests were voluntary; while in later times, the priesthood required tithes, first fruits, and portions of sacrifices.[2] The more advanced forms of the cult were seen as being reflected in P and 1–2 Chronicles, as opposed to 1–2 Kings. Thus, P was given a postexilic date, closer to the time of the Chronicler.

A key element in Wellhausen's scheme centered around the identity and significance of the tabernacle. P was considered late because it reflected a fulfillment of the centralization agenda in D. Whereas D commanded the centralization of the cult, P presupposed the existence of such unity. Thus, P rested on the result which was the aim of D, clearly making P a later source. In addition, the tabernacle of the wilderness, depicted in P, was not considered a prototype of the Jerusalem temple (to appear in P's future), but rather, was understood to be a copy of the temple.[3]

Kaufmann countered Wellhausen's view by pointing out that the tabernacle could not be representative from the time of the Second Temple because the ark, cherubim, *urim* and *tummim* of the tabernacle are all missing from Second Temple accounts. Also, in regard to centralization, Kaufmann clarified that D required ritual slaughter to be performed at the central place of worship chosen by God. However, nonritual slaughter for food could take place anywhere (Deut 12:15–16). In contrast, P makes no such allowance. Therefore, if P and its tabernacle reflected the Second Temple period, those outside of Jerusalem could not have eaten meat without great difficulty.[4] Friedman explains:

2. Hildebrand, "Summary of Recent Findings," 129–30; Wellhausen, *Prolegomena*, 28–38 (locations of sacrifice), 59–71 (character of sacrifices), 83–107 (character of festivals), 141–52 (priestly divisions), 153–58 (priestly tithes).

3. Wellhausen, *Prolegomena*, 34–35, 37.

4. Kaufmann, *The Religion of Israel*, 180–84.

"Rather, in Kaufmann's view, the Priestly Tabernacle must correspond to the local sanctuaries of numerous Israelite towns, it reflects the opposite of centralization, and P therefore was composed prior to Josianic reform."[5] In addition, the paschal sacrifice described in Exod 12:2–20 depicts a home sacrifice, which must pre-date the centralization of D. Also, in contrast to Wellhausen's scheme, Kaufmann observed that Israel's neighbors in early times held festivals according to fixed times and with fixed rites, rather than according to agricultural spontaneity. Thus, similar practice was considered conceivable for early Israel.[6]

Contrary to the notion that priestly divisions were a late development, Kaufmann argued that the distinction between priests and Levites actually existed well before the exile.[7] Regarding the tribe of Levi, Kaufmann stated:

> The tribe was divided into two groups: priests—who served actively in temples, and Levites—who, though qualified, did not hold priestly office (Judges 17:12f.; I Kings 12:31). This division is pre-exilic.
> The various traditions regarding the origin of the Aaronic priesthood and the sacerdotal tribe of Levi agree on one point: from the beginning, there was a fundamental contrast between the priestly family (the Aaronids) and the tribe.[8]

The opposition between Aaron and the zealot Levites in the story of the golden calf (Exod 32 [JE]; Deut 9–10) served as evidence of early priestly divisions. This conflict eventually resulted in the separation of roles between the two groups. The Levites were distinguished by their role of having charge over and guarding the sacra, especially the ark.[9]

The role of the Levites involved the physical transport of the tabernacle. This role was performed until the tabernacle was no longer a mobile sanctuary, that is, until the permanent temple was built in Jerusalem.[10] Accordingly, Kaufmann stated that the Levites passed from the scene when the building of the sanctuary was complete (since their role of guarding the ark had ended). Kaufmann concluded, "By

---

5. Friedman, *Exile and Biblical Narrative*, 45.
6. Ibid.; Kaufmann, *Religion of Israel*, 178 (fixed festivals), 179 (paschal sacrifice).
7. Kaufmann, *Religion of Israel*, 193–200.
8. Ibid., 197.
9. Ibid., 197–98.
10. Milgrom, *Studies*, 24–29.

later times there were no Levites in the temples. Hence, they are scarcely mentioned in the pre-exilic literature. In common usage, Levite became synonymous with priest. Only the old priestly writings preserved a record of the ancient Levites."[11] A sudden reappearance of the Levites was prompted by the concerns of the restoration during the postexilic period. Foremost among these concerns was restoration of the proper form of the cult, for which the priestly writings served as a guide. In accordance with P's system, the Levites were employed to guard against the dangers of contact with the holy. Furthermore, in order to abide more fully by the Torah, Levites were needed for the restoration of the proper sacred hierarchy. Thus, the desire to fulfill the commands of the Torah motivated the renewal of the Levitical class in postexilic times. This occurred in spite of the fact that Levites had no proper function in the new community, at first.[12] Thus, Kaufmann explained the progression of the divisions among the priesthood, and demonstrated that priestly divisions were not limited to the exilic period and beyond.[13]

From such foundations established by the views of Wellhausen and Kaufmann, the debate over the date of P has continued to evolve. Arguments in defense of an early date for P appear to take more seriously the possibility that the sacrificial cult was actually performed as depicted in the Torah and for the purposes described in the Torah. This view seeks evidence for the earliest realistic practice of the cult as described in P and the earliest evidence for the existence of P's tabernacle, which serves as a central focus of the cult. In contrast, those who defend a late date tend to see in P a programmatic justification for the promulgation of the cult in later periods of Israel's history. Both views

---

11. Kaufmann, *Religion of Israel*, 199.

12. Ibid., 199–200. Kaufmann notes that the Levites were eventually assimilated into the singers and porters (ibid., 200, n. 14). I am grateful to Jacob Milgrom for pointing to 1 Chr 23:24–32 as evidence of the new role for Levites after there was no longer need for transporting the tabernacle (see especially v. 26). Accordingly, it should be clarified that the reason Levite became synonymous with priest after the temple was built was not because there were no Levites around the temples, as Kaufmann stated. Rather, the key to their absence in other literature at this time is found in the recognition that such literature is marked by common usage. That is, outside of the priestly sectarian documents, Levite became synonymous with priest.

13. Coote and Ord also recite a history of Priestly factions that dates back to the early monarchy. Coote and Ord, *In the Beginning*, 32–34.

require historical reconstruction which includes some speculation due to the lack of comprehensive historical data.

Arguments defending a late date typically understand the program of P as a response to the situation of the postexilic community and Persian rule. For example, J. G. Vink contends that the dispersion of Israel was the catalyst for an emphasis on the purity of the cultic community with Palestine as its central focus. Behind the program of P, and the related mission of Ezra, was the influential Persian policy to make Palestine a stronghold of its empire (based on religious [cultic] cohesion).[14] Gottwald explains that a restored and functioning Jewish community in Palestine following the exile required civil order and a legitimate cult. Civil order was provided by the Law under Persian imperial administration, and the cult was established by means of a system of sacrificial and ritual holiness. Due to the absence of political autonomy for the restored community, those who dominated the cult gained considerable power. Accordingly, the priests, who were custodians of the cult system, wielded political, economic, and ideological power. In the midst of priestly factions competing for leadership rights, the Aaronid priests emerged with firm political and economic power in part by certifying their claims through alignment with the P document.[15] In addition to serving as justification for priestly rights, P's final form was likely prompted by the postexilic rebuilding of the temple. Thus, Gottwald sees two important functions in P for the restoration community following the exile: 1) P served as "a suitable *charter for the reestablished temple*," and 2) it "served as *ideological justification for the power play of the Aaronic priests*."[16]

Levine adds that the attempt to rebuild the temple would naturally stimulate the desire to codify cultic procedure and project the contemporary situation into earlier accounts of Israelite history (in order to

14. Vink, "Date and Origin," 143–44.

15. Gottwald, *Hebrew Bible*, 461–62. Gottwald explains that due to the historical disruptions since the late seventh century, a number of priestly factions existed which competed for leadership rights over the renewed cult. In the end, one group emerged victorious, while lesser groups were relegated to secondary positions in cult administration. This victory was secured in part by gradations in priesthood instituted after the exile. These gradations were validated by tracing the limited legitimate priestly line to Aaron. All other priestly groups were lumped together as Levites and demoted to support roles within the cult.

16. Ibid., 479.

summon Mosaic authority). A motivating factor behind the program of the exiles was the desire to legitimize their right to re-establish and maintain control over former estates. He explains this phenomenon in relation to the use and significance of the term אחזה. This term is found only in P within the Pentateuch, and outside the Pentateuch only in material that is later than P (Josh 21–22; Ps 2:8; Ezek 40–48). The term describes a "holding" granted to a non-native tenant. Leviticus 25 and 27, which contain laws regarding the rights of those who own such holdings, can be understood as legitimation of the claims of the returning exiles over the holdings which they were now reappropriating. Levine claims that such a system of land tenure was surely incompatible with the period of the monarchy in Israel. Thus, the priestly writers projected the system back into the pre-monarchical tribal period when God was the only king. Yet, in actuality, the period of conquest and settlement did not fit such a system of land tenure any more than did the monarchic period. Therefore, Levine concludes that the system of land tenure reflected by the term אחזה is most appropriate to the period of the return of the exiles. The priestly writers translated the propaganda of the Edict of Cyrus into theology, and thereby legitimized the reappropriation of estates with religious authority.[17]

Responses to such arguments that support a late date for P highlight the speculative nature of the debate. In contrast to those who see a late programmatic purpose in P, the concern for the purity of the cultic community need not be restricted to the postexilic period and the rebuilding of the temple. It is equally plausible, that the purity of the cult would have been emphasized during the establishment of the first temple and as part of an original concern to document cultic procedures. Thus, P can be considered the charter for the first temple rather than the second temple. As for the influence of Persian policy, it is understandable that the Persians would not want to grant political sovereignty to the returning exiles, and thus, would lend stability to the area by promoting unity based on the cult. However, such a policy may have drawn upon existing and previously documented traditions of the cult, rather than newly generated writings. That is, Persian policy may have appealed to existing religious traditions from the history of Israel as a basis for cohesion.

17. Levine, "Late Language in the Priestly Source," 71–82. It should be noted that Levine argues that the legal sections of Ezek 40–48 are postexilic (ibid., 72).

Likewise, the contention that P represents the *"ideological justification for the power play of the Aaronic priests"* appears inconclusive. Such a view of P interprets the cultic regulations as a system of temple taxes and sacrificial tribute appropriated by the Aaronic priests for the (corrupt) purpose of promoting their own wealth and power. In contrast, it may just as readily be argued that P represents a genuine charter for legitimate cultic procedure and is concerned with maintaining purity for the temple and among the people of God.

In response to Levine's argument regarding the term אחזה, Avi Hurvitz credits M. Paran with the observation that a distinction in meaning can be made between the use of אחזה in P and its use in Chronicles–Nehemiah. In P, the term carries a rural, agricultural connotation, and is accompanied by ארץ and שׂדה. In contrast, in Nehemiah and Chronicles, the term maintains a close affinity to עיר.[18] Hurvitz notes that, because Levine did not take this distinction into account, his interpretation of the use of the term אחזה is highly suspect.[19] Furthermore, Levine's contention that the system of land tenure implied by the term אחזה (as expressed in Lev 25 and 27) is most appropriate to the postexilic situation is not conclusive, since an equally plausible (and perhaps less strained) application is evident. Knohl sees the laws of Lev 25 as part of "a wide-ranging agrarian and social reform whose aim is the rehabilitation of a social class whose financial status had been eroded and who had been uprooted from their land."[20] The need for such reform, along with other concerns addressed by the Holiness Code, can be attached to the situation prominent during the reigns of Ahaz and Hezekiah. The prophets who prophesied during this period demonstrate clear evidence of social and financial polarization which led to the uprooting of farmers from their land, with some being sold into slavery. In addition, during this period, the northern kingdom of Israel

---

18. Hurvitz, "Dating the Priestly Source," 95–96, citing M. Paran, "Literary Features of the Priestly Code—Stylistic Patterns, Idioms, and Structures" (Ph.D. diss., Hebrew University of Jerusalem, 1983), 218–19. Furthermore, Hurvitz contends that the term אחזה can be understood as a priestly technical term, used exclusively in priestly circles. The equivalent of אחזה found in early and late non-priestly writings is נהלה ("inheritance," "property"). Therefore, the absence of אחזה from non-priestly, pre-exilic texts does not necessarily imply that it is a late term. Hurvitz, "Dating the Priestly Source," 91–92.

19. Hurvitz, "Dating the Priestly Source," 97 n. 42.

20. Knohl, *Sanctuary*, 205.

collapsed with the result that many were exiled from their land.²¹ The program reflected in Lev 25 represents a reform which eliminates "all slavery within Israelite society and assures the agrarian rehabilitation of dispossessed farmers."²² Accordingly, the system of land tenure implied by the term אחזה may be understood in relation to the situation during the period of Hezekiah.

Hildebrand supplements the arguments for an early date for P, with the observation that the danger of approaching the sanctum, which is frequently referred to in P, is also reflected in early sources (1 Sam 6:19–20; 2 Sam 6:6–9). In addition, the Ugaritic epic of King Keret describes the dwelling place of El in similar terms as P's tabernacle, that is, "letter for letter the same as in Hebrew (*mškn* and *'hl*)."²³ Even the description of the physical structure was similar, thereby making a structure such as P's tabernacle appropriate to antiquity.²⁴

In response to the foundational concern that the legislation in P is not reflected in preexilic biblical works, Menahem Haran suggests that P did not become exposed to the public until Ezra's time. He asserts that P was composed in the preexilic period, but was publicized as part of the complete Pentateuch by Ezra. The priesthood had a unique quality in preexilic times as a "distinctive, semi-esoteric group." Thus, P lived a sectarian existence before Ezra (limited to the sect of the priesthood). It existed in the backstage of history and remained an isolated property in the hands of the priestly circle, making little or no impression on the community outside of that circle.²⁵ Ezra's activity, however, brought P into public exposure. "When Ezra turned the canonized Torah into the foundation-stone of Jewish life, he included in this Torah 'hidden scrolls'—priestly writings which by then had already been in existence for almost three centuries."²⁶

In an earlier article, Chayim Cohen cited an interesting Akkadian text which supports the theory of secret priestly scrolls. He pointed to

---

21. Knohl, *Sanctuary*, 206.

22. Ibid., 217.

23. Hildebrand, "Summary of Recent Findings," 131; cf. Ginsberg, *The Legend of King Keret*, 23 (KRT B, Col. 3, ll. 18–19).

24. Hildebrand, "Summary of Recent Findings," 131.

25. Haran, *Temples*, 8, 11–12; idem, "Behind the Scenes," 327–28; and idem, "Character of the Priestly Source," 135–37.

26. Haran, *Temples*, 12.

an Akkadian parallel which had been used in support of an argument acknowledging P as the special sole possession of the priests in the preexilic period.[27] Cohen cites a certain colophon of three lines (ll.33–35), which have been translated as follows:

> 21 is their number; secrets of Esagil.
> Whoever is for Bel must not show
> (them to anyone) but the *šešgallu*
> priest of the Temple Etusa.[28]

This colophon instructs the priests to keep secret the contents of the text. Cohen lists the following additional parallels between the Akkadian text and P.

1. Both contain a call to artisans for temple work (ll.190–195; Exod 36:2–3).
2. Both texts contain instructions for fashioning objects for the temple (ll.201–8; Exod 25:17–21).
3. Both contain cleansing rituals (ll.353–63; Lev 16:15–16, 27–28, 30).[29]

The conclusion implied by this data is that P shares the same genre of ritual texts as the Akkadian tablet. Thus, since the Akkadian text was kept secret, it is possible that P could have existed in the preexilic period and was also kept secret.[30]

---

27. Cohen, "Was P Secret," 39. The argument is based on Kaufmann's contention that the legal corpora of the Torah were composed and fixed prior to the formation of the Torah book. Kaufmann argued that the dividing line between the composition of the Torah law codes and the beginning of their incorporation into the Torah as a whole was the period of Josiah's reform inspired by Deuteronomy. Later, the crisis of the exilic period prompted the culmination of the task begun by the Deuteronomist, i.e., the compilation of the law corpora into the Torah book. Kaufmann, *Religion of Israel*, 172, 210–11.

28. Cohen, "Was P Secret," 40.

29. Ibid., 41–43. See "Temple Program for the New Year's Festival at Babylon," translated by A. Sachs (*ANET*, 331–34).

30. Cohen, "Was P Secret," 44. P may not have been intentionally kept hidden or secret (or utopian in character) in the preexilic period. However, it was predominantly a concern of the priesthood and was expressed in priestly technical language. Thus, originally serving as a priestly legal manual, P would not have had noticeable impact upon the common populace or in common historiography.

Zevit points to socio-historical evidence which adds to the growing argument for the preexilic date of the priestly material. The priestly tithe laws of Num 18:21–28 provided for the needs of the Levites who worked as judges, administrators, cultic functionaries, and laborers, but had no agricultural lands. Nine-tenths of the annual tithe was kept by the Levites and the remaining tenth was given to the priests by the Levites.[31] This tithe law appears in contrast to that of Deut 14:27–29 which provides a tithe to the Levites only every third year. Noth concluded that the tithe law of Num 18 "was practiced in a late period which can no longer be precisely determined."[32] However, Zevit clarifies that the tithe law of Deut 14:27–29 is understood in relation to the Josianic reform. The reduced status for the Levites may be explained by developments over a prolonged period, including: 1) the reduced territory over which the monarchy and clergy in Jerusalem had control after the successful revolt of the northern tribes, 2) the resultant loss of many Levitical cities (after the defection of the northern tribes), and 3) the closing of the high places in the period of the Josianic reform. This reconstruction implies that the P tithe law of Num 18 derives from a period at least *prior* to Josiah's reform (i.e., before the reduction of Levitical status). This is proven if it *cannot* be shown with equal plausibility that the tithe law could be understood within the history of the postexilic period. By pointing to the continued reduction in status of the Levites into the postexilic period, Zevit demonstrates that indeed the Levitical tithe law of Num 18 is *not* equally applicable to the postexilic period, and therefore must be understood within the early (preexilic) setting.[33]

Literary comparison between P and other biblical books provides further evidence in support of an early date for P. Hildebrand points to evidence which implies an early date when P is compared to the biblical Historical Books. Priestly expressions reflected in Josh 14:1—21:40, which contains a similar arrangement of material as that in Num 26–36, imply that P may have preceded the Joshua text. In addition, 1 Sam 14:32–35 refers back to Lev 19:26, and priestly ritual expressions are found in 2 Kgs 12:5–17 (Eng., 12:4–16) and in 2 Kgs 16:10–16. These

---

31. Zevit, "Converging Lines of Evidence," 485–87.
32. Noth, *Numbers*, 137.
33. Zevit, "Converging Lines of Evidence," 487–92.

examples suggest that the writer(s) of such texts in Samuel and Kings had access to P accounts which must have been extant earlier.[34]

Ties between P and Ezekiel have long been recognized by scholars. The similarities between the two works suggest that one is dependent upon the other. Friedman contends that it is more natural to expect that a prophet would quote from the Torah, rather than the reverse. Consequently, he cites examples from Ezekiel which refer back to Torah (Ezek 7:26; 22:26; 43:11; 44:5, 23). Friedman also observes that it is striking that Ezekiel's temple design appears to have no impact on P, despite P's central concern for the temple. This implies that Ezekiel must have been later than P.[35] Hildebrand adds more specifically that passages in Ezekiel which appear to refer to passages in Leviticus include: Ezek 22:26 which alludes to Lev 10:10, Ezek 20:11 which alludes to Lev 18:5, and portions of Ezek 34 which allude to some passages in Lev 26. This would require that P was extant earlier than Ezekiel.[36] Furthermore, despite the common assertion that Ezek 40–48 contains the law code from which P is an outgrowth, Haran argues that the historical cross-section represented in P is earlier than Ezek 40–48, and P demonstrates more originality than Ezek 40–48. Thus, Ezek 40–48 appears as an outgrowth of P.[37] Finally, Klostermann points to the dependence of Ezek 20 upon Lev 26 with the observation that Ezek 20:23 relates that the Lord had previously sworn to the children of Israel in the wilderness that they would be scattered among the nations. In light of how Ezek 20 appears to summarize much of the Holiness Code, v. 23 appears to be a clear reference to Lev 26 (see especially v. 33). He concludes that Ezekiel and his audience must have had the Holiness Code (of the priestly literature) in hand.[38]

In relation to Deuteronomy, Friedman observes that P at times pursues the same interests as the Deuteronomistic tradition; while at other times, P engages in polemic against D. Therefore, it appears that P compositions mostly occurred concurrently with the Deuteronomistic

---

34. Hildebrand, "Summary of Recent Findings," 137.
35. Friedman, *Exile and Biblical Narrative*, 61, 63–64.
36. Hildebrand, "Summary of Recent Findings," 136.
37. Haran, "Behind the Scenes," 327.
38. Klostermann, *Der Pentateuch*, 385.

composition.³⁹ Hildebrand also cites traces of priestly views in D, but interprets them, not as concurrent with, but rather, as preceding D. For example, Deut 24:8–9 appears to allude to priestly law regarding leprosy in Lev 13–14. Also, the statements in Deut 4:16–18, 25, 32 appear to reflect earlier priestly idioms.⁴⁰ Milgrom strengthens this line of argument by stating that "there is not one demonstrable case in which P shows the influence of D."⁴¹ In contrast, D certainly reflects the prior existence of P. Milgrom explains that the phrase כאשר צוה/נשׁבע/דבר ("according as he commanded/swore/spoke") is the formula used in D to indicate its source. Three of the cases in which this phrase is used, point to P as the source: 1) Deut 24:8 points to Lev 13–14; 2) Deut 29:12 (Eng., 29:13) points to Gen 17:7–8; Exod 6:7; Lev 26:12; and 3) Deut 10:9; 18:1–2 point to Num 18:20.⁴² Furthermore, D's dependence upon P can be seen in relation to D's listing of the dietary laws. Milgrom contends, "finally, all eighteen verses of D's diet laws can be shown to be a borrowing from and alteration of Lev 11 . . . , which proves that D had before it the present MT of Lev 11."⁴³ Zevit offers further evidence for the priority of P with the observation that Deut 1:20–46 reflects the P redaction of the spy story in Num 13–14 and its later summary in Num 32:8–13. He contends that a similar situation can be found in other narratives in Deuteronomy which parallel JEP accounts.⁴⁴

Proponents of an early date for P strengthen the argument by means of more reliable *linguistic* data and thereby tip the scales in fa-

---

39. Friedman, *Exile and Biblical Narrative*, 65–70.

40. Hildebrand, "Summary of Recent Findings," 136–37.

41. Milgrom, *Leviticus 1–16*, 9.

42. Ibid., 9. Levine counters Milgrom's argument with the contention that the formula which Milgrom claims points to a prior source, merely reflects a basic doctrine of priestly ideology, i.e., that all of the instructions of the cult were directly commanded by God. Therefore, the formula כאשר צוה/נשׁבע/דבר is actually integral to priestly ideology and does not point to earlier sources. Thus, it could be argued that what Milgrom sees as prior sources may actually be later compositions intended to supply foundation or justification for earlier instructions. Levine, review of *Leviticus 1–16*, 282–83. If Levine's response is accepted, it throws the discussion back into a stalemate at this juncture. That is, one might argue either direction: D reflects dependency on P based on the phrase in D which points to its prior source; or P represents a later response to D created to provide justification for instructions in D.

43. Milgrom, *Leviticus 1–16*, 10.

44. Zevit, "Converging Lines of Evidence," 503–10.

vor of recognizing the composition of P in relation to preexilic times.⁴⁵ After establishing a relative date of composition based on terminology, the pursuit of historical reconstruction can take place with greater confidence.

Before describing the significant work which has been done on priestly terminology, two challenges to the linguistic data must be addressed. Cross argues that archaizing tendencies in P demonstrate its date within the exilic period. He contends that a number of archaic terms appear in early biblical documents, fall out of use for a period of time, and then reappear in P with a more narrow technical meaning. Some such terms also reappear in other exilic materials.⁴⁶ Cross concludes in relation to these archaisms in P that: "inasmuch as these terms take on new or restricted force in Priestly usage, we can distinguish the archaic from the archaizing and pursue Priestly influences."⁴⁷ For example, Cross cites the use of שכן and משכן as technical terms in P referring to the Glory or covenant presence of the Lord. This usage is also found in Ezekiel and in the sixth century material of Zechariah. This can be distinguished from the original archaic use of שכן in reference to the "tenting of" the Lord (Deut 33:12, 16; 1 Kgs 8:12; Ps 68:17, 19). Similarly, other priestly technical terms found in Ezekiel and Second Isaiah are used to augment this argument that P should be dated to the sixth century: כבוד ("glory"), נשיא ("leader"), שדי (proper name), ברא ("to create"), and תהו ("chaos").⁴⁸

Hurvitz provides three main arguments which refute the accusation of archaizing on the part of the priestly writer. He points out first, that the technicalities of P make the use of obscure archaisms inconceivable. The realm of the cult laws demanded concrete and accurate terminology. The use of outdated terms which were not current in the contemporary language would result in ambiguity and confusion for

---

45. Milgrom explains that linguistic data provides the most trustworthy approach to identifying the date of P. Historical studies, involving historical reconstruction, rely too heavily on speculation, while comparative studies are unable to demonstrate exactly when possibly early priestly institutions among neighboring cultures may have been introduced into Israel. Studies based on terminology, however, provide control through the datable standard of the life span of priestly terms. Milgrom, *Leviticus 1–16*, 3; also idem, *Leviticus 17–22*, 1334.

46. Cross, *Canaanite Myth*, 322–23.

47. Ibid., 323.

48. Ibid., 323–24.

the reader. The second point reveals the inconsistency in the argument of those who hold a late date for P and accuse P of archaizing. If P is late, used archaic language, and avoided all contemporary priestly terms, then P would be isolated from the other exilic and postexilic works. This contradicts, however, the thesis of those who argue for a late date based on the affinities which P demonstrates with other late literature. Consequently, how could P be late due to linguistic affinities with other late works and, at the same time, be filled with archaisms, and thereby, lack linguistic affinities with other late works?[49] Finally, even if P did intend to write in archaic style, it is difficult to believe that P was so successful in removing every trace of contemporary language from the work. This is based on the observation that, "in the 100 or so chapters of the Priestly sections in the Pentateuch, no one has so far shown unequivocal instances of linguistically late elements—either in technical or narrative contexts."[50]

Milgrom adds to the refutation of archaizing in P with evidence regarding the use of the term עבדה. This term denotes "physical labor" in P, but in postexilic texts its meaning changes to "cultic service." The term עבדה is applied in P to the Levites. Their עבדה is confined to the physical transport of the tabernacle. The Levites, however, are forbidden, on pain of death, to officiate in the service of the cult (Num. 18:3). In contrast, postexilic texts confine the application of the term עבדה to priests alone. This is because for postexilic texts the term now means "cultic service." Thus, if P were late and guilty of archaizing, it would never apply עבדה to Levites as it does, for Levites are forbidden to officiate in cultic service.[51] Milgrom sums up the contradiction as follows: "No postexilic writer could have used 'ăbōdâ in its earlier sense of 'physical labor' when it flatly contradicted the meaning it had in his own time. His readers would have been confused, nay shocked, to learn that 'cultic service,' exclusively the prerogative of priests and fatal to non-priests, had been assigned to the Levites."[52]

---

49. Hurvitz, "Evidence of Language," 50–51.

50. Ibid., 52.

51. Milgrom, *Studies*, x; idem, *Leviticus 1–16*, 7; idem, "Priestly Source," 459.

52. Milgrom, *Leviticus 1–16*, 8; see also idem, "Priestly Source," 459; and idem, *Studies*, x. For the detailed research concerning the occurrences of עבדה in the Bible, see: ibid., 18–45.

A second challenge to linguistic arguments in support of an early date for P comes in the form of Polzin's study of the grammar and syntax of priestly materials.[53] Through the investigation of grammatical-syntactic features, Polzin developed a profile for "Late Biblical Hebrew" (i.e., "LBH," postexilic Hebrew) based on characteristics taken from Chronicles, and a contrasting profile for "Classical Biblical Hebrew" ("CBH") based on the linguistic features of a sampling of JE, the court history in 2 Samuel and 1 Kings, and a sampling of Dtr. After developing this second profile, Polzin concluded that, not only did these three sets of material present a homogeneous linguistic picture, they also stood in marked contrast to the LBH of the Chronicler. Next, Polzin pursued an analysis of P in order to plot its chronological location in relation to the two linguistic profiles representing LBH and CBH. His analysis of P revealed four key grammatical-syntactic features which clearly belong to LBH as represented by the Chronicler. At the same time, Polzin discovered two unique features in P which are not typical of either LBH or CBH. Finally, the analysis showed that P also demonstrated seven features which corresponded specifically to CBH. Polzin's interpretation of this data is that P demonstrates signs of linguistic change reflecting a move away from CBH. The four features in P which correspond to LBH indicate that P must be later than JE, the Court History and Dtr.[54] The four linguistic features which indicate a move within P toward LBH are as follows:

---

53. The discussion in this chapter has focused predominantly on arguments related to the legislation in P. In contrast, Polzin's analysis is based on narrative material in P. Nevertheless, since I also view the narrative in P as preexilic, Polzin's argument will be evaluated here in the midst of the linguistic discussion.

54. Polzin, *Late Biblical Hebrew*, 15–16, 27–84, 90–96.

1. Use of the prospective pronominal suffix plus l^e plus substantive, to show possession.
2. Preference for construing singular collectives in the plural.⁵⁵
3. A mixture of 3fpl suffixes ending in *mem* or *nun*. (A feature of LBH is that 3fpl suffixes show a merging with 3mpl suffixes.)
4. Density of the use of the infinitive absolute. (Like 1–2 Chronicles, P uses the infinitive absolute much less frequently than JE, the Court History, or Dtr.)⁵⁶

Polzin concludes from this data that, "These four features illustrate the beginnings of a transition from classical BH, as we know it from JE, the Court History, and Dtr., toward LBH as it is exemplified in the Chronicler's language."⁵⁷ Polzin's data and his interpretation of it place the language of P between that of JE, the Court History, and Dtr., and that of the language of 1–2 Chronicles. P represents a period in which the language was in transition. This period roughly corresponds to that of the exile.

In response to Polzin's grammatical-syntactic analysis, Rendsburg presents a convincing rebuttal. Specifically, Rendsburg disputes the evidence of the four features which Polzin claims link P to LBH. The first feature, regarding the use of the prospective pronominal suffix plus le plus substantive to show possession, is not a characteristic of LBH.

---

55. Polzin states that the Chronicler almost always construes singular collectives as plurals. He then cites the following chart of data for evidence showing that P corresponds to the Chronicler in this feature:

Corpus	Ratio (collectives construed as *singular: plural*)
JE	7:2
Court History	27:23
Dtr.	4:3
P^g	9:10

Polzin, *Late Biblical Hebrew*, 98. It can be seen that P hardly corresponds to the Chronicler. Admittedly JE, the Court History, and Dtr all construe collectives as singulars slightly more often than as plurals, while P construes them slightly more often as plurals. However, P certainly does not correspond to the claim that the Chronicler almost always construes collectives as plurals. Rather, the ratio appears more to be 50/50, which corresponds more closely to JE, the Court History, and Dtr.

56. Ibid., 98–99.
57. Ibid., 99.

This feature appears in Phoenician, Aramaic, Akkadian, and Ethiopic texts. Furthermore, Polzin neglects to cite many other instances of this feature in CBH, including a number of early passages. Thus, Rendsburg concludes that this feature is characteristic of both early and late Biblical Hebrew, and does not necessarily link P to LBH.[58]

The second feature, regarding the preference for construing singular collectives in the plural, is likewise a weak argument for linking P to LBH. Polzin himself cites evidence of the use of this feature in CBH. The Chronicler's preference for this feature may simply be a matter of personal style. Even Polzin's own chart listing the occurrence of this feature demonstrates that P aligns more with the early literature as opposed to the Chronicler's work.[59]

The third feature, regarding 3rd fem. pl. suffixes ending in *mem*, actually occurs throughout the Bible. Rendsburg cites evidence of its use throughout the Pentateuch, in Dtr., and the Prophets. Thus, this feature is also not a characteristic of LBH.[60]

Finally, Polzin claims that the decreased use of the infinitive absolute is a characteristic of LBH on the basis of its limited use in 1–2 Chronicles. However, Polzin admits that the book of Esther, contemporary to 1–2 Chronicles, demonstrates frequent use of the infinitive absolute. He explains that this is an archaizing tendency on the part of the author of Esther, and that 1–2 Chronicles represents living LBH. Rendsburg counters, however, that 1–2 Chronicles is based on earlier material while Esther is clearly from the Persian period. Therefore, it could just as easily be concluded that Esther represents living LBH, and 1–2 Chronicles is guilty of archaizing. Thus, this feature also fails to link P to LBH.[61]

Having refuted the above challenges, a look at the distinct terminology in P and its distribution in the Hebrew Bible consolidates the argument for an early date of composition. To begin, Rendsburg offers three points of linguistic evidence which point to an early date for P:

---

58. Rendsburg, "Late Biblical Hebrew," 67.
59. Ibid., 67, 74; see chart in note above.
60. Ibid., 69.
61. Ibid., 67–68.

1. Use of the "third person common dual suffix—(h)m." Thirty of the 43 occurrences of this feature appear in early works. P has the highest concentration of any single work with 9 occurrences. The dual survives from Egypto-Semitic which is on its way out. P's frequent use of the dual places it early.
2. Use of the "third person common singular independent pronoun הוא." The epicene הוא is used only in the Pentateuch (when used for the feminine pronoun, it is pointed הִוא). P aligns itself with the rest of the Pentateuch by using this unique grammatical feature.
3. The absence of borrowed Persian words in P. The Chronicler's work and Daniel contain a number of borrowed Persian words. P and the Pentateuch contain none of these borrowings.[62]

Hurvitz adds a study of nine terms or word pairs which distinguish P from the late works of 1–2 Chronicles, Ezra, Nehemiah, and Ezekiel. Following is a summation of this research.

1. יחש ("genealogy") and התיחש ("to be enrolled by genealogy") appear only in 1–2 Chronicles, Ezra, and Nehemiah, while they are absent from preexilic biblical literature and from P. In similar contexts P uses alternative terms deriving from the roots ספר, שפח, ילד, פקד.
2. The Chronicler makes use of the term התנדב ("to offer freewill offerings"), while P never employs the hithpael form of this root.
3. The term חפה ("to cover") is found in 1–2 Chronicles and rabbinic literature as a parallel to the priestly term צפה ("to overlay"). In addition, temple and tabernacle descriptions in 1–2 Kings and in the Pentateuch use צפה to the exclusion of חפה.
4. The term בוץ ("byssus", a fine linen) is restricted to the late writings, while the equivalent term שש appears in early and late texts. In the early literature, שש appears in contexts corresponding to those where בוץ would be expected. שש (used in P) turns out to be the older equivalent of בוץ.
5. Ezekiel and 1–2 Chronicles use the technical term הדיח in reference to washing sacrifices. This term never appears in P, but

62. Ibid., 77–80.

rather the term רחץ appears in its place. The exclusive use of רחץ in P reflects an age prior to the term's absorption into its later equivalent, הדיח.

6. The genealogical formula מ. . . ומעלה ("from *x* years old and upward") is found in P and sometimes in 1–2 Chronicles and Ezra. However, P is unaware of the later deviation to this formula which appears only in 1–2 Chronicles and Ezekiel, that is, מ. . . ולמעלה.

7. The formula סביב סביב ("around") is found only in Ezekiel and 1–2 Chronicles in the Bible. The preexilic works of 1–2 Samuel and 1–2 Kings use the shorter term סביב in place of the longer formula. P uses the shorter preexilic term exclusively.

8. The term עזרה ("enclosure") is used only in 1–2 Chronicles and Ezekiel in the Bible, and appears to have gradually replaced the earlier term חצר which appears in P, as well as 1–2 Kings, 1–2 Chronicles, and Ezekiel.

9. The expression קבל + דם is found in 1–2 Chronicles and in the Mishnah. It is the technical formula used for "catching the blood of the sacrifice." P, however, is unfamiliar with this expression and uses instead the expression לקח + דם.[63]

In another article, Hurvitz adds the evidence of the priestly term עדה ("congregation"), which appears in biblical texts indicative of the preexilic period.[64]

This research demonstrates a linguistic distinction between P and the works of Ezekiel, 1–2 Chronicles, Ezra, and Nehemiah. Though Ezekiel, 1–2 Chronicles, Ezra, and Nehemiah may use terminology from earlier times as well as later terms, P exclusively prefers the earlier terminology. Thus, P is independent of the later literature and is unaware of the "special priestly terminology characteristic of the exilic and post-exilic writings."[65]

Milgrom adds to the linguistic evidence gathered by Hurvitz and strengthens the argument for an early date for P. He reinforces the argument that עדה is an early term by observing that it is replaced in later literature by its synonym קהל ("congregation," "assembly").

---

63. Hurvitz, "Evidence of Language," 26–45.
64. Hurvitz, "Language of the Priestly Source," 87.
65. Hurvitz, "Evidence of Language," 47.

Milgrom states: "indisputably post-Biblical books totally eschew עדה in favor of קהל."[66] Within the biblical corpus, קהל appears throughout, while עדה, present in preexilic texts, disappears from postexilic biblical texts. Significantly, עדה does not appear at all in Deuteronomy or in Ezekiel. Furthermore, עדה carries the technical meaning "the people's assembly," and appears as a political body with legislative and judicial functions. In contrast, in preexilic texts, קהל does not appear with this technical sense, and never participates in legislative or judicial functions. However, in postexilic literature, קהל replaces עדה in its technical usage. This is evident in Ezekiel where קהל is used twelve times with the technical meaning of עדה.[67] In some of the Ezekiel passages קהל serves a judicial function, as only עדה did in preexilic texts. The technical use of קהל becomes predominant in postexilic literature, and thus, takes over the function previously attributed to עדה.[68] This leads to the conclusion that עדה eventually disappeared from linguistic usage, and that "the עדה of pre-exilic texts has been transferred to the post-exilic קהל."[69] Milgrom dates the use of the technical term עדה in relation to the period of the judges. "The last incident where all of Israel is led by the עדה is the internecine war with Benjamin (Judg 19–21), a time when Israel had no national leader or שופט."[70] After that point, עדה appears only twice more, in the book of 1 Kings (1 Kgs 8:5; 12:20). The first reference is suspect, and in this instance the עדה only serves in an honorary capacity. The second reference in 1 Kings describes an עדה of the northern tribes who were not bound by the dynastic principle of the monarchy of the Davidic covenant. Thus, עדה was a body which functioned during the tribal period in order to address trans-tribal issues. However, when the monarchy was established there was no longer a need for the עדה, which subsequently disappeared.[71]

---

66. Milgrom, *Studies*, 4.

67. Milgrom, *Studies*, 4–9. Milgrom lists Ezek 16:40; 17:17; 23:3, 46, 47; 32:22, 23; 38:4, 7, 13, 16.

68. Ibid., 9–10. Milgrom cites the judicial practice of city officials (קהל) participating in the hand-laying ceremony in 2 Chr 29:20, 23, 28, 30, 31. In P, this function is carried out by the זקני העדה (Lev 4:15).

69. Ibid., 10.

70. Ibid.

71. Ibid., 11.

A similar pattern of usage can be seen with respect to the synonyms used to refer to "the tribe," that is, מטה and שבט. Having presented the same type of meticulous research, Milgrom concludes by associating the phenomenon of this word pair with the previous one. He states, "the conclusion is therefore inescapable that by the end of the first commonwealth מטה fell out of the linguistic currency and שבט was exclusively employed."[72] The term מטה was the authentic word used for the tribe during the premonarchic period. Taken together, מטה and עדה are absent from biblical literature dated after the ninth century.[73]

The same pattern can be seen in the word pair, אלף (and its equivalent בית אבות) and משפחה, synonyms for "clan" or "family." The leadership of Israel is only associated with אלף, as with מטה and עדה of the previous word pairs. Thus, אלף is the more ancient term.[74] Milgrom draws the conclusion that the use of these three distinctively priestly terms (אלף and מטה and עדה) reflects premonarchic times:

> Each priestly term is attested only in early pre-exilic texts and is found in construct with Israel's leaders, an indication that it reflects a living institution, whereas its synonym is non-specific and becomes a technical term only after the priestly term disappears from use. Since these three synonym pairs refer to societal units of early Israel, it is safe to conclude that they reflect Israel's socio-political organization in pre-monarchic times.[75]

Milgrom continues the argument with a word pair associated with the priestly doctrine of repentance. He argues that P expresses repentance with the term אשם, rather than the prophetic term שוב. The distribution and use of these two terms leads to the conclusion that P devised its terminology with respect to its doctrine of repentance before the term שוב became the standard idiom for repentance. Therefore, priestly legislation concerning sacrificial expiation (which has repentance at its base) is preexilic in origin.[76]

As evidence of the distribution of this word pair, Milgrom observes that the term שוב with the meaning of repent does not occur in

---

72. Ibid., 13.
73. Ibid. 14–15.
74. Ibid., 15.
75. Ibid., ix.
76. Ibid., x; and Milgrom, *Leviticus 1–16*, 5.

early narratives at all. However, the term occurs often with this meaning in prophetic and postexilic works. It is clear therefore, that שוב was the standard word for "repent" in postexilic times. In contrast, P uses other synonyms, such as אשם, for repentance, but not שוב. Furthermore, אשם is found only in P.[77]

As additional evidence of the antiquity of this term, Milgrom explains that the priestly doctrine of repentance corresponds with that of other early literature. According to the early literature, repentance cannot fully erase sin and its consequences. Likewise P maintains that repentance mitigates the force of a deliberate sin, converting it to an unintentional sin, but still requires sacrificial expiation. This is a step removed from the prophetic doctrine in which repentance can actually wipe out sin. Thus, the priestly law describes a time before the prophetic concepts penetrated the cult. Milgrom concludes that the sacrificial system in P must be preexilic.[78]

The cumulative effect of the evidence gathered by Hurvitz and Milgrom regarding the distribution of the above word pairs comprises a strong argument for the antiquity of P. The impact of this evidence is even greater in consideration of Milgrom's contention that there are a total of twenty-two such word pairs as those discussed here. "The replacement of P terms by others indicates not only that the former belong to an earlier age but also that their cumulative effect—twenty-two attestations in all—makes it unlikely that their absence in late Hebrew is purely an accident."[79]

---

77. Milgrom, *Studies*, 63–64. It should be noted that Ezekiel is included among the prophetic texts to which Milgrom points regarding the use of שוב with the meaning of repent. Milgrom, *Leviticus 1–16*, 5. The significance of this is that Ezekiel shares with P the sociological milieu of priests. Thus, the counter argument, that the distinction in the terminology for "repentance" between P and (later) prophetic works is based on diverse sociological settings rather than on historical development of terminology, is refuted.

78. Milgrom, *Studies*, 64–65. For the detailed argument regarding the priestly doctrine of repentance and the corresponding concepts in the early literature, see ibid., 47–62.

79. Milgrom, *Leviticus 1–16*, 5. Milgrom further adds to the *terminological* argument for an early date, evidence regarding the antiquity of priestly *institutions*. See Milgrom, *Numbers*, xxxiii–xxxv.

Sanctuary and Cult Initiated at Shiloh

The predominant identification of God as YHWH in the priestly legislation suggests that an understanding of the origins of YHWH worship may lend further insight into the provenience of P. Upon reviewing extra-biblical evidence, Karel van der Toorn concludes that, outside of Israel, there is no persuasive indication that YHWH was worshipped in the West Semitic world.[80] He then points to a number of biblical texts that preserve the memory of a topographical link between YHWH and the mountain area south of Edom.

> In these theophany texts Yahweh is said to come from Seir, from "the field(s) of Edom" (Judg. v 4; note the correction in Ps. lxviii 8 [ET lxviii 7]). According to the Blessing of Moses Yahweh comes from Sinai, "dawns from" Seir, and "shines forth" from Mount Paran (Deut. xxxiii 2). Elsewhere, he is said to come from Teman and Mount Paran (Hab. iii 3). The reference to "Yahweh of Teman" in one of the Kuntillet 'Ajrud inscriptions is an extra-biblical confirmation of the topographical connection.[81]

Van der Toorn contends that all of the places named in these texts are in or near Edom, and he points to additional extra-biblical evidence supporting this topographical connection. Such evidence led van der Toorn to the conclusion that "*Yahweh* became a major god in Israel as a result of Edomite-Midianite influence."[82] In an earlier work, Cross does not press the same conclusion but does state in regard to the name YHWH: "The earliest appearance of what appears to be the independent form of the name is found in fourteenth and thirteenth-century lists of South Palestinian (Edomite) place-names."[83] Furthermore, Cross suggests that YHWH may have been originally a cultic name of the patron deity of "the Midianite League in the south."[84]

---

80. Van der Toorn, "Saul and Israelite Religion," 537–38. He takes issue with Stephanie Dalley's suggestion (and others) that YHWH was worshiped as a major God in Hamath in the eighth century (Dalley, "Yahweh in Hamath," 21–32). Van der Toorn, "Saul and Israelite Religion," 537 n. 49.

81. Van der Toorn, "Saul and Israelite Religion," 538; see also, Emerton, "New Light on Israelite Religion," 3, 9–10.

82. Toorn, "Saul and Israelite Religion," 538–39.

83. Cross, *Canaanite Myth*, 61.

84. Ibid., 71.

Despite the southern location of Edom in relation to Israel, van der Toorn suggests that the Edomite influence regarding the worship of YHWH may have actually originated in the north. He presents evidence supporting the idea that an Edomite-Midianite cult may have been established in Israel by Edomite elements who settled in the north. Van der Toorn's investigation suggests that Saul chose YHWH as the state deity of Israel, at the beginning of the united monarchy, based on Edomite connections in Saul's background. The evidence further leads to the proposition that Edomite groups settled in the north around Gibeon, and possibly as far as Gilead, as early as 1200 B.C.E.[85]

Van der Toorn's thesis prompts the possibility that this same Edomite influence may have been responsible for the origin of the worship of YHWH as reflected in the earliest strata of P, stemming from Shiloh. If Edomite settlers were evident from Gibeon to Gilead, then Shiloh certainly could have fallen under their influence. Accordingly, Yahwism may be traced back, not only to Saul, but to the priestly leadership in Shiloh before the monarchy. This Yahwistic tradition was later brought to Jerusalem, as the Shiloh sanctuary gave way to the Jerusalem temple.[86] This proposition offers a picture of the origins of P and the worship of YHWH, and presents a contrast to the picture of the origins of the worship of El Shaddai as reflected in the priestly narrative in Genesis.[87]

The tabernacle tradition in P lends further insight into the historical setting of priestly legislation. Despite Cross' contention that the priestly writers stemmed from a later period, he argues that "Priestly tradition must be deemed an important historical witness to the Mosaic age."[88] Among the materials in P reflecting antiquity, the description of the tabernacle stands out. Its transmission can be traced back to the historical development of the cult in the wilderness period. From there,

---

85. Van der Toorn, "Saul and Israelite Religion," 520–25, 539–42.

86. Donald Schley argues that Gen 49:10–12 and Jer 7:12–15; 26: 6–9 reflect the appropriation of Shiloh's cultic heritage to Jerusalem, i.e., Jerusalem succeeded Shiloh as "the place where Yahweh had caused his name to dwell" (Schley, *Shiloh*, 186–87).

87. This contrast will be elaborated further in the discussion of the provenience of the priestly narrative in Genesis, later in this work.

88. Cross, "The Tabernacle," 52.

the tabernacle can be traced to its establishment at Shiloh during the period of the Judges.[89]

Ancient sacred tent traditions serve as parallels which illuminate possible origins for the priestly tradition of the tabernacle. Cross points to the Arabic *qubbah* institution among Semites, while Richard Clifford finds a parallel, even closer in time and culture, in the Canaanite tent of El.[90] Such shrines might be considered prototypes for the Mosaic tent of meeting.

Cross sees the culmination of the priestly tabernacle tradition in the tent of David. While the Mosaic tent likely reflected its Semitic prototypes with a simplistic character, the priestly writers would have drawn their tradition from the most elaborate stage of the institution, that is, the Davidic "Tent of Yahweh." This, in part, serves to explain the lavishness of the tabernacle description, for, based on the wealth of the Davidic court, the Davidic tabernacle would have been richly and ornately constructed. Rather than a fabrication of later times or as an anachronism of the First or Second Temple, the tabernacle tradition reflects the development of the tabernacle institution from its wilderness beginnings to the establishment of David's tent. The acacia wood and curtains of red leather reflect the desert tradition, while the aspect of the tent as a portable temple reflects Canaanite connections, and some of the cultic furnishings and decorations suggest Phoenician influence. Thus, elements of the priestly tradition of the institution of the tabernacle can be seen in progression to its highest development in the Davidic "Tent of Yahweh."[91]

Haran describes the ancient tradition behind the tabernacle in relation to a nomadic dwelling. "It is a type of dwelling in its own right, reflecting, in its structure, nomadic or semi-nomadic conditions, and has a basis in the early stages of Israelite history, prior to the settlement in Canaan."[92] A tabernacle (משכן) was a variation of a tent (אהל),

---

89. Ibid., 54–57.

90. Ibid., 59–61; Clifford, "The Tent of El," 221–27.

91. Cross, "The Tabernacle," 56, 63–65. Cross affirms that some influence of the Solomonic temple upon the priestly description of the tabernacle cannot be denied. His point, however, is that the priestly description of the tabernacle does touch authentic traditions which antedate the temple.

92. Haran, *Temples*, 195. Haran argues that the tabernacle, as literally described in P, is mostly imaginary and never actually existed. Nevertheless, he affirms that the P

and the two dwellings are described in parallel in some instances. Thus, shepherds are described in connection with using tabernacles (Song 1:8); while the "people of the East" are depicted as living in tents in one instance (Judg 6:3–5), and as camped in tabernacles in another (Ezek 25:4). The two types of dwellings are described in parallel in Num 24:5; Isa 54:2; Jer 30:18; and Ps 78:60. Most significantly, tabernacles are also mentioned in Israel's wilderness camp (Num 16:24, 27; 24:5; Ps 78:28). In the wilderness setting, the Lord's tabernacle is set apart simply as larger and more splendid than any other (Lev 17:4; Num 16:9; 17:28). Thus, the form of P's tabernacle, depicted as a portable shrine carried around in the wilderness, is consistent with historical possibility.[93]

In distinction from the Jerusalem temple, Haran sees the foundation of the tabernacle tradition in P as derived from a shrine legend. According to the narrative account, the tabernacle is built at Sinai, carried through the wilderness, brought to Canaan, and finally stationed at Shiloh. Once it is stationed at Shiloh, P contains no indication of the removal of the tabernacle to any other site.[94] Thus, Haran identifies the tabernacle in P as follows: "Therefore, the conclusion cannot be avoided *that the legend contained in P is that of the Shiloh shrine.*"[95] "This legend is based on the belief which the priestly writers shared with all those who had earlier transmitted it, that the house of God at Shiloh was brought from Sinai after having been erected there on divine

---

tabernacle does reflect an ancient authentic tradition. The ancient tradition has been embellished through the magnificent descriptions of gold, silver, bronze, and dyed wool; all of which Haran claims to be fictitious for the setting of the wilderness period. This magnificent description reflects the temple of Solomon's period, which was not a tabernacle at all. Haran, "Shiloh and Jerusalem," 14–17; idem, *Temples*, 189, 195.

93. Haran, "Shiloh and Jerusalem," 18–19; idem, *Temples*, 195–96. Zevit argues the uncertainty of the historicity of the tabernacle described in Exodus as a portable shrine constructed in Sinai. His arguments focus on the geographic availability of the timber required for the construction of the tabernacle. Zevit, "Timber for the Tabernacle," 136–13. It may be true that the materials described in Exodus could not have been used for the construction of a sanctuary carried in Sinai. However, the Exodus description could be considered a retrojection of a portable shrine associated with Shiloh (built in Palestine) back into the wilderness period. This is similar to the suggestion by Haran, which Zevit dismisses because such a reconstruction of tabernacle traditions cannot be attached to specific texts. In any case, Zevit's contention denies the historicity of a tabernacle built in the wilderness, but not one built in Palestine around Shiloh.

94. Haran, "Shiloh and Jerusalem," 19–20.

95. Ibid. 21.

instruction."[96] The final form of the Shiloh legend in P has been recast with Jerusalemite dress. The magnificent descriptions of the tabernacle including precious materials are retrojections of Solomon's temple onto the older legend of the Shiloh shrine. Thus, the P authors, having cast P in literary form at a time when the Shiloh shrine no longer existed, turned the shrine legend into an artistic monument within the context of the Jerusalem temple.[97] The result of Haran's thesis is a pre-exilic date for the writing of P, in light of the description of the ancient tabernacle legend cast in the form of the glory of the First Temple.

Cross and Haran both deny that P's tabernacle is merely a retrojection of the First or Second Temple into the wilderness and early settlement periods. Rather, each recognizes early tabernacle traditions which have developed over time in relation to later influences such as the Davidic tent of Yahweh and the temple of Solomon. Milgrom appears to take such early traditions even more seriously as historical witnesses to P's tabernacle, thereby bringing further insight into the initial setting from which priestly legislation emerged.

Milgrom observes that after the end of P's history, the tabernacle is set up at Shiloh (Josh 18:1). This is independently affirmed at 2 Sam 7:6-7. The narrative of 1 Sam 1-3 depicts a temple at Shiloh, suggesting that the tabernacle may have been brought to reside beside the temple. This is supported by archeological evidence and data from the biblical Historical Books which describe the prominence of Shiloh. Information from these sources depict Shiloh as a prominent transtribal religious center during the premonarchic period.[98]

As evidence for the history of Shiloh as a cultic center, Israel Finkelstein describes a significant period of cultic activity there, beginning from the Middle Bronze II age (i.e., pre-Israelite sacred traditions are apparent). Evidence suggests the existence of a shrine or sanctuary as early as the Middle Bronze period. Furthermore, a cult site appears to have existed at Shiloh during its uninhabited period of Late Bronze I. This isolated cult site at Shiloh in the period following Middle Bronze III must have continued the tradition from the Middle Bronze Age. Based on the lack of human habitation at the site during this period,

---

96. Haran, *Temples*, 200.
97. Haran, "Shiloh and Jerusalem," 23-24; idem, *Temples*, 203.
98. Milgrom, *Leviticus 1-16*, 30-31.

Finkelstein concludes that Shiloh served solely as a cult place in the Late Bronze Age. This was followed by a period of inactivity at Shiloh beginning in the Late Bronze IIA period. The Iron Age I, however, once again yielded considerable evidence that activity in Shiloh portrayed the site as a cult center. During the early Iron I period, it appears that the Shiloh sanctuary served the Israelite population in the central hill country and vicinity. Finkelstein proposes that the sanctuary may have represented a genuine architectural construction.[99] Such archaeological data supports the recognition of Shiloh as a center for cultic activity prior to, and during, the premonarchic period of Israel.

Milgrom adds evidence from the biblical Historical Books in support of the prominence of Shiloh. The Historical Books testify that the tabernacle (tent of meeting) was set up in Shiloh (Josh 18:1; 19:51), and that the Ark was kept there (1 Sam 4:3). These writings also reflect evidence that oracular decisions were offered at Shiloh (Josh 18:10; 19:50–51; 21:2–4; 1 Sam 14:3). In addition, Shiloh was depicted as a administrative and military center (Josh 18:9; 22:12; Judg 21:12).[100]

The archaeological depiction, in conjunction with that of the biblical Historical Books, corresponds to the presuppositions of P which prescribe a central sanctuary with the ark and cultic paraphernalia. Furthermore, P does not claim that its tabernacle is the only legitimate place of worship. Thus, though Shiloh may serve as a transtribal religious center for festivals and annual pilgrimages, it is also a regional sanctuary among others (e.g., Mizpah: Judg 11:11; 20:1; 21:5, 8; 1 Sam 7:5–6; and Bethel: Judg 20:18, 23, 26–27).[101]

Milgrom further supports the identification of P's tabernacle with a local shrine at Shiloh with clues taken from sacrificial procedures described in Leviticus. The first involves the person afflicted with chronic genital discharges (Lev 15:13–15). The requirement for this person and other bearers of severe impurity demands that they reach the sanctuary in one day's journey. This would be impossible if P's tabernacle were identified with the Jerusalem temple of the monarchy. However, it is possible to fulfill the requirement if the tabernacle is understood as

---

99. Finkelstein et al., *Shiloh*, 377, 381–84. Though an Iron Age I sanctuary was not found in the excavations, Finkelstein discusses its likely location at the site (ibid., 384–85). Finkelstein, *Archaeology of the Israelite Settlement*, 211–34.

100. Milgrom, *Leviticus 1–16*, 31.

101. Ibid., 31–32.

a *regional* sanctuary (among others) at Shiloh. The second sacrificial pericope to which Milgrom points involves the thanksgiving offering described in Lev 7:11–15. This offering was originally cooked and eaten on the sanctuary grounds. In contrast, Lev 10:14 presents a polemic against this older practice, and allows the offering to be eaten in any clean place. The explanation for this contrast is the recognition of two strands in P. Leviticus 10:14 reflects P-editors reworking the older practice in order to conform to newer temple regulations. The older practice reflects the pre-temple tradition at Shiloh (which is attested at Shiloh according to 1 Sam 2:13–14).

Milgrom's third pericope comes from Lev 7:31, 33. This passage stipulates that the right thigh of a sacrifice is due to the officiating priest, while the breast is to go to the entire priestly staff. The P-editors can be seen again in Lev 9:21; 10:15 according to which the thigh is now assigned to all the priests. A similar situation is seen in Milgrom's final pericope, that is, Lev 7:9–10. Here the cooked cereal offering is due the officiating priest, while the raw cereal offering is assigned to all the priests. Leviticus 2:3, 10 reveal the editors' hands as now the cooked and raw portions go to the entire priesthood. The explanation for these editorial changes is again found in the transition from local sanctuary to temple. The prescriptions giving the stipends only to the officiating priest reflect a sanctuary staffed by a single priestly family (such as Eli and sons at Shiloh, 1 Sam 1–3). However, the editors' additions reflect the pressures of the temple environment. At the temple, the priesthood expands to many families, and thus pressure builds to share the priestly portions of sacrifices with all the priests. Milgrom's point in regard to these last three sets of texts, which demonstrate editorial activity within P, is that the earlier strands of these passages must originate in a sanctuary prior to the Jerusalem temple.[102]

Milgrom concludes that P's tabernacle reflects both a pre-Hezekian (pre-centralization) Jerusalem temple and the Shiloh sanctuary. The original P texts (P^1) reflect sacrificial procedures which stem from Shiloh. Later P-editors (P^2) reworked these texts as in-house adjustments in response to the move from the single-priestly-family sanctuary to the multiple-priestly-family temple. Still later, the major P redaction identified as H takes place in reaction to the momentous crisis at the

---

102. Ibid., 32–33, 418–19.

end of the eighth century (i.e., the influx of refugees from the northern kingdom and the prophetic rebuke of social injustices in the land). This places P, with both of its strands (and the major redaction of H) in pre-exilic times. Accordingly, the composition of the texts of P can be dated no later than the middle of the eighth century, that is, approximately 750 B.C.E.[103]

Limitations of Unifying Themes

The distinction between narrative and legislation in P is further evident in discussions regarding the *intent* of the priestly literature. For example, Wellhausen stressed that the focus of P is the cultic legislation of the Sinai material, while Elliger emphasized that the theme of P is found in the promise of land derived from the priestly narrative (P^g).[104] I contend that Exod 6 marks the boundary for the division between priestly narrative and that which is predominantly legislation. Proposed unifying themes within the priestly literature fail to bridge this disjunction at Exod 6, thereby affirming the original independence of these two components of P. Though unifying themes have been suggested, each fails to demonstrate consistent development across both of these elements of the Priestly source, beyond redactional expansions.

Ralph Klein's proposal that the concept of God's memory reveals a unified intention developed across the growth of P illustrates this point. He argues that the narrative of P reflects an emphasis on God's memory especially in relation to the everlasting covenants with Noah and Abraham. P's message is that God continues to remember the promise to Noah with the assurance that the world and life in it will continue, even for the exiles in Babylon. Likewise, God's memory is demonstrated in the keeping of the covenant with Abraham in which God promised "to be God" to Abraham and his descendants. This covenant was remembered in the exodus from Egypt, through God's dwelling with Israel in the sanctuary, and through the gift of land as an everlasting possession. P calls the exiles to hold fast to these covenants based on their partial fulfillment in the past. The exilic audience is called to see themselves in the situation described at the end of the P narrative, as Israel on the verge of entering and possessing the promised land. For P, the ideal cul-

103. Ibid., 34.
104. See Klein, "Message of P," 58.

tic community will make possible the ongoing fulfillment of the two everlasting covenants. That is, the functioning of a proper priesthood and sacrificial system will serve to awaken God's memory, reminding God of the promises, and result in acts of deliverance.[105] Klein's study of the word *zikkārôn* ("memorial") prompted his understanding that cult activities served as signs stimulating God's memory.

> Cult objects and cult activities, therefore, were designed to stimulate God's memory, which is virtually synonymous with his acts of intervention. Just as the rainbow served in P^g as a stimulus to God's memory and action (Gen. 9) so in the expanded priestly writing the cult was to bring Israel to the remembrance of Yahweh. God's memory of his people, in both P^g and P^s, serves as the catalyst that makes real the salvation implicit in the everlasting covenants.[106]

This scheme distinguishes between P's message to the exilic situation (expressed in P^g) and to that of the restoration (expressed in P^s). For the exiles, God's memory (stimulated by the rainbow) will lead to deliverance and action to fulfill the covenant promises. In the following period of restoration, proper practice of the sacrificial cult will secure God's continued commitment to the covenant promises, manifested especially through God's dwelling in the tabernacle and the land.[107]

Klein's argument recognizes early and late components within the priestly literature, yet contends that the theme of God's memory provides a theological continuity across such elements. This implies that later redactors or supplementers would have developed the theme from earlier compositions within P. Accordingly, the theme of God's memory in relation to the covenants with Noah and Abraham (P^g) is further developed through later supplementation, in relation to cultic objects and activities (P^s). This scheme maintains the distinction between priestly narratives (particularly in Genesis) and priestly legislation, as separate strata within the priestly literature. Accordingly, the unifying theme appears to represent a redactional expansion. However, the issue is complicated by the possibility that a still later redactor introduced the theme which brought together the two strands of P. That is, were the

---

105. Ibid., 60–64.
106. Ibid., 65.
107. Ibid., 62–63, 66.

legislative supplements to P written with the theme of God's memory (taken from P^g) in mind, or did a separate redactor, such as H, bring the two P strands together by imposing the unifying theme across both? The issue is further obscured by the relative dates assigned to the various priestly components. Klein assumes the traditional sequence of P^g followed by the legislative supplements labeled P^s, with H considered earlier than P^s, and possibly earlier than P^g.[108] In contrast, I propose that P as a legal manual (encompassing much of P^s) represents the earliest priestly strata, followed by the narratives in Genesis (most of P^g), with H understood as the redactor who brought the priestly literature into its latest form. This does not deny the presence of the theme of God's memory within P, but it does question it as an original theme unifying the components of the priestly literature.

The most significant objection to this unifying theme is that it reduces the understanding of the entire sacrificial cult to that of a sign for stimulating God's memory to act on behalf of the people of Israel. This diminishes the rich role assigned to sacrifices and offerings in regard to such important concepts as atonement and purgation. The study of the word *zikkārôn* is insightful, but is not applied to every cult object and activity as Klein seems to imply. It falls short as a comprehensive theme representing the intent of the priestly legislation.

Campbell finds a unified message of hope for the exiles based on P's emphasis on the orderliness of God and the sign of the Sabbath. This is evident in the creation account, as well as the structure of the P text.[109] P's message to the exilic community is that the world is not chaotic, and the fate of the exiles lies within this order ordained by God. The one sign of assurance that is left for the exiles, after temple and liturgy, king and court, and land and seasons are all gone, is the crown of the creation account, that is, the Sabbath. This distinguishing mark of the people of Israel is left to the exiles for maintaining contact with

---

108. Ibid., 58, 66.

109. Campbell, *Study Companion*, 76. The orderly structure of the text includes the following elements: the arrangement of ten generations between creation and the flood, ten generations between Noah and Abraham, and the ten *toledoth* formulas. In addition, Campbell points to the arrangement of six days and a seventh at creation, as well as six days and a seventh before Moses ascended Sinai (Exod 24:16). He also notes P's care for dating events by year, month, and day, as well as providing ages for persons.

the orderly, creator God.¹¹⁰ P's message promotes assurance that God's promises will not fail, and God's presence will not depart. Such assurance is evident in the orderliness which God has ordained.

> This is P's message to his people. Just as God has set the world in order, ordained toward Sabbath, so too God has set Israel on the road toward Canaan, the promised land. God, the creator, has the power to achieve it. Israel's unbelief can delay the accomplishment of God's will; it cannot deflect God from it. God's love for Israel is unconditional; it will not bow to rejection. God's presence is set in Israel's midst; it will not be withdrawn.¹¹¹

The weakness in Campbell's scheme is that it fails to recognize that the priestly literature reflects more than one concept with regard to the Sabbath. That is, the Sabbath carries a different connotation for P than it does for H. It is the hand of H that developed the Sabbath theme taken from the narratives in Genesis (specifically, the creation account), while legal material in P gives different expression to the notion of the Sabbath. Consequently, the concept of Sabbath does not serve to provide a unified theme within the priestly literature. Furthermore, the legal material in P could not serve to provide a message of hope for the exiles based on maintaining religious identity through an emphasis on keeping the Sabbath. This is because not only does P lack an emphasis on the type of Sabbath observance which could be kept during exile (i.e., simple prohibition of work), but on the contrary, P describes a Sabbath observance that required sacrificial service (which could not occur in exile without the temple) and *work* (at least with respect to the priests who served at the temple)!¹¹²

Gottwald also sees a unified theme running throughout the priestly literature in terms of a Priestly emphasis on order over chaos. Continuity can be seen beginning with how God overcame chaos in creating the world, and then conquered chaos again with Noah's ark, and finally God defeated the chaos of sin by means of the tabernacle and its

---

110. Ibid., 69, 77.

111. Ibid., 82.

112. See Knohl, *Sanctuary*, 162–63. The distinction between P and H regarding their views of the Sabbath will be further elaborated later in this work, in relation to the discussion of H's redaction of the priestly literature. I am indebted to Jacob Milgrom, who pointed out to me that P could not emphasize Sabbath work prohibitions because the Priests worked on the Sabbath at the temple.

surrounding cult. The concern behind this scheme can be understood as a stabilizing strategy to preserve the exilic community in the midst of its disorienting (chaotic) period of exile and restoration. The cultic system served a primary role in addressing this concern by helping to establish a distinct self-perpetuating and self-correcting community. Accordingly, the sacrificial system, in conjunction with the purity laws, reflects a priestly conceptual world which was highly rationalized and orderly. The detailed instructions regarding sacrifices and dealing with impurity comprise a balanced classification system. A breach in the regulations governing this system, exposing one to uncleanness and death, would subvert the order of the world. Habitual exposure in this regard would have to be rectified by proper ritual.[113]

Coote and Ord further expand on such an emphasis on order in the sacrificial cult. They also see a unified message between the narrative of P in Genesis and the legal material focused on the temple, the sacrificial cult, and the laws regulating certain aspects of social justice. The foundation for this unified theme is in the creation account itself. "The categories and structures established in Genesis 1 constitute the spring from which everything in the priestly reconstruction of history flows, the seed from which all grows, the bud from which all blossoms."[114]

Coote and Ord explain that the key characteristic of the created entities in Gen 1 is movement, made possible by being alive. To stay alive, a creature has to eat and hold its blood. Accordingly, the disposition of blood becomes the foundational element in the rites of the priesthood. In addition, priests were concerned with the oversight of proper food consumption, particularly the consumption of meat. Part of the created order was the assignment of food, specifically plants, for eating. Accordingly, animals were not to eat each other, so that blood was not shed. This demonstrates that eating meat was not a part of the original order. However, following the cleansing of the earth through the flood, God established a covenant with Noah (and with all flesh) allowing the eating of meat so long as the blood was properly disposed. In addition, a later covenant with Moses further restricted what kinds of meat were to be considered clean for consumption. It was the priests' function to oversee these regulations and distinguish between clean and unclean

---

113. Gottwald, *Hebrew Bible*, 473, 477–78.
114. Coote and Ord, *In the Beginning*, 50.

meat. Since the priests ate much of what was brought to the altar for sacrifice, they not only controlled the nation's meat supply, but also gave themselves access to large quantities of meat. Coote and Ord conclude that Gen 1 and the priestly literature that develops from it represent the tradition of an ascendant priesthood. This priesthood assumed control over cultic sacrifice and the luxury of eating much meat. Both of these elements are traced to the function of the proper disposal of blood in order to maintain the principle of order established by God at creation. This was all supported by the priestly rationale that reinforced the popular notion that the temple was the place of God's presence, and therefore the place to bring offerings for divine blessing. The priests described the world as established with a pervasive and abiding order from creation. For the priests every form of disorder must be managed. In the priestly scheme the epitome of disorder was loose blood, a manifestation of the loss of life.[115] The sacrificial cult governed loose blood and thus signified the resolution of disorder.

> The priestly cult offered to govern loose blood, to restore the flow of blood to its prescribed place in the framework of the created order, and in so doing to signify also the resolution of other social experiences of disorder, through sacrifices specified for such purposes as purgation, pacification, compensation, and reparation. The motif that underlies the entire roster of sacrifices is thus the restoration of the order created by God, as revealed in the priestly cult.[116]

At the core of the issue of order was the concern for social order. The purposes which individual sacrifices served included gifts to God, expiation, atonement, purification, and dealing with guilt and reparation.[117] All of these, which related to social concerns, were tied to a world order in the priestly literature. "The account of creation in Genesis 1 provided the theoretical basis for managing law and order, misdeed and reparation, through a cult whose highlight was elite consumption of meat."[118]

---

115. Ibid., 54–59, 66, 107–8.
116. Ibid., 108.
117. Ibid., 108–12.
118. Ibid., 113.

The theme of orderliness in P, which is mentioned by Campbell, Gottwald, and Coote and Ord does seem to reflect an aspect of the style of the priestly literature. The organization, detail, and structure of elements like the creation account, the genealogical data, and the sacrificial instructions reflect a tendency on the part of the priestly writers to be organized and thorough. This tendency may be shared by more than one priestly school, and thus may be reflected in the various priestly documents. To conclude, however, that a theme of cosmic order was established in the creation account and is reflected within the entire priestly cult reaches beyond the evidence of the text.

As with Campbell's notion of Sabbath, Coote and Ord overlook distinctions between P and H in relation to the disposal of blood. Admittedly, the restrictions regarding the disposal of blood might be traced back to the original constraint that only plants were to be designated for food (Gen 1:29–30; thus, no blood was to be shed for eating), and to the later stipulation which allowed the eating of meat so long as the blood was drained and not eaten (Gen 9:3–4). However, such blood restriction is reflected most directly by the hand of H, rather than P. H explicitly reflects the concern of avoiding the blood because it is the life of a creature (Lev 17:10–11; cf. Gen 9:4). This implies a possible connection between the priestly school of H and the P narratives in Genesis. The same connection, however, is not so clear with regard to the cultic legislation in P itself which prescribes the blood manipulation by the priests.

Furthermore, it does not appear that the instructions regarding blood in P are based on a rationale concerned with restoring the flow of blood to some prescribed place according to the created order. In contrast, the word דם ("blood") does not even occur in the creation account of Gen 1. Nor is there any direct discussion in Gen 1 regarding the proper place of blood (to which blood is to be restored) in the created order. In addition, the priestly disposal of blood does not prescribe a particular place to where blood is to be restored (assuming there was a corresponding instruction in the creation account), except that it be poured out at the base of the altar. This does not reflect the picture of the created order which, according to Coote and Ord's description, stipulates that blood rightly belongs in the flesh of creatures in order to keep them alive, and hence, moving. The priestly cult makes no attempt to restore blood to such a place. A common understanding regarding the pouring out of blood at the base of the altar is that such blood is returned to God, not some element (or creature) in God's creation.

Finally, Coote and Ord's contention that the management of *all* of the law and sacrifices in P find their theoretical base in the order established with the creation account is beyond the evidence of the text. Too many themes and concepts are introduced in the legal material that have no real antecedent in the creation account (e.g., various sacrificial rites, impurity instructions, the tabernacle, etc.). The terminology of the creation account is not reflected in the legal material of P. Rather, the legal material has distinct terminology and a distinct focus. Admittedly, some terminology has been taken from the creation account, and developed in isolated passages within the legal material. However, it appears that such development is restricted to the redaction by H, and does not reflect the original intent of P.[119]

Traditional Priestly Themes

Themes commonly discussed in relation to the priestly literature include covenant and the promise of land. Three significant covenants are recorded in the priestly literature. The first two covenants are readily identified as the covenants with Noah (Gen 9:8–17) and Abraham (Gen 17). The third covenant clearly relates to Sinai, yet is not as easily assigned to a specific pericope in P. Cross identifies the third covenant with formulae spread throughout the Sinai material in P, from Exod 19 to Num 10:10. He adds that the Sinai covenant is anticipated in P at Exod 6:2–9, and effectively concluded with the closing exhortation enumerating blessings and curses in Lev 26:3–45.[120]

It is evident that the theme of covenant in P is expressed most explicitly in the narrative material up to Exod 6. For, as Cross argues, the third covenant (the only one appearing after Exod 6) is never explicitly defined in P, but rather is identified with formulae spread throughout the Sinai material. The actual covenant ceremony is not even recorded in P.[121] This disjunction between the second and third covenants is further evidenced by the apparent shift in theme which takes place between the second and third covenants. As pointed out by Cross, and

---

119. See the discussion of H's redaction of the priestly literature later in this work.
120. Cross, *Canaanite Myth*, 297.
121. See Campbell, *Study Companion*, 72.

Brueggemann and Wolff, the themes of the promise of fruitfulness and multiplication, and of possession of the land, tie the covenants together.[122] However, this is explicitly true only for the first and second covenants. As Brueggemann and Wolff demonstrate, the blessing of fruitfulness and multiplication is introduced at the creation account, is expressed throughout the narrative material of P in Genesis, and appears for the last time within the introduction to Exodus. In fact, Brueggemann and Wolff claim that the confessional formula regarding fruitfulness and multiplication does not appear in P's rendition of the Mosaic era, likely due to the emphasis on legal material there.[123] This theme is thus confined to P material preceding Exod 6. A shift in theme occurs with the Sinai material that emphasizes the "tabernacling" presence of God.[124] Most telling in regard to the disjunction between the second and third covenants is the use of the word ברית ("covenant") itself. Though this term is the word for covenant in the first two covenants (Noah and Abraham), it is not used by P at all in the material following Exod 6. Rather, the appearances of the word ברית in the priestly literature following Exod 6 can all be attributed to H.[125]

Sue Boorer sees the purpose of P as that of providing hope to the exiles in the form of the promise of future restoration based on the fulfillment of the Abrahamic covenant and the promise of land. She explains that P presents an overview of Israel's history from creation to the situation of the Babylonian exile. However, P reinterprets the traditions of the major periods of the history of Israel in order to provide a basis of hope for the exiles. Consequently, Boorer interprets the stages of the wilderness sojourn in P as corresponding to major periods in Israel's history as follows:

> sojourn in the wilderness of Sin = traditional wilderness period
>
> sojourn in wilderness of Sinai = occupation of Canaan/monarchy

---

122. Cross, *Canaanite Myth*, 296; Brueggemann and Wolff, *Vitality*, 37–38, 103–7.

123. Brueggemann and Wolff, *Old Testament Traditions*, 107. Cross points out that the promise of fruitfulness and multiplication also appears at Lev 26:9 (Cross, *Canaanite Myth*, 296). However, this is clearly within H, rather than P.

124. Cross, *Canaanite Myth*, 298–300.

125. For the attribution of the appearances of the term ברית ("covenant"), in the priestly literature following Exod 6, to H, see Knohl, *Sanctuary*, 141–42; Gottwald, *Hebrew Bible*, 203.

sojourn in wilderness of Paran up to Jericho = exilic period[126]

Boorer argues that P emphasizes the Abrahamic covenant, and ignores the Davidic covenant. This is because the Davidic covenant of an everlasting dynasty for the house of David, along with the promise of God's eternal dwelling in the temple, was devastated by the destruction of the exile. Accordingly, P presents the traditions of the monarchic period at Sinai as part of the wilderness sojourn. Thus, the monarchic period is not seen as the fulfillment of the promise of land, but rather is another step on the way to the possession of the land which has not yet been fully gained. Likewise, the exile is a stage on the journey to the fulfillment of the covenant, promising land. Consequently, P affirms that the exile has not negated the promise of land. The Abrahamic covenant still stands, and is yet to be fulfilled.[127]

Klein's critique of Boorer's analysis further demonstrates the disjunction between the covenant theme (emphasizing the promise of land, and the theme of fruitfulness and multiplication) and the Sinai material. As Klein rightly objects, Boorer's analysis effectively excludes all aspects of the cult, priesthood, and sacrifices (detailed in the Sinai account) from any significance in the theme and theology of P.[128] The implication of her scheme is that the Sinai material does not convey the promise of land and fruitfulness (taken from the Abrahamic covenant), but rather is representative of the monarchic period which is invalidated by the exile. Once again the deep significance of the sacrificial system in relation to the foundational concepts of atonement, purgation, and the presence of God are completely overlooked.

This brief analysis of two traditional themes in P suggests two separate focuses corresponding to separate components of P. The P narrative in Genesis up to Exod 6 centers around the themes of covenant, promise of land, and the blessing of fruitfulness and multiplication. Following Exod 6, these themes are developed only in a secondary manner. The shift in P to the Sinai material introduces a shift in theme. The predominantly legal material following Exod 6 is concentrated on the presence of God, the temple, and the sacrificial cult.

---

126 Boorer, "Kerygmatic Intention," 12–13.

127. Ibid., 14–17.

128. Klein, "Message of P," 59–60.

Central Focus on Tabernacle and Cult

The Tabernacle and the Presence of God

Based on the assertion that P properly defined is made up of the legal material in Exodus through Numbers, a review of the content of the core legislation within P reveals the central concerns of the source. As described previously, the core of P consists of the Sinai legislation from Exod 25 through Num 10. This material is focused on the following elements:

1. Construction of the tabernacle, its furniture, and the priestly garments
2. Consecration of the priests
3. Sacrificial laws and the first sacrifices
4. Purity laws
5. Instructions, including the roles of priests and Levites, and the ordering of the camp

It is clear that the central focus in P is the tabernacle and its surrounding cult. Another way to describe the topics listed above is as follows: the construction of the tabernacle and its furniture, the consecration of the priests who serve at the tabernacle, the laws regarding the sacrifices offered at the tabernacle, the purity laws which serve to keep the tabernacle from defilement (cf. Lev 15:31), instructions for the priests and Levites who serve in relation to the tabernacle, and the ordering of the camp around the tabernacle.

The rest of the P material (in Exod 6–24, and Num 11–36) consists mostly of brief narratives and itineraries which serve to frame the central legislation and provide the appropriate historical setting. This surrounding material also includes some additional legislation which appears as supplementary to the core of P. The original intent of the P source, however, must be discerned from the bulk of its content, which is clearly focused on the tabernacle and its surrounding cult.

Appropriately, Noth finds the focus of the theology of P within the Sinai material. He argues that P presents an ideal cultic order by portraying it as having been realized in antiquity. In part, P is an etiology of the postexilic Jerusalem cult. P expresses the proper system for the worship of God in contemporary postexilic times with concessions to the pre-monarchic traditions including a mobile tabernacle, the ark in the Holy of Holies, and the twelve tribes camped around the sanctuary. More than just an etiology, however, Noth finds in the purpose of P a desire to present a program for the future. That is, P wished to present a corrective to the dominant views of worship with a concern for bringing reform. P's program of a proper cult centered around the sanctuary and God's presence in relation to it.[129]

Stripping away the unnecessary attempt to interpret P in relation to the exilic circumstance reveals P's theological intent in relation to the presence of God, the sanctuary, and proper cult. Rather than an etiology of the postexilic cult, or a program for the future, P constitutes the original cultic program established around the tabernacle and eventually the First Temple.

Cross rightly observes that the heart of the Sinai covenant in the view of the Priestly writer was the "tabernacling" presence of God (Exod 29:45–46; Lev 26:11–13). The Sinai covenant, the cult, and its law, served to make possible God's dwelling among Israel, resulting in the possibility of full redemption for Israel.[130] Cross expresses the priestly theological understanding behind the third covenant, which embraces the legal material in P, with these words: "The entire cultic paraphernalia and cultus was designed to express and overcome the problem of the holy, transcendent God visiting his pervasively sinful people."[131]

This major theme is initially portrayed at the climax of the construction of the tabernacle. After all of the elaborate and detailed instructions regarding the construction of the tabernacle and its furniture have been carried out, the climactic moment is described in Exod 40:34–35: "And the cloud covered the tent of meeting, and the glory of the Lord filled the tabernacle. And Moses was not able to enter the tent of meeting, because the cloud settled upon it, and the glory of the Lord filled the tabernacle." Thus, P's central feature, the tabernacle, represents the presence of God.

This is further illustrated by the significance of the phrases לפני יהוה ("before the Lord" or "the presence of the Lord") which appears throughout the P material. In relation to P, Milgrom describes this phrase

---

129. Noth, *Pentateuchal Traditions*, 240–46.
130. Cross, *Canaanite Myth*, 298–300.
131. Ibid., 299.

as referring to the area of the tabernacle "within the sacred precincts," or possibly "the outer court area." The phrase can appear as equivalent to פתח אהל מועד ("the opening of the tent of meeting"), which defines the area in the outer court between the entrance and the altar. The equivalence of these two phrases is evident by their apposition in Lev 14:11, 23; 16:7.[132] The significance of defining the forecourt of the tabernacle as being literally "before the Lord" is the underlying understanding that the presence of the Lord is within the inner sanctum of the tabernacle itself. This is affirmed in that, not only is the outer court "before the Lord," but the altar of incense that stands in the holy place (shrine) of the tabernacle is also described as being "before the Lord" (Lev 16:12). This implies that the presence of the Lord is understood to be within the holy of holies (adytum) itself. The presence of God as depicted in the tabernacle is most explicit in the instructions regarding the Day of Atonement. Leviticus 16:2 records the Lord's instructions to Aaron, through Moses, including the warning that God will appear in the cloud over the mercy seat, which is in the holy of holies.

The priestly writer not only establishes the presence of the Lord in the tabernacle, but furthermore, records an elaborate cult aimed at maintaining that presence. This is best illustrated in the purpose of the great annual purgation rite of the tabernacle on the Day of Atonement (Lev 16). The goal of this annual purgation is to cleanse and rid the tabernacle of all sins and impurities (Lev 16:16, 20–21) so that God's presence will not abandon the tabernacle. This is necessary because God cannot abide impurity, and therefore the aim of the Day of Atonement is "to make possible God's continued presence among his people."[133] As illustrated by the Day of Atonement, a major concern of the sacrificial cult, and the central theme for P, is maintaining the purity of the tabernacle in order to secure the continued presence of God in the midst of the community of Israel.

Divine and Human Relationships

Another foundational theme implicit in P is the concern for personal holiness, especially reflected in relationship to God and neighbor. In

---

132. Milgrom, *Leviticus 1–16*, 150, 155, 209–10. Noth identifies "before the Lord" as simply the location of the holy place. Noth, *Leviticus*, 22.

133. Wenham, *Leviticus*, 228. Also, Milgrom, *Studies*, 81–82.

relationship to God, P describes this concern as the need for cleansing from sin and impurity. Based on the same rationale regarding the tabernacle (i.e., God cannot abide impurity), the children of Israel must also be cleansed. The purity regulations and sacrificial cult provide for such cleansing. As a result, God abides in the cleansed sanctuary, and among a clean people. The purification offering (חטאת) is the primary means by which contamination from sin and impurity is purged. Thus, the relationship with the Divine is sustained.[134]

The relationship between God and persons is not simply one of preserving the Divine presence through cleansing and purity. The sacrificial cult includes the communication of positive expressions such as giving thanks, conveying satisfaction in the accomplishment of a vow, and the spontaneous giving of a free-will offering. All of these are expressed through the well-being offerings (שלמים). In P, these offerings are presented in response to joyous motivations. Thus, contact with God through the sacrificial cult is understood as truly relational.[135] It has been suggested that the well-being offering originally constituted a meal shared by God and the worshipers, based on the fact that not all of this sacrifice was offered on the altar, but some was eaten by the participants in a sacrificial meal.[136] This portrays a picture of intimate relationship between the Divine and the worshiper through shared table fellowship. It must be clarified, however, that P was very intentional about avoiding any imagery which implied that the sacrificial cult was intended to satisfy the needs of the Divine such as providing daily food.[137] Nevertheless, the image of the sacrificial meal does communicate the significance of relationship between God and people, a concept which is included within the priestly theology. Kaufmann has argued that the well-being offering does not constitute a meal whereby a person is elevated to equal association with God, but rather the

---

134. See Milgrom, *Leviticus 1–16*, 49–50; idem, "Priestly Source," 457–58. For elaboration of the ways in which the priestly legislation addresses personal sin and impurity, see Milgrom, *Numbers*, 444–47; idem, *Leviticus 1–16*, 365, 373–78; Noth, *Leviticus*, 37, 124.

135. Milgrom, *Leviticus 1–16*, 49; idem, "Priestly Source," 457. De Vaux offers similar descriptions of the three motives or occasions for well-being offerings (thanksgiving, free will, and vow). His initial description is rather solemn, but he later mentions the joyous aspect of the sacrifice. Vaux, *Studies*, 33, 35, 37.

136. Noth, *Leviticus*, 31.

137. Knohl, *Sanctuary*, 131–35; Kaufmann, *Religion of Israel*, 111.

human participant is pictured as a guest of the Lord, whose consumption of the offering symbolizes nearness to God. Thus, the emphasis is not mystical union *with* God, but joy *before* the Lord.[138]

The reparation offering (אשם) is particularly concerned with offenses directly related to God's name or the property of God (Lev 5:15).[139] This offering also reveals an ethical aspect of priestly theology. Milgrom explains that the association of this offering, and that of the purification offering, with the concept of "feeling guilt" bears ethical consequences. The resultant expiation of the sacrifice depends on the remorse of the sinner and the reparation the sinner brings to the one offended and to God. The case described in Lev 5:20–26 (Eng. 6:1–7) illustrates the significance of this offering. In regard to one who falsely swears an oath in relation to defrauding another, rectification would include the restoration of property with an additional fine. Such action, subsequent to feelings of guilt (remorse), makes the person eligible for sacrificial expiation in regard to the false oath (an intentional crime against God normally not eligible for atonement; Num 15:30–31). This illustrates how the priestly doctrine of repentance provided for the conversion of an intentional sin into an inadvertent sin in order to make it eligible for sacrificial expiation.[140] The key lies in sincere repentance and the required ethical action of reparation.

Besides the purification, well-being, and reparation offerings, two others remain, as recorded in P. Milgrom states that the full rationale for these remaining two offerings is unclear.[141] It appears that the burnt offering (עלה) has a function similar to that of the purification offering in that it too is said to make atonement on behalf of the offerer (Lev 1:4; 16:24). De Vaux argues that initially the burnt offering was an act of homage to God through the unreserved offering of a gift.[142] Such a concept certainly fits the overall theme of relationship with God expressed through the sacrificial cult, by including the characteristic of humble adoration.

---

138. Kaufmann, *Religion of Israel*, 111–12.

139. For a discussion of the common confusion between the reparation offering and the purification offering, see de Vaux, *Studies*, 98–102.

140. Milgrom, *Leviticus 1–16*, 50, 365; idem, "Priestly Source," 458.

141. Milgrom, *Leviticus 1–16*, 49; idem, "Priestly Source," 457.

142. De Vaux, *Studies*, 37.

Finally, the grain offering (מנחה) often appears as a supplementary offering, along with a libation, in accompaniment to burnt offerings (Lev 23:12–13, 18; Num 28:9, 11–14, 19–21, 27–29, 31; 29:2–4, 6, 8–11, 13–34, 36–38). Norman Snaith suggests that the grain offering can plainly carry the meaning of a "gift," or "tribute," similar to the burnt offering.[143] Gary Anderson's work provides some helpful clarity in this regard. In P, מנחה is used specifically or technically with the meaning "grain offering," while other sources in the Bible use it in the generic sense of sacrifices in general (Gen 4:3–5; 1 Kgs 18:29, 36; 2 Kgs 3:20; Mal 1:10, 11, 13) or with the secular meaning "gift," or "tribute" (Gen 32:21–22 [Eng. 20–21]; 2 Sam 8:2; Ps 72:10; Zeph 3:10; 2 Chr 9:24). The different meanings of the term do not necessarily imply a historical development of its usage. Rather, the various meanings could co-exist. This is because the priestly circles would have used the term in a technical sense in order to precisely categorize and identify various offerings. Such precision was not a concern of the common populace; so the generic use of the term would have continued outside of priestly circles. This explanation suggests that the "grain offering" in P may have been a specific category of gift offerings brought to the temple by worshipers.[144]

To summarize, all of the offerings which comprise the sacrificial cult in P contribute to the maintenance of positive relationships between God and the children of Israel. The cult deals with sin and impurity so that God's presence can abide in the sanctuary in the midst of the community of Israel; it brings expression to the joyous communication of thanksgiving, accomplishment, and free will contributions; and it promotes repentance and restitution in matters of wrongdoing against God and fellow Israelites.

Reverence for Life

The priestly writers were not only concerned with divine and human relationships, but also with a reverence for life in general. This aspect of priestly theology is especially implicit in the purity laws. Milgrom explains that the impurity regulations are included within the priestly ritual complex which only makes sense as a symbolic system. He points out that the sources of impurity in P are specifically designated

---

143. Snaith, "Sacrifices," 309, 314–16.
144. Anderson, *Sacrifices and Offerings*, 29–32.

to represent a particular priestly rationale. There are three sources of impurity designated in P: 1) a corpse, 2) scale disease, and 3) genital discharges. Milgrom notes that only certain types of scale disease were declared impure. In addition, genital discharges were specified to the exclusion of other bodily secretions, such as mucus, perspiration, urine, or feces. The reason for such specificity with regard to the sources of impurity lies in the common denominator which they all share, that is, the representation of death. This common factor reveals the priestly rationale. There is no question that a corpse represents death. Similarly, the particular types of scale diseases described in P are those which give the appearance of death. The scale diseases which afflict humans give the appearance of approaching death through the highly visible wasting away of the body. In a related manner, the impurity laws single out moldy fabrics and houses infested with fungus, not because they have scale disease, but because they give the appearance of it. Finally, the genital discharges of semen from men and blood from women also represent death. That is, the loss of these elements, which in themselves signify life forces, represents death. Milgrom concludes that the impurity regulations symbolically call Israel to choose life by means of obedience to these commands of God. This system is also partly a polemic against the attribution, on the part of Israel's neighbors, of impurity to demonic forces. Thus, the objective of the impurity system is to focus an emphasis on "life" through obedience to God, while separating Israel from the pagan beliefs of other nations who attribute many of the circumstances of life to demonic influences.[145] Milgrom states this objective as follows: "Despite all of the changes that are manifested in the evolution of Israel's impurity laws, the objective remains the same: to sever impurity from the demonic and to reinterpret it as a symbolic system reminding Israel of the divine imperative to reject death and choose life."[146]

In sum, the theological intent of P centers on the tabernacle and the sacrificial cult. The priestly writers were concerned with codifying the means by which the presence of God could be maintained through a system of sacrifice and purity. The same system served to enable right relationships with God and neighbor. In addition, the cult presented in P promotes a foundational concern for a genuine reverence for life.

---

145. Milgrom, *Leviticus 1–16*, 45–47; idem, "Priestly Source," 456.
146. Milgrom, *Leviticus 1–16*, 47; idem, "Priestly Source," 456.

PART TWO

P^N: A Northern Priestly Component

3

The Composition of P^N

OUR INVESTIGATION TO THIS POINT HAS DEMONSTRATED A SIGNIFICANT distinction between that which has been traditionally understood as P narrative in Genesis (up to Exod 6) and the legal material attributed to P in Exodus–Numbers. In contrast to P legislation in Exodus–Numbers, the content of the priestly associated narratives in Genesis has no direct relation to the temple, the sacrificial cult, or the related laws in P. Thus, the distinct content and focus of the material traditionally attributed to P in Genesis constitutes another line of demarcation between that material and P itself. For the sake of convenience, I designate the material normally attributed to P in Genesis (up to Exod 6) with the sign P^N.[1]

The unique structure and terminology of P^N serve to confirm its original distinction from P. The content of P^N includes the use of specific formulas and phrases which are rarely, if ever, repeated in the rest of the Hebrew Bible. In addition, the structure of the document reflects an exclusive outline which defines its parameters. An intentional link between P^N and P occurs at Exod 6. This link brings P^N within the sphere of the priestly literature. The redactor who composed this link provided a transitional appendix to P^N in addition to Exod 6, and thereby attached P^N to the rest of the priestly literature.

---

1. I use the letter "P" because we are dealing with material that has traditionally been designated as part of the Priestly source and does show signs of having been redacted in relation to other priestly strata. I use the superscript "N" in order to distinguish this material from P itself and to acknowledge the northern provenience which this material appears to reflect.

The Content of P^N

P^N is a document which consists mainly of the creation account in Gen 1, a version of the flood story, the Abrahamic covenant of Gen 17, and some brief narratives regarding the transmission of the Abrahamic covenant through the patriarchal generations; all tied together by genealogical notices. Genesis 17 serves as a central turning point in P^N. The P^N material prior to Genesis 17 provides a brief prehistory leading up to the Abrahamic covenant (i.e., creation of humanity, acknowledgment of sin and God's reaction to sin [the flood story], and genealogical links from the first human to Abraham). Genesis 17 then provides a turning point at which the focus of the narrative narrows from a universal to a more specific perspective. Both the creation account and the covenant with Noah bear universal implications. The creation account describes the origins of humanity, and the covenant with Noah constitutes a universal promise not to destroy the earth again. The covenant introduced in Gen 17, however, narrows the focus of the narrative to the individual Abraham and his descendants. P^N material following Gen 17 focuses primarily on the transmission of this covenant through the generations of the patriarchs. This passing-on of the covenant further narrows the scope of the narrative by focusing attention on a particular line of descendants, specifically Isaac, Jacob, and Joseph (Ephraim and Manasseh).

A primary means of identifying the content of P^N is that of tracing the characteristic terminology and themes that tie the work together. The writing begins with the creation account in Gen 1—2:4a. The genealogy of Gen 5 is tied to this creation account through phrases found in Gen 1:27–28, which are repeated in 5:1b–2 ("God created humankind, ... male and female he created them, and he blessed them"), and phrases in Gen 1:26 repeated in 5:3 ("in his likeness, according to his image").[2]

P^N's version of the flood story is also linked to the creation account by means of a number of repeated phrases and echoes as described in the following list:

---

2. Noth, *Pentateuchal Traditions*, 17 n. 42; see also, Campbell and O'Brien, *Sources*, 24 n. 5.

1. The imagery of Gen 7:11; 8:2a ("fountains of the deep," and "floodgates of the sky") echoes the picture implied in Gen 1:6–8 (with waters above and below the firmament).
2. The repetition of the phrase למינהו ("after its kind") in Gen 6:20; 7:14 recalls its use in Gen 1:12, 21, 25.
3. The designation of food in Gen 1:29–30 is echoed in Gen 6:21 and 9:3 ("it shall be food for you").
4. The terminology used to designate the living things created in Gen 1:20–21, 24–25 is reflected in Gen 7:14, 21; 8:17; 9:2.
5. The description of the ark "on the surface of the water" (על־פני המים —Gen 7:18) echoes that of the movement of the Spirit of God in Gen 1:2.
6. The dominion of humans over the animals set forth in Gen 1:26, 28 is echoed in Gen 9:2.
7. Gen 9:6 repeats the terminology from the making of the human, בצלם אלהים ("in the image of God") as described in Gen 1:27 (cf. 1:26).
8. A key concept which ties all of P^N together is the repetition of the phrase found in Gen 1:22, 28, that is, פרו ורבו ("be fruitful and multiply"). In the flood story, this phrase is found in Gen 9:1, 7 (cf. 8:17).[3]

Following the flood account, brief patriarchal narratives are evident as P^N texts due to echoes of the key concept (#8 in the above list) of the "fruitfulness and multiplication" of those with whom God has established a covenant. This theme is repeated throughout the rest of P^N as follows:

1. Gen 17:2, 6 in relation to Abraham (and Ishmael in response to Abraham's plea, 17:18, 20).
2. Gen 28:3 where Isaac passes a blessing on to Jacob.
3. Gen 35:11 in which God appears to Jacob as he did to Abraham in chapter 17.
4. Gen 47:27b referring to Jacob in Egypt.
5. Gen 48:4 in which Jacob recounts the promise to Joseph.[4]

---

3. Campbell and O'Brien, *Sources*, 25. Campbell and O'Brien note the echoes between the creation and flood accounts in n. 9(2)(3) of their recreated P document. See also, Emerton, "Priestly Writer," 386.

4. See Emerton, "Priestly Writer," 387.

In each of these passages this theme of abundance is revealed by the presence of the two verbs פרה ("to be fruitful") and רבה ("to multiply").

This notion of increase and abundance is already anticipated in the patriarchal stories at Gen 13:6, 11b–12abα in which the possessions of Abram and Lot are too great for the land to bear. The same dilemma is described between Jacob and Esau at Gen 36:6–7. A picture of this ongoing abundance is also seen at Gen 46:6–7 which describes Jacob and all his descendants moving to Egypt. Each of these passages can be identified with P^N by means of the development of this distinctive theme.

The central text of Gen 17 in P^N introduces a few other unifying phrases which identify P^N passages following Gen 17. At the beginning of this passage (Gen 17:1b), God reveals himself to Abram as אל שדי. This title appears as P^N's characteristic designation for God. P^N introduces the title at Gen 17:1b and repeats it at Gen 28:3; 35:11; 43:14a; 48:3. All of these occurrences of this title, except one (43:14a), appear in conjunction with the previously identified key theme of abundance.

A final occurrence of אל שדי in P^N appears within the Testament of Jacob (Gen 49:25).[5] The original independence of the various sayings in the Testament of Jacob has long been recognized.[6] The unique character of the Joseph blessing in particular (Gen 49:22–26) has been observed by Dillmann, and von Rad identifies vv. 25b–26 as an ancient form of a fertility blessing.[7] Consequently, due to the appearance of both the characteristic title אל שדי and theme of abundance (expressed as a fertility blessing in vv. 25–26, and reflected in the form of פרה in v. 22), the blessing of Joseph (Gen 49:22–26) in the Testament of Jacob can be attributed to P^N.

John Emerton points out further connections establishing a unity within the material which is here identified as P^N. Each of these connections also stems from the central P^N text of Genesis 17. The command requiring Isaac's circumcision and the promise of Isaac's birth

---

5. That is, אל שדי appears in this verse according to a few medieval manuscripts, the Samaritan Pentateuch, the Septuagint, and the Syriac translation. David Biale points out that the Masoretic ואת is less convincing contextually than ואל. Biale, "El Shaddai in the Bible," 244 n. 14; see also Dillmann, *Genesis*, II:477–78.

6. See Kuenen, *Hexateuch*, 240; Fohrer, *Introduction*, 66; Rad, *Genesis*, 421.

7. Dillmann, *Genesis*, II:473; Rad, *Genesis*, 428; see also Biale, "El Shaddai in the Bible," 248.

(Gen 17:12, 21) are fulfilled in Gen 21:2, 4. The theme of the promise of the land set forth in Gen 17:8 is reflected in Gen 28:4; 35:12. The phrase ארץ מגרים ("land of sojournings") is taken from Gen 17:8 and is repeated in 28:4; 36:7; 37:1; and Exod 6:4.[8] Finally, the promise describing Abraham as the father of many nations and projecting the rise of kings among his descendants (Gen 17:4–6, 16) is reflected in Gen 28:3; 35:11.[9]

Interspersed among the passages which make up P^N are the genealogies, lists, itineraries, and birth and death notices which traditionally have been argued as characteristic of P. Whybray contends that there is no link between these passages and the narrative of P, and that, since it is the nature of this kind of material to be formal, schematic, and arid; no characteristic narrative style of P should be deduced from such material (genealogies, lists, notes of dates and ages, headings, summaries, and itineraries).[10] Such an argument, however, does not exclude genealogies and lists from being included as part of P^N. Furthermore, it can be said that P^N demonstrates a concern to communicate the formal information contained in such material, and therefore has a tendency to include genealogies, lists, itineraries, and birth and death notices within its writing. This tendency itself may be considered characteristic of P^N. Finally, the identification of such material with P^N becomes even more evident upon recognizing its contribution to the unique structure of P^N (as detailed later in this chapter).

A listing of the passages which have been identified above as P^N, along with those of related themes and terminology, reveals the following index of the content of P^N:

Genesis:

1—2:4a
5:1–28, 30–32
6:9–22

---

8. Emerton, "Priestly Writer," 387. Emerton includes Gen 47:9 in his list of occurrences of the phrase "land of sojournings." However, the complete phrase does not occur in that verse. The occurrence in Exod 6:4 is part of the transition which a redactor composed in order to tie P^N to the rest of the priestly literature, as will be discussed below.

9. Ibid., 387.

10. Whybray, *Making of the Pentateuch*, 59–60.

7:6, 11, 13–16a, 18–21, 24
8:1–2a, 3b–5, 7, 13a, 14–19
9:1–17, 28–29
10:1–7, 20, 22–23, 31–32
11:10–27, 31–32
12:4b–5
13:6, 11b–12aba
16:1a, 3, 15–16
17:1–13, 15–27
21:2–5
25:7–8, 11a, 12–17, 19–20, 24–26
28:1–5
31:18[11]
35:6 (cf. 48:3), 9–13 [12], 15, 22b–29
36:1–7
37:1–2a
41:46a
43:14a
46:6–27
47:27b–28
48:3–6
49:22–26, 33b

The above index of P^N corresponds to a traditional rendering of the narrative of P in Genesis, with a few significant differences. Using Campbell and O'Brien's synthesis and presentation of Noth's work as a standard depiction of the conventional identification of P in Genesis, the following additions and deletions have been made in delineating the content of P^N:[13]

11. A fragment of the Jacob story may be missing, that is, the narration of his time in Paddan-aram and how he acquired wives and property. This missing fragment would appear between the material in 28:5 and 31:18.

12. Regarding the term עוד ("again") in v. 9: Dillmann claims that this word refers back to 28:11ff. (J). Thus, the word was inserted here by a redactor when P and J were brought together in the Pentateuch (Dillmann, *Genesis*, II:305; see also Rad, *Genesis*, 339).

13. Campbell and O'Brien, *Sources*, see "Index of Biblical Passages by Source," 260. For comparable indices of the priestly texts, see Campbell, *Study Companion*, 87–91 (this appendix lists the P texts as identified by Noth, Elliger, and Lohfink); McEvenue,

1. Additions:

    Genesis 25:24-26a—The birth notice of Jacob and Esau. P^N shows a distinct interest in genealogies and birth and death notices. Given the importance of Jacob's role in the document, his birth notice is expected.

    Genesis 43:14a—This is clearly part of P^N as evidenced by the use of P^N's unique designation for God, אל שדי. Along with Gen 41:46a, this verse constitutes the remaining fragment of P^N's account of the Joseph story.[14]

    Genesis 49:22-26—The blessing of Joseph is included due to the appearance of the title אל שדי in conjunction with the theme of abundance, as described earlier.

2. Deletions:

    Genesis 17:1, 8, 14—These verses are actually not to be deleted (except for verse 14, which is all H). I have listed them here merely to point out that they have been modified by H. The H redactor has inserted the divine name יהוה, which is foreign to P^N, into verse 1. This insertion constitutes part of the intentional link by which H attaches P^N to P. In addition, the phrase והייתי להם לאלהים ("I shall be their God") in verse 8 has been inserted by H. Verse 14 reflects the characteristic כרת formula used by H and has apparently been inserted in order to apply the כרת formula to the command regarding circumcision. A discussion of the H redaction of the priestly literature is presented later in this work.

    Genesis 19:29—There is no foundation for this reference to appear in the narrative of P^N. The story of the destruction of the cities is completely missing in P^N. It may be conceded, as with the Joseph story, that this is the only fragment of P^N's account of the destruction of the cities which remains after the compilation

---

Interpreting the Pentateuch, 173–74 (this appendix lists the priestly narrative); and Friedman, *Exile and Biblical Narrative*, 141–47.

14. This appears to be one of the few instances in which an account from P^N has been mostly omitted in the process of compilation with JE. See Noth, *Pentateuchal Traditions*, 14; Campbell and O'Brien, *Sources*, 34 n. 31. In keeping with the character of P^N, the Joseph account was probably a brief narrative relating only the bare essentials of the story in order to explain the presence of Joseph in Egypt and the eventual movement of Jacob and his descendants to Egypt.

of the pentateuchal sources.¹⁵ However, this story has no particular significance for P^N in relation to its themes or interests.

Genesis 21:1b—The use of the name for God, יהוה, here is uncharacteristic of P^N. This verse also has no foundation in P^N, for the promise to Sarah recorded in Gen 18:1–15 is not included in P^N. This entire verse is unnecessary to P^N, as verse 2 picks up the narrative by itself.

Genesis 23:1–20; 25:9–10; 49:1a, 29–33a; 50:12–13—I concur with Rendtorff (and others) who hold that the story of the purchase of the cave at Machpelah is not part of the priestly material.¹⁶ I presume that the other references (listed here, outside of chapter 23) have only been attached to P because they each refer back to the story of chapter 23.¹⁷ Thus, there is no reason to include them in P (or, in this case, P^N).

Genesis 26:34–35; 27:46; 28:6–9—The story of Esau's Hittite wives, Rebekah's dissatisfaction with them, and Esau's subsequent taking of a wife from the daughters of Ishmael appears independent of P^N. In fact these narratives contradict P^N's notice of Esau's wives, as listed in the descendants list for Esau (36:2–5).

According to the texts of Gen 26:34 and 28:9 the wives of Esau were:

- Judith, daughter of Beeri the Hittite
- Basemath, daughter of Elon the Hittite
- Mahalath, daughter of Ishmael, sister of Nebaioth

In contrast, P^N lists the following as Esau's wives:

- Adah, daughter of Elon the Hittite
- Oholibamah, daughter of Anah, granddaughter of Zibeon the Hivite
- Basemath, Ishmael's daughter, sister of Nebaioth

---

15. Noth suggests this verse was originally connected to Gen 13:6, 11b–12aba; *Pentateuchal Traditions*, 13.

16. Rendtorff, *Problem of the Process*, 154–56; Eerdmans, *Komposition der Genesis*, 20–22. The account of Abraham's purchase of the cave (Gen 23) is said to be characteristic of P due to its legal interests. However, Rendtorff points out that only a single verse (23:17) reflects legal style. In addition, the account is a profane story with no mention of God, unlike other legal texts. Whybray, *Making of the Pentateuch*, 60.

17. See Eerdmans, *Genesis*, 21.

Not only is there a distinction in names, but also the only name common to the two lists of wives is attributed to different fathers. Furthermore, it is not simply a mixing of fathers' names, but of heritage as well. In one list Basemath is the daughter of a Hittite, while in the other she is the daughter of Ishmael (a wife whose heritage Esau sought in contrast to the Hittite women who upset his mother). Clearly, the two lists do not belong to the same source.

Genesis 33:18a—This isolated reference has been attributed to P due to the presence of the designation "Paddan-aram."[18] This designation is hardly characteristic of P, as it is traditionally defined, for the term never appears outside of Genesis. Within Genesis, it may simply serve as a common designation. There is no compelling reason to attribute it solely to P. As part of the P^N text this verse is awkward and unnecessary, interrupting the flow of the narrative. P^N flows naturally from 31:18 to 35:6. These two references both include P^N's characteristic emphasis of marking the abundance of people and/or possessions when moving from one place to another. Such emphasis is missing from 33:18a (which also describes movement from one place to another). It is true that Paddan-aram does appear in P, but it also appears in what must be other source material; for example, Gen 28:6–9 (as noted just above, this pericope contradicts material in P^N).

Genesis 36:8–14—The secondary character of this pericope is evident by the fact that it is redundant in relation to the immediately preceding material (Gen 36:1–7). Both describe the genealogy of Esau.

Terminology of P^N

A closer examination of the unique terminology in P^N further reveals the original independence of this document. A major theme for P^N, as identified previously, is the "fruitfulness and multiplication" of those with whom God has established covenant. The verbs, פרה ("to be fruitful") and רבה ("to multiply"), which define this theme, are used together in parallel almost exclusively in P^N. These two verbs appear in parallel fifteen times in the Hebrew Bible. Ten of those occurrences appear in

---

18. Campbell and O'Brien, *Sources*, 32 n. 27, 33 n. 28; Driver, *Introduction*, 135 ("Paddan-Aram" is listed here by Driver among the terms characteristic of P).

P^N.[19] The other five instances of these two verbs used in tandem appear either in references that refer directly back to the associated theme in P^N, or in references that appear to draw upon this theme from P^N for a related purpose.

The first two appearances of these verbs in parallel, outside of P^N, occur in H. The first use by H occurs at Exod 1:7 as part of the appendix to P^N, which was composed by H in order to link P^N and P.[20] Exodus 1:7 clearly echoes the use of these verbs in P^N by describing the increase in number of the children of Israel. The second reference using these two verbs together in H occurs at Lev 26:9. Here again, H echoes the theme from P^N in relation to the increase in number of the children of Israel. In this case the theme is presented as part of a promise conditioned upon obedience to God's commandments, and as a confirmation of God's covenant (Lev 26:3, 9). This confirmation refers to the covenant with Abraham and his descendants as described in P^N (Gen 17:1–8). This is evident, not only from the repetition of the abundance theme (Lev 26:9; cf. Gen 17:2, 6), but also from the repetition of the promise "to be God" to the people (Lev 26:12; cf. Gen 17:7–8). Thus, this reference in H clearly draws from the P^N text of Gen 17.

The final three occurrences of פרה in combination with רבה are found in Jer 3:16; 23:3; and Ezek 36:11. Each of these texts speak of the increase of the children of Israel as part of the future hope of restoration proclaimed by the prophets after the devastation of the fall of the kingdoms of Israel and Judah. The appearance of the verb pair in these instances clearly echoes its use throughout P^N. The prophets draw upon the promise of God connected to the covenant with Abraham in order to proclaim hope in a time of crisis. Thus, it appears that these prophetic texts are dependent upon the earlier text of P^N.

In every instance, this verb pair refers to an increase in number of people (or, in two instances, an increase in number of animals; Gen 1:22; 8:17). Initially, the concern is the population of the newly created world (Gen 1:22, 28). This concern is repeated after the flood (Gen 8:17; 9:1, 7). Then, within the central text of P^N (Gen 17), this concern is focused upon God's covenant with Abraham and his descendants (Gen 17:1–6, 20). Finally, this concern is passed on specifically to the children

19. Gen 1:22, 28; 8:17; 9:1, 7; 17:20; 28:3; 35:11; 47:27b; 48:4.

20. The appendix to P^N is made up of Exod 1:1–7, 13–14; 2:23–25. The redactionary work of H in relation to P^N is presented more fully later in this work.

of Jacob/Israel; first when they are developing as a new people (Gen 28:3; 35:11; 47:27; 48:4; Exod 1:7; Lev 26:9), and secondly when they are given a new hope for restoration following exile (Jer 3:16; 23:3; Ezek 36:11). These two verbs in parallel are found nowhere else in the Hebrew Bible; most significantly, they do not appear in tandem in P (i.e., outside of Genesis or H). The theme is developed in P^N, is echoed in H, and finally echoed again in three verses of the Prophets, but is otherwise never expressed in P. This observation adds weight to the identification of P^N as a document originally independent of P.

The terminology used to refer to God in the priestly literature further establishes the independence and character of P^N. The full title, אל שדי, used in P^N to refer to God, appears only seven times in the Hebrew Bible (Gen 17:1b; 28:3; 35:11; 43:14a; 48:3; Exod 6:3; Ezek 10:5). Of these occurrences, only Ezek 10:5 appears outside of P^N.[21] A clear distinction is evident between P^N and P due to the complete disjunction between the two documents in regard to addressing God. P^N never refers to God as יהוה, and P never refers to God as אל שדי. That this signifies originally independent sources, rather than an intentional transition in reference to God within a single source, is evident by the clear redactional interruption evident at the seam between P^N and P. Exodus 6 is the transitional text that serves to link P^N to P. It is precisely at this point that the identity of God is explicitly transferred from אל שדי to יהוה (Exod 6:2–8). This transitional text reveals the hand of the priestly editor H.[22]

Since the burning bush account is attributed to JE (Exod 3:1–15), and if Exod 6:2–8 is rightly attributed to H, then a supposed unified P (including narrative in Genesis and legal material in Exodus–Numbers) would suddenly, without explanation, change its reference to God from אלהים/אל שדי to יהוה. The reader of P would be confused when the reference to God was suddenly changed without reason or explanation. In fact, the reader may wonder if a second deity had suddenly become the focus of the text. It does not suffice to claim that P simply presumed the

---

21. As a note of interest, Ezek 10:5 is the only occurrence of אל־שדי, with a maqqēp. As will be discussed in relation to the date and setting of P^N, Ezekiel uses the term אל־שדי with a different meaning than that found in Genesis. The occurrence at Exod 6:3 is part of the transition which the H redactor composed in order to tie P^N to the rest of the priestly literature.

22. H's redaction of the priestly literature will be discussed later in this work.

JE account (at Exod. 3:1–15), because JE makes use of the term יהוה in reference to God in accounts well before the burning bush narrative. Thus, if P were composed with dependence upon JE, any attempt to create an intentional distinction between the references used for God before and after the revelation to Moses would be futile. The reader would wonder why P had used אל שדי at all, when the supposedly adjacent JE text referred to God as יהוה even before the revelation to Moses at the burning bush.[23] Consequently, it becomes apparent that P (legal material in Exodus–Numbers) and P[N] (narratives in Genesis traditionally associated with P) were originally independent documents. H brought the two documents together and provided an explanation for, and transition between, the two references for God in the priestly writings.

Another thematic phrase that can be included within terminology unique to P[N] is ארץ מגרים ("land of sojournings"). This phrase occurs only six times in the Hebrew Bible. Four of the occurrences appear in P[N] (Gen 17:8; 28:4; 36:7; 37:1). The fifth occurrence appears in the transitional text of Exod 6 (vs. 4), which links P[N] with P. The only other occurrence in the Hebrew Bible is in the book of Ezekiel (Ezek 20:38).[24]

The unique death notice used in P[N] contributes to the terminology which demonstrates the independence of P[N]. In reporting the deaths of the patriarchs Abraham (and his son Ishmael; Gen 25:8, 17), Isaac (Gen 35:29), and Jacob (Gen 49:33), P[N] uses the formula: ויגוע וימת ויאסף אל־עמיו ("and he expired and died and was gathered to his people"). This complete formula appears only in these four verses in the Hebrew Bible.[25] Thus, this particular formula for indicating a person's death is unique to P[N].

---

23. See Koch, "P—Kein Redaktor," 464–66.

24. The resemblance between Ezekiel and the priestly literature is commonly recognized (See Driver, *Introduction*, 130). This is the third instance in this discussion in which unique P[N] terminology appears in Ezekiel (Ezek 36:11; 10:5; 20:38). In light of the argument that Ezekiel is dependent on the priestly literature (as discussed previously), it appears that P[N] was attached to P and became associated with the priestly literature before the time of Ezekiel.

25. The death notice for Jacob/Israel stands out by virtue of missing the verb וימת (he died). Perhaps this is a symbolic gesture whereby the author seeks to imply that Jacob indeed "expired and was gathered to his people," but Israel lives on as the community that carries on the covenant passed down through the patriarchs.

The genealogical data recorded in P^N also sets apart this source from others. As described below, the use of the *Toledoth* book and the *toledoth* formula are unique to P^N. The regular pattern for genealogical entries, taken from the *Toledoth* book and used by P^N, is not found elsewhere in the Hebrew Scriptures. Similarly, the *toledoth* formula (אלה תולדות), used as a framing device, is exclusive to P^N. [26]

Another designation unique to P^N is the particular way in which this source reports a person's age. Apparently, the most common method of reporting someone's age in the Hebrew Bible is by means of the phrase בן־ ‪ ‬שנה (lit., "a son of X years").[27] A much less common form of designating one's age is the phrase ימי שני חיי (lit., "the days of the years of one's life").[28] A third method of designating one's age appears only in P^N. It is simply the use of the phrase ויהיו ימי ‪ ‬ ("And the days of X were"), or ויהיו כל־ימי ‪ ‬ ("And all the days of X were"). This particular wording appears thirteen times in the Hebrew Bible.[29] Each instance is within P^N, and constitutes an element of terminology found only in P^N.

Also unique to P^N is the recording of birth announcements in conjunction with the age of the father at the time of the birth. This is evident as part of the pattern of the genealogical entries taken from the *Toledoth* book and recorded by P^N at Gen 5:1b–28, 30–32; 11:11–26. Each new generation in the *Toledoth* book is introduced in conjunction with the age of the corresponding father. Similarly, the three birth announcements in P^N, apart from the *Toledoth* book, are also recorded in conjunction with the age of the corresponding father: Abram was eighty-six when Ishmael was born (Gen 16:16), Abraham was one hundred when Isaac was born (Gen 21:5), and Isaac was sixty when Jacob and Esau were born (Gen 25:26). I am not aware of any other instances in the Hebrew Bible in which the birth of a child is announced in di-

---

26. In addition to the 10 occurrences in P^N, the *toledoth* formula appears only at Num 3:1; Ruth 4:18; and 1 Chr 1:29. Numbers 3:1 is an insertion attributable to H. The isolated references in Ruth and 1 Chronicles constitute the only other appearances of this formula in the Hebrew Bible. These two instances merely serve to introduce independent genealogical lists, and do not comprise any connected framework.

27. For example: Gen 7:6; 26:34; Exod 7:7; Lev. 27:3; Num 14:29; Deut 31:2; Josh 14:10; 2 Sam 5:4; 1 Kgs 22:42; 2 Chr 22:2; Jer 52:1; etc.

28. Gen 25:7; 47:8, 9, 28; 2 Sam 19:35 (Eng. v. 34). A shortened version of this phrase, שני חיי, appears at Gen 23:1; 25:17; and ימי שני appears at Eccl 6:3.

29. Gen 5:4, 5, 8, 11, 14, 17, 20, 23, 27, 31; 9:29; 11:32; 35:28.

rect relation to the age of the child's father.³⁰ This seems to be a unique characteristic of P^N.

The precise wording of another phrase that appears to be unique to P^N is זרעך אחריך ("your seed after you"). This particular phrase appears only eight times in the Hebrew Bible. Six of those occurrences designate the descendants of Abraham (Gen 17:7, 8, 9, 10) and Jacob (Gen 35:12; 48:4) in relation to the Abrahamic covenant. The only other two occurrences of this particular wording appear in relation to God's promise of a dynasty for the line of David (2 Sam 7:12; 1 Chr 17:11).³¹

The unique use of terminology in P^N as described above, contributes significant evidence to the recognition of the original independence of this document in relation to the rest of the priestly literature. Most of the terms and phrases which have been discussed are found only in P^N. The rare exceptions to this are found in clearly distinct material outside of the priestly literature. The following chart, which organizes the content of P^N according to like material, highlights P^N's characteristic use of terminology and the tendency to include formal information (genealogies, lists, itineraries, birth and death notices):

Toledoth Formula:

Gen 2:4a—Heavens and the earth
Gen 6:9—Noah
Gen 10:1—Sons of Noah
Gen 11:10—Shem
Gen 11:27—Terah
Gen 25:12—Ishmael
Gen 25:19—Isaac
Gen 36:1—Esau
Gen 37:2a—Jacob

---

30. In only one other passage does it appear that the age of the father is recorded in the same verse as the birth announcement of a child. However, in this instance there may be some question as to whether the age of the father is intended to be associated with the time of his taking a wife, or the time of the birth of the child: 1 Chr 2:21.

31. The Chronicles text clearly borrows from its earlier source in the 2 Samuel text. The 2 Samuel text may reflect a dynasty motif from a document stemming from the court of Solomon. See McCarter, *II Samuel*, 224–25. Perhaps then, P^N has taken this phrase from a known dynastic motif, and applied it to the promise of God to the patriarchs.

Narrative Material:

- Creation account: Gen 1—2:3
- Noah, and the Flood Story: Gen 6:10-22; 7:6, 11, 13-16a, 18-21, 24; 8:1-2a, 3b-5, 7, 13a, 14-19; 9:1-17, 28-29
- Abrahamic covenant: Gen 17:1-13, 15-27
- God blesses Isaac: Gen 25:11a
- Isaac blesses Jacob, and sends him to Paddan-Aram (covenant recited): Gen 28:1-5
- God blesses Jacob (covenant repeated): Gen 35:6, 9-13, 15
- Fragment of Joseph story in Egypt: Gen 43:14a
- Jacob repeats to Joseph (Ephraim and Manasseh) the blessing which he received from God (covenant recited): Gen 48:3-6
- Joseph's blessing: Gen 49:22-26

Genealogies:

- Adam to Noah's sons: Gen 5:1-28, 30-32
- Shem to Abram: Gen 11:11-26

Descendants Lists:

- Sons of Noah: Gen 10:2-7, 20, 22-23, 31-32
- Sons of Ishmael: Gen 25:13-16
- 12 sons of Jacob: Gen 35:22b-27
- Sons of Esau: Gen 36:2-5
- Sons of Jacob who went to Egypt: Gen 46:8-27

Itineraries (along with theme of abundance):

- Migration of Terah and family to Haran: Gen 11:31-32
- Migration of Abraham and his abundance to Canaan: Gen 12:4b-5
- Abraham and Lot separate due to abundance: Gen 13:6, 11b-12aba
- Migration of Jacob and his abundance back to Canaan: Gen 31:18
- Jacob and Esau separate due to abundance: Gen 36:6-7
- Jacob settles in Canaan: Gen 37:1
- Joseph before Pharaoh: Gen 41:46a

- Migration of Jacob and his abundance to Egypt: Gen 46:6–7
- Jacob fruitful in Egypt: Gen 47:27b–28

Birth Notices:

- Birth of Ishmael: Gen 16:1a, 3, 15–16
- Birth of Isaac: Gen 21:2–5
- Birth of Jacob and Esau: Gen 25:20, 24–26

Death Notices:

- Death of Abraham: Gen 25:7–8
- Death of Ishmael: Gen 25:17
- Death of Isaac: Gen 35:28–29
- Death of Jacob: Gen 49:33b

Structure of P^N

The use of genealogies in P^N goes beyond merely the inclusion of formal data. P^N uses the *Toledoth* book and a formula derived from the book as structural devices to organize the entire document. The *Toledoth* book refers to a source containing genealogies which follow a particular pattern for each entry. P^N includes the entries from this source which list the genealogical data from Adam to Terah. Thus, the *Toledoth* book is evident only in Gen 5 and Gen 11:10–26. The consistent pattern of the genealogical entries from the book is not found in the Hebrew Bible outside of these two lists. The *toledoth* formula, on the other hand, refers to the heading which P^N uses to organize and frame the P^N narrative. This formula is simply: אלה תולדות _ ("these are the generations of X").[32] P^N has apparently devised this formula from the heading of the *Toledoth* book which begins: זה ספר תולדת ("this is the book of the generations").[33]

---

32. See Cross, *Canaanite Myth*, 301–5; Fohrer, *Introduction*, 183.

33. See, Noth, *Pentateuchal Traditions*, 235. Noth prompted this thought with the statement that the *toledoth* formula (P's superscriptions) is an occasional imitation of the *Toledoth* Book.

P^N's Use of the Toledoth Book

Gerhard von Rad suggested that זה ספר תולדת ("this is the book of the generations") designates the beginning of the actual *Toledoth* book (Gen 5:1).[34] Following this title is the genealogy from Adam until the three sons of Noah: Shem, Ham, and Japheth (Gen 5:3–32). This genealogy was composed with a very definite pattern. Each genealogical entry is worded in three sentences as follows:

A) ויחי־X, Y שנה ויולד את־Z

B) ויחי־X אחרי הולידו את־Z W שנה ויולד בנים ובנות

C) ויהיו כל־ימי־X, V שנה וימת

A) "And X lived Y (number) years, and became the father of Z.

B) And X lived, after becoming the father of Z, W (number) years, and became the father of (other) sons and daughters.

C) And all the days of X were V (number) years, and he died."

This pattern is very consistent in chapter five of Genesis, so that any variation is quite noticeable. The first break in the pattern appears in the very first genealogical entry, regarding Adam (Gen 5:3–5). Here the hand of P^N is evident acting upon this first entry of the *Toledoth* book. Instead of simply naming the son of Adam, P^N adds the description that Adam's son was born בדמותו כצלמו ("in his likeness and according to his image"). By adding this phrase, P^N links the beginning of the *Toledoth* book to the creation account which uses the same terminology to describe how the first human was made in the image and likeness of God (Gen 1:26). Aside from this insertion, the entry for Adam follows the pattern of the genealogical entries from the *Toledoth* book with the exception of a couple of minor variations which appear to reveal the distinct style or concern of P^N. Since P^N has already disrupted the pattern in the first entry, the particular style of P^N becomes noticeable in the rest of the initial entry. Instead of the usual wording in the second sentence of the pattern [B], ויחי־__ אחרי הולידו את־__ ("And X lived, after

---

34. Von Rad, *Genesis*, 70. See also Wenham, "Priority of P," 241–42.

becoming the father of Z, . . .")], P^N writes: ויהיו ימי־אדם אחרי הולידו את־ שת ("And the days of Adam were, after becoming the father of Seth, . . ."; Gen 5:4). Thus, it appears that P^N prefers to designate a person's life span by means of the phrase ויהיו ימי־_ ("And the days of X were").[35] That P^N intends the same meaning by this distinct wording is apparent when the phrase אשר־חי ("which he lived") is added to the third sentence of the pattern (C), in the case of the Adam entry (Gen 5:5). Thereby, P^N indicates that the phrase "the days of someone" is synonymous with the phrase "someone lived" (a certain number of years).

Accordingly, if the phrase ויהיו ימי־_ ("And the days of X were") indicates the hand of P^N, then the third sentence of the pattern (C) in each of the normal genealogical entries in Gen 5 may have been added by P^N. That is, P^N simply summed up the years a person lived before and after they became the father of the son indicated in the entry, then recorded that total number of years, and finally stated that the person died. In this way, P^N left most of the entries of Gen 5 untouched, except to finish each entry with a notice of the total life span of the individual, and a statement that the individual died. This suggestion is affirmed by examining the genealogical entries found in the other genealogy in P^N taken from the *Toledoth* book, that is, Gen 11:10b–26. These entries follow the same pattern as that described for Gen 5, except that none of them includes the third sentence of the pattern (C), that is, ויהיו כל־ימי־ _ שנה וימת ("And all the days of X were V years, and he died."). Thus, in the case of the genealogy found at Gen 11:10b–26, P^N chose to leave the entries as they were, and not to add the summation of each individual's life span along with a notice of death.

The second major disruption which P^N creates in the pattern of the genealogical entries of Gen 5 occurs in the entry concerning Enoch (Gen 5:21–24). The first sentence of the Enoch entry (A) is normal with regard to the pattern described above (Gen 5:21). In the second sentence (B), however, instead of stating that "Enoch lived, after becoming the father of Methuselah, three hundred years," P^N inserts that Enoch "walked about with God" three hundred years after becoming the father of Methuselah (Gen 5:22). Then, after adding the summation of Enoch's life span to the entry (Gen 5:23), P^N writes a different death

---

35. Recall the previous discussion of this phrase in relation to terminology unique to P^N (i.e., P^N's preferred means of designating one's age).

notice for Enoch's entry: "And Enoch walked about with God, and he was not because God took him" (Gen 5:24).

A third disruption to the pattern occurs within the genealogical entry for Lamech (Gen 5:28–31). This entry contains all the usual elements (all three sentences; A, B, C) of the genealogical pattern as described above. The entry is interrupted with an insertion, which if removed, leaves the pattern in its normal state. The entry begins with the usual pattern regarding the first sentence (A), except instead of naming the son to whom Lamech became a father, the entry is changed to merely state that Lamech became father to בן ("a son") (Gen 5:28). Then the insertion states that this son is named Noah and he will bring rest from the labors caused by the ground which the Lord cursed (Gen 5:29). The insertion is clearly alien to P^N. This is evident because the insertion refers to God as יהוה which is uncharacteristic of P^N, and the insertion refers to the cursing of the ground which is linked to the J creation account in Gen 3.[36]

The final disruption to the normal pattern of the genealogical entries found in Gen 5 occurs in the final entry, regarding Noah. This entry only contains the first sentence of the pattern (A); however, instead of naming one son to whom Noah became father, the entry names three sons. It appears that the *Toledoth* book may have originally named only Shem as the son of Noah in this entry. This is due to the fact that the following genealogical entry (after Noah) designates only Shem, as recorded in Gen 11:10–11. At that point the genealogical entries continue, without major disruption, in accordance with the pattern described above. Although, as mentioned previously, the entries in Gen 11:10b–26 appear in their original form, and do not include P^N's summation of years lived, along with a notice of death (sentence C of

---

36. Wenham affirms: "It is universally agreed that v 29 is a J passage" (Wenham, "Priority of P," 243). He also argues that the disruption in v. 3 may be attributed to J, based on the use of the phrase, "and he called his name..." Thereby, Wenham states that J appears to have edited elements at the beginning and end of the genealogy in Gen 5. This contributes to his thesis that P served as a source for J rather than *vice-versa*. I concur that J appears to have inserted v. 29 into the genealogical entry concerning Lamech, and thus appears to have edited this entry (as incorporated in P^N). However, it is not conclusive that the same is true for the disruption in v. 3. As described above, the changes in v. 3 appear to come from the hand of P^N and do not show signs of J. Wenham's only evidence for attributing v. 3 to J is a phrase which he notes appears a number of times elsewhere in Genesis, though not exclusively in J texts.

the pattern). Thus, it appears that the *Toledoth* book originally listed genealogies from Adam to Terah (Gen 5:1a, 3–32; 11:10b–26). Between the entries regarding Noah and Shem, we find the insertion of P^N's brief narrative regarding the Flood.

The hand of P^N changed the genealogical entry recorded in Gen 5:32 from naming Shem as the son of Noah, to naming all three sons of Noah. This change served as a transition for the insertion of the flood story which P^N introduces by means of the *toledoth* formula naming Noah: אלה תולדת נח ("these are the generations of Noah"; Gen 6:9). Noah is then described as a righteous and blameless man who "walked about with God," just as Enoch was described as one who walked about with God (Gen 6:9; cf. 5:22, 24). The following verse (Gen 6:10) repeats the genealogical statement that Noah became the father of Shem, Ham, and Japheth (cf. Gen 5:32). This creates an intentional link between the preceding genealogical entries (Gen 5:3–32) and the story of the flood.[37]

P^N's flood story ends with the familiar pattern that was repeated throughout the genealogical entries in Gen 5:

B) ויחי־נח אחר המבול שלש מאות שנה וחמשים שנה

C) ויהיו כל־ימי־נח תשע מאות שנה וחמשים שנה וימת

> B) "And Noah lived, after the flood, three hundred and fifty years.
>
> C) And all the days of Noah were nine hundred and fifty years, and he died." (Gen 9:28–29)

In this case, however, the genealogical entry pattern includes only the second (B) and third (C) sentences of the pattern as P^N normally employed it in Gen 5. The first sentence (A) of this particular genealogical entry (regarding Noah) appears just before the flood, at the end of the genealogical listing in Gen 5 (i.e., at v. 32). Thus, the flood story is enveloped within the last entry of the genealogical list in Gen 5. That is, the entire P^N flood story is inserted between the first (A) and second

---

37. In contrast to Friedman's argument that this repetition demonstrates that two separate strata of priestly work are evident here. Friedman, *Exile and Biblical Narrative*, 78–79.

(B) sentences of the genealogical entry regarding Noah (Gen 5:32 and 9:28–29).[38] This can be illustrated as follows:

> A) "And Noah was five hundred years old, and Noah became the father of Shem, Ham, and Japheth" (Gen 5:32).
>
> *The Flood Account (Gen 6:9–22; 7:6, 11, 13–16a, 18–21, 24; 8:1–2a, 3b–5, 7, 13a, 14–19; 9:1–17).*
>
> B) "And Noah lived, after the flood, three hundred and fifty years.
>
> C) And all the days of Noah were nine hundred and fifty years, and he died." (Gen 9:28–29).

The connection which P^N creates between the genealogical entry begun in Gen 5:32 and the flood account is further evident from the summation of Noah's age at the end of the flood story. P^N states that Noah was nine hundred and fifty years when he died (Gen 9:29). In accordance with the third sentence (C) of the genealogical entry pattern, this is normally the summation of the years before and after becoming the father of the son specified in an entry. In this case, the entry begins by stating that Noah was five hundred when he became father to his three sons (Gen 5:32), and further indicates that Noah lived three hundred and fifty years after "the flood" (Gen 9:28; the flood has taken the place of the three sons of Noah in the genealogical entry). From this, it appears that Noah lived a total of eight hundred and fifty years. The missing one hundred years are taken from the midst of the flood story where it is said that Noah was six hundred when the flood waters began (Gen 7:6). Thus, the summation of Noah's years before the flood and his years after the flood equals nine hundred and fifty years (Noah's age when he died; Gen 9:29).

P^N solidifies the tie between the genealogy of Gen 5 and the flood account by making clear to the reader that "the flood" is to be identified with the position of the three sons of Noah in the genealogical entry regarding Noah. This is initially accomplished by the repetition of the first sentence (A) of the Noah genealogical entry (originally recorded

---

38. See von Rad, *Genesis*, 68. The first line of this genealogical entry for Noah (Gen 5:32) expresses the age of Noah using the more common phrase בן _־שנה (lit., "a son of X years"). This further demonstrates the disruption of the original Noah entry from the *Toledoth* book.

at Gen 5:32) *within* the flood account (at Gen 6:10, after P^N introduced the flood account at Gen 6:9). The absence of Noah's age is significant in this repetitive entry (Gen 6:10). The transition between the three sons of Noah and "the flood" continues at Gen 7:6 in which the first sentence (A) of the Noah genealogical entry is echoed a third time. This time, however, Noah's age *is* given, in conjunction with when the flood waters came (were born?) upon the earth. The transition from the three sons of Noah to "the flood" is completed at Gen 9:28–29. Here "the flood" has taken the position of the three sons in the second sentence (B) of the genealogical entry regarding Noah (Gen 9:28).

The next entry from the *Toledoth* book (after Noah and the flood) identifies Shem and his son, and begins at Gen 11:10b. Following this entry, the genealogical pattern described previously is followed from Shem to Terah (without P^N's insertion of the summation of age and a death notice for each entry).[39] At the last entry, concerning Terah, P^N intervenes in a similar manner as with the flood account. Here, however, the insertion is simply the short account of the migration of Terah and his family to Canaan. As with the earlier genealogical entry for Noah, Terah is said to have become the father of three sons (Gen 11:26). The next verse contains P^N's introduction to the short account of Terah's migration (Gen 11:27a). Next, similar to the flood account, P^N repeats the notice of Terah becoming the father of three sons (Gen 11:27b). This repetition is inserted within the account of Terah's migration to Canaan (Gen 11:27, 31) in order to tie together this account with the preceding genealogical list. Finally, the notice of Terah's age and his death closes the account of the migration to Canaan (Gen 11:32). Thus, as the flood is enveloped by the genealogical entry of Noah, so the short account of Terah's migration (Gen 11:27, 31) is enveloped within the genealogical entry of Terah (Gen 11:26, 32). The notice regarding the death of Terah also closes P^N's use of the *Toledoth* book. Its familiar pattern for genealogical entries is not found again in the Hebrew Scriptures.

---

39. Wenham notes that the pattern for the opening line (A) is slightly varied in the first three genealogical entries (vv. 10b, 12, and 14). However, beginning with the entry at v. 16 the pattern from chapter 5 is followed closely. Wenham, "Priority of P," 242.

P^N's Use of the Toledoth Formula

The use of the *toledoth* formula in P^N not only marks Gen 17 as a central feature of the document, but also organizes the work into distinct sections. The formula serves as a framework for the document. The first appearance of the formula constitutes a concluding statement for the creation account which begins the document, and the final appearance of the formula introduces the account of the final patriarch (Jacob) whose death notice concludes P^N.

Cross has identified the *toledoth* framing device as the formula אלה תולדות, and observes the following twelve appearances of this formula: Gen 2:4a; 5:1; 6:9; 10:1; 11:10, 27; 25:12, 19; 36:1, 9; 37:2; and Num 3:1.[40] Of these twelve, Cross notes that two are secondary: Gen 36:9 is redundant in relation to 36:1 (both mark the generations of Esau), and Num 3:1 is conflated with a following genealogy headed by the formula אלה שמות.[41] Furthermore, we observe that the appearance of the exact wording of the formula excludes Gen 5:1 from the list of headings. Thus, the original formula appears at Gen 2:4a; 6:9; 10:1; 11:10; 11:27; 25:12; 25:19; 36:1; and 37:2a. In accordance with the content of P^N as listed previously, Gen 17 appears as the only substantial narrative within the central *toledoth* section of P^N. That is, the *toledoth* heading designating the family of Abraham (beginning with Abraham's father, Terah; Gen 11:27) is enveloped by four *toledoth* sections prior to the one designating Terah, and four *toledoth* sections following the one designating Terah. Thus, Gen 17 appears highlighted as a central point in the framework of P^N. The *toledoth* formula serves not only to identify this central portion of the document, but also, outlines the entire work and contributes to the identification of its parameters.

The first appearance of the *toledoth* formula occurs at the end of the creation account (Gen 2:4a). Here the object of the formula is the heavens and the earth. Normally, the formula appears *before* a descendants list, or *before* a story about the person (or about descendants of the person) designated by the formula. In this first case, however, the creation account itself must be told before a record of its account can be formally stated. This fosters the image that the creation must come into existence before it is possible for anyone to record its history of origin.

---

40. Cross, *Canaanite Myth*, 301–5.
41. Ibid., 302 n. 33, 308 n. 47.

Thus, the first appearance of the *toledoth* formula appears immediately following the creation account. Included within this first section of P^N appears P^N's initial use of the *Toledoth* book whose opening statement (Gen 5:1a) comprises the introduction from which the *toledoth* formula was devised. The following material in this first section of P^N consists of genealogical data from Adam to Noah's sons.

The second section of P^N begins with the second appearance of the *toledoth* formula itself (Gen 6:9). Here the formula designates Noah and introduces the flood account. This section closes with the death of Noah (Gen 9:29).

The third appearance of the *toledoth* formula (Gen 10:1) designates the sons of Noah and opens the next section of P^N, which is comprised simply of a descendants list of Noah's sons.[42]

---

42. This list is often identified as the priestly portion of the "Table of Nations" (Gen 10:1–7, 20, 22–23, 31–32). It interrupts the continuous flow of P^N's use of the *Toledoth* Book, evident in Gen 5 and 11:10–26, as described previously. Cross suggests that P split up the *Toledoth* Book in this fashion in order to separate the era of creation (Gen 1) from that of Noah (Gen 6–9), and the era of Noah from that of the Patriarchs (Gen 12 and following; Cross, *Canaanite Myth*, 301). The place of the Table of Nations (Gen 10), however, appears redundant in that it seems to parallel the genealogy of Gen 11:10–26 (esp. Gen 10: 22, 31; Cross, *Canaanite Myth*, 301; Friedman, *Exile and Biblical Narrative*, 79). Dillmann's comments, however, contend that the priestly (A = P in Dillmann's scheme) portion of the Table of Nations "is not superfluous in view of ch. xi. 10ff., but necessary" (Dillmann, *Genesis*, I: 312). That is, chapter 10 provides an expected presentation of the significance of the sons of Noah in relation to the generations of the *nations* after the flood. This universal emphasis is distinct from the concern picked up in Gen 11:10–26 which focuses more specifically on generations leading up to Terah, Abraham, and eventually to Israel.

Von Rad points out that the Table of Nations reflects the political-historical viewpoint of its time, and appears to point to a picture of the seventh century (von Rad, *Genesis*, 140–44). Along similar lines, Westermann observes that the sons of Japheth listed at Gen 10:2–3 represent nations which did not become known to Israel until the seventh century. Westermann, *Genesis 1–11*, 503–6. If this is the case, then Gen 10:1–7, 20, 22–23, 31–32 might be considered a later insertion in relation to P^N (which I will argue dates to the eighth century B.C.E.). Consequently, original P^N would not have included the disruption caused by the Table of Nations, but would have flowed coherently from the first half of the *Toledoth* Book (Gen 5 with the insertion of the flood account enveloped in the last entry) ending with Noah, to the second half of the use of the *Toledoth* book (Gen 11:10–26) beginning with Shem. The original structure of P^N would still reflect a central turning point at Gen 17, with four occurrences of the *toledoth* formula before the Abrahamic covenant (Gen 2:4a; 6:9; 11:10, 27) and four occurrences after the covenant (25:12, 19; 36:1; 37:2a).

The next appearance of the *toledoth* formula designates Shem (Gen 11:10). It introduces the section of P^N which incorporates the second part of the *Toledoth* book as it is found in P^N (genealogies from Shem to Terah).

The fifth appearance of the *toledoth* formula designates Terah (Gen 11:27) and introduces the brief account of the migration of Terah and his family to Canaan. At this point, P^N no longer makes use of the *Toledoth* book itself. Apparently, the *Toledoth* book concluded with the genealogical entry regarding Terah, or the rest of the book was lost. P^N continues this section, introduced by the *toledoth* formula designating Terah, by continuing the migration account of Terah's family. The emphasis shifts, however, from Terah to his son, Abram (Gen 12:4b–5). As recorded in Gen 11:31–32, the family originally headed out for Canaan, but only made it as far as Haran, where Terah died. Genesis 12:4b–5 directly picks up the account by indicating that Abram, the son of Terah, continued the journey from Haran to the land of Canaan. This section includes the central feature of P^N, the Abrahamic covenant (Gen 17). The section closes with P^N's death notice regarding Abraham.

The next section of P^N opens with the *toledoth* formula which designates Ishmael (Gen 25:12). This brief section simply contains a descendants list regarding the sons of Ishmael, and closes with P^N's death notice regarding Ishmael.

The seventh section of P^N is introduced by the *toledoth* formula which designates Isaac (Gen 25:19). This section includes narrative regarding the birth of Isaac's sons, and an account that highlights Jacob as the heir of the Abrahamic covenant (see esp. Gen 35:9–13). This section concludes with a descendants list regarding the sons of Jacob, and P^N's death notice regarding Isaac.

The following section opens with the *toledoth* formula which designates Esau (Gen 36:1). The *toledoth* formula regarding Esau is followed by a descendants list of the sons of Esau, and a brief notice regarding the abundance of Jacob and Esau.[43]

The final section of P^N begins with the *toledoth* formula which designates Jacob (Gen 37:2a). This section contains an account of Jacob and his sons, including their move to Egypt, and the important passing

---

43. Regarding the secondary character of the appearance of the *toledoth* formula at Gen 36:9, see Cross, *Canaanite Myth*, 302 n. 33, 308 n. 47.

of the covenant blessing to Joseph (Gen 48:3–6). The section concludes with a death notice regarding Jacob.

Following is an outline of the complete structure of PN in accordance with the description above:

—The Priestly creation account; Gen 1—2:3

I. Toledoth Formula (Heavens and the earth); Gen 2:4a
   —Heading of Toledoth book; Gen 5:1a
   —Genealogy (Adam to Noah's sons); Gen 5:1b–28, 30–32

II. Toledoth Formula (Noah); Gen 6:9
   —The flood account; Gen 6:10–22; 7:6, 11, 13–16a, 18–21, 24; 8:1–2a, 3b–5, 7, 13a, 14–19; 9:1–17, 28–29

III. Toledoth Formula (Sons of Noah); Gen 10:1
   —Descendants list (Sons of Noah); Gen 10:2–7, 20, 22–23, 31–32

IV. Toledoth Formula (Shem); Gen 11:10
   —Genealogy (Shem to Terah's sons); Gen 11:11–26

V. Toledoth Formula (Terah); Gen 11:27
   —Migration of Terah and family to Haran; Gen 11:31–32
   —Migration of Abram and abundance to Canaan; Gen 12:4b–5
   —Abundance of Abram and Lot forces separation; Gen 13:6, 11b–12aba
   —Birth of Ishmael to Abram; Gen 16:1a, 3, 15–16
   —Abrahamic covenant; Gen 17:1–13, 15–27
   —Birth of Isaac to Abraham; Gen 21:2–5
   —Death notice: Abraham; Gen 25:7–8, 11a

VI. Toledoth Formula (Ishmael); Gen 25:12
   —Descendants list (Sons of Ishmael); Gen 25:13–16
   —Death notice: Ishmael; Gen 25:17

VII. Toledoth Formula (Isaac); Gen 25:19
   —Birth of Jacob and Esau; Gen 25:20, 24–26
   —Isaac blesses Jacob, reflecting abundance and covenant; Gen 28:1–5
   —Migration of Jacob and abundance back to Canaan; Gen 31:18
   —God blesses Jacob as heir to Abrahamic covenant; Gen 35:6, 9–13, 15

—Descendants list (12 sons of Jacob); Gen 35:22b–27
—Death notice: Isaac; Gen 35:28–29

VIII. Toledoth Formula (Esau); Gen 36:1
—Descendants list (Sons of Esau); Gen 36:2–5
—Abundance of Jacob and Esau causes separation; Gen 36:6–7
—Jacob settles in Canaan; Gen 37:1[44]

IX. Toledoth Formula (Jacob); Gen 37:2a
—Joseph before Pharaoh; Gen 41:46a
—Fragment of Joseph story in Egypt; Gen 43:14a
—Migration of Jacob and his abundance to Egypt; Gen 46:6–7
—Descendants list (Sons of Jacob who went to Egypt); Gen 46:8–27
—Jacob fruitful in Egypt; Gen 47:27b–28
—Jacob repeats to Joseph the covenant blessing; Gen 48:3–6
—Joseph's blessing emphasizing abundance; Gen 49: 22, 25–26
—Death notice: Jacob; Gen 49:33b

Exodus 6: Redactional Link between P and P^N

The redactional transition which serves to link P^N to P includes three significant passages: Exod 1:1–7, 13–14; Exod 2:23–25; and Exod 6. The first two texts serve to bridge the gap between P^N which ends with the death of Jacob and the formal transitional link to P at Exod 6. Exodus 1:1–7, 13–14 and Exod 2:23–25 extend themes from P^N by repeating the unique terminology of "fruitfulness and multiplication" (Exod 1:7), and by recalling God's covenant with Abraham stemming from Gen 17 (Exod 2:24). These two passages also provide the foundation for the main transitional link of Exod 6 by establishing the major incentive for God's revelation in Exod 6, that is, the harsh labor which the Egyptians imposed on the children of Israel (Exod 1:13–14), the resultant cries of the children of Israel (Exod 2:23), and the response of God in remembering the covenant (Exod 2:24–25). This incentive for God's revelation to Moses is verified at Exod 6:5. This verse constitutes a response to the

---

44. Each of the *toledoth* sections, beginning with the *toledoth* of Terah/Abraham, concludes with a death notice, except for the *toledoth* of Esau. The redaction of the Esau *toledoth* by the hand of H will be discussed later. Perhaps the death notice for Esau was lost in the process of that redaction.

situation of harsh labor described in Exod 1:13–14 and 2:23–25, and echoes the terminology of those two passages as follows:

1. Exod 6:5—אני שמעתי את־נאקת בני ישראל ("I have heard the groaning of the children of Israel"); cf. Exod 2:24—וישמע אלהים את־נאקתם ("God heard their groaning").
2. Exod 6:5—Use of a hiphil form of the verb עבד in describing the labor which the Egyptians forced on the children of Israel; cf. Exod 1:13 (also cf. the use of the related noun, עבדה, in Exod 1:14; 2:23).
3. Exod 6:5—ואזכר את־בריתי ("And I have remembered my covenant"); cf. Exod 2:24—ויזכר אלהים את־בריתו ("And God remembered His covenant").

The parallel terminology between Exod 1:13–14; 2:23–25 and Exod 6:5, as well as the foundation which Exod 1:1–7, 13–14; 2:23–25 lays for the revelation to Moses in Exod 6 (especially in relation to v. 5) suggests that these passages all stem from the same hand.[45]

Exodus 6 serves as the intentional link or transition between P[N] and P itself. This is initially evident by recognizing that Exod 6 refers back to the center of P[N] (the Abrahamic covenant at Gen 17) and points forward to the work of P. A priestly redactor thus ties the tradition reflected in P[N] into the P source itself. The key to this link is the transition from recognizing God as אלהים/אל שדי to recognizing God as יהוה.

P[N] reflects a tradition that recognizes God as אל שדי and אלהים, in contrast to P, which clearly identifies God as יהוה. P's preference for יהוה is evident not only in P's command formula וידבר יהוה אל־משה, but also throughout P. It appears that a priestly redactor composed Exod 6 in order to attach P[N] to P and to identify the God of P[N] with the God described in P. If the same author had composed both works, then only one of the divine names would be expected throughout, and the transitional link in Exod 6 would be unnecessary.[46] This is substantiated by

---

45. I contend later in this work that H is the redactor responsible for Exod 6. In light of the connections just described, Exod 1:1–7, 13–14; 2:23–25 should also be assigned to H.

46. It is commonly argued that the switch in divine names may be an intentional device on the part of the priestly writer to highlight the significance of the divine revelation to Moses. Accordingly, God is known as אלהים up until God reveals the divine name יהוה to Moses. This could be considered an intentional transition within one and the same source, P. Such an argument would be reasonable if the explanation of the

the distribution of the use of the divine names in the two documents. Especially significant is the one unique appearance of יהוה in the context of P^N (see below).

Klaus Koch substantiates the view that Exod 6:2–8 is a turning point in P. He sees it as a coordinating point within P between the patriarchal material up to the oppression in Egypt and the deliverance-from-Egypt account up to Sinai. Koch confirms that, in the P stratum, the divine name יהוה is used for the first time in place of אלהים at Exod 6.⁴⁷ However, there is actually one verse where this occurs prior to Exod 6, that is, Gen 17:1:

ויהי אברם בן־תשעים שנה ותשע שנים וירא יהוה אל־אברם ויאמר

אליו אני־אל שדי התהלך לפני והיה תמים

> And Abraham was 99 years old when the Lord (יהוה) appeared to Abraham, and said to him, "I am *El Shaddai* (אל שדי), walk before me and be blameless."

This is the only occurrence of יהוה in all of the traditionally accepted P material in Genesis. This material clearly prefers אלהים when referring to God. This exception in Gen 17:1 must be an insertion of the divine name by the priestly redactor who combined the work of P and P^N.⁴⁸ The insertion is made to further link Gen 17 to Exod 6. It does not picture a contradiction, for God does not appear to Abraham as יהוה, but only as אל שדי. The name יהוה is only inserted in the mouth of the

---

transition (Exod 6) were also written by the same author (P). However, the text which explains the transition in divine names (Exod 6) appears to be the work of the priestly redactor H (as will be argued later in this work). Thus, the unity of the two texts which refer to God with diverse titles is called into question. Without Exod 6 (written later by H), the supposed unified P contains no account of the divine revelation to Moses of the name יהוה. Thus, the designation for God would change within the document without any explanation.

47. Koch, "P—Kein Redaktor," 462–63.

48. As evidence that J edited P, Wenham argues that Gen 17:1a ("The LORD appeared to him") constitutes J's editorial introduction to the chapter. Wenham, "Priority of P," 249. Wenham affirms that this introductory remark is secondary to the rest of Gen 17, and lists other J texts which utilize the Niphal of ראה in the same manner as in Gen 17:1a (The LORD *appeared* to him). I agree with the secondary character of Gen 17:1a, but I submit that the hand of H is reflected here, rather than J. The use of the phrase, "The LORD appeared to X" is not unique to J, and thereby does not seem distinctive of J material (cf. Deut 31:15; 1 Kgs 9:2; 2 Chr 7:12).

narrator, and serves to identify the God referred to in this passage as the same God described in the P material to which this passage within its source (P[N]) is now being attached (via the link of Exod 6).

The transition of divine names which unites P[N] to P is further evidenced by the unique phrase, וידבר אלהים אל־משה ("And *Elohim* said to Moses"). This formula appears only once in the Hebrew Bible, at Exod 6:2. It mimics the 91 occurrences of the phrase וידבר יהוה אל־משה ("And YHWH said to Moses"), which appears throughout P and aids in the identification of the parameter of P (as described previously). The unique version of this phrase in Exod 6:2 serves to highlight the transition between אלהים and יהוה, and link P[N] to P.

This transition regarding the name by which the God of Israel is to be known is not carried out simply to replace one term for the Divine with another. Rather, the concern here is to bring the traditions of one community of worshipers in line with another community of worshipers. There is not only a transition from the use of אלהים to יהוה, but in addition, the two terms are combined in a unique phrase of identification for the deity: אני יהוה אלהיכם. As expected, this unique phrase first occurs within P materials at the transitional chapter of Exod 6 (verse 7). It then recurs inserted throughout P as a characteristic of the redactor who attached P[N] to P. Thus, the priestly literature (as redacted by H) does not reflect a transition from one divine reference to another, but rather reflects the joining of two references for God.

The movement toward יהוה is most explicit in Exod 6:2–3:

וידבר אלהים אל־משה ויאמר אליו אני יהוה:

וארא אל־אברהם אל־יצחק ואל־יעקב באל שדי ושמי יהוה לא

נודעתי להם:

> 2) And God spoke to Moses, and said to him, "I am the Lord (יהוה). 3) And I appeared to Abraham, to Isaac, and to Jacob as El Shaddai (אל שדי), but (by) my name, YHWH (יהוה), I did not make myself known to them.

The reference to the revelation of אל שדי refers most explicitly to Gen 17, but also to each of the other four occurrences of this divine title which unite the patriarchal material in P[N].[49] The transition also trig-

---

49. Gen 28:3; 35:11; 43:14a; 48:3.

gers the recognition of אלהים (main designation for God in P^N) as יהוה, which is the name by which God is known in P.⁵⁰

Koch supports the argument that P is an independent document, and not a redaction of JE, by reference to this new revelation of God's name in Exod 6:2–3. If this were a P redactional passage within the Pentateuch, Exod 6:2–3 would come too late, for God has already revealed himself as יהוה in Exod. 3:13–15. In addition, it would be difficult to explain why the P redactor allows the apparently clear movement from Exod 2:24–25 to Exod 6:2–8 to be disrupted by Exod 3–4. Furthermore, the superseding of the manifestation of אל שדי to the Patriarchs by the proclamation of the name יהוה commencing with Moses, is difficult to explain as a P redactional element within the pentateuchal sources. Given the importance of the divine name, יהוה, the statement of Exod 6:3 would be a "direct slap in the face" to the JE strand which presupposes the name יהוה throughout the patriarchal history and before. Even the self-introductory formula, אני יהוה, was announced to the patriarchs in JE (Gen 15:7; 28:13). Koch concludes by questioning how a redactor, who copied and commented on Genesis and incorporated without objection the name יהוה many times, could then imply that all of that material does not presuppose a knowledge of the name יהוה on the part of the Patriarchs.⁵¹

Accordingly, Koch convincingly demonstrates the distinction between JE and P as separate sources. However, this does not clarify why the priestly writer would resort to a different divine name in the primeval and patriarchal periods than that used in the period of the exodus from Egypt and beyond. Koch mentions that the transition in names serves to coordinate the two different epochs in the history of Israel, and thereby help structure the Pentateuch.⁵² In contrast to Koch, however, the change within the content of the history itself seems sufficient to mark the two epochs, that is, from family groups free in Canaan to a small multitude oppressed in Egypt. Furthermore, as noted previously, without the work of the redactor who added Exod 6 (H), P by itself would have no explanation for the transition of divine references, or

---

50. Koch, "P—Kein Redaktor," 463.
51. Koch, Ibid., 464–66.
52. Ibid., 462.

even any account of the revelation to introduce the new divine name יהוה.

Upon clarifying the redactionary work of H (to be presented later in this work), it becomes apparent that Exod 6 serves to join P^N and P. In P^N God is recognized as אלהים and אל שדי, while P refers to God as יהוה. The priestly redactor composed Exod 6:2–8 in order to identify the two divine titles as referring to one and the same Deity, and to attach the two corresponding works. Thereby, the priestly redactor brought those who follow the P^N tradition into subjection to the legal requirements set forth in P.

4

The Provenience and Intent of P^N

THE NORTHERN PROVENIENCE OF P^N IS SUGGESTED BY THE CLIMAX OF the thematic emphasis on the Abrahamic covenant. The transmission of the Abrahamic covenant is clearly a major theme in relation to the intent of P^N. Two key texts relating this theme suggest a northern provenience for P^N. Genesis 35:9-13 relates the passing of the covenant to Jacob in a direct revelation from God. Within this text, just before relating the covenant, God explicitly changes Jacob's name to Israel. Thus, it is not Jacob who receives the covenant and its blessings, but rather, Israel, after whom the northern kingdom is identified.[1]

---

1. The identification of the northern kingdom as "Israel" has been considered a late (exilic or later) development. However, there is evidence that suggests that the northern kingdom may have been recognized by the name "Israel" during the eighth and possibly as early as the ninth century. The Moabite Stone (ca. 840–820 B.C.E.) refers to "Omri, king of Israel" as the one who humbled Moab. "The Moabite Stone," translated by W. F. Albright (*ANET*, 320). A line within the annals of Shalmaneser III, regarding the fight against the Aramean coalition (858–824 B.C.E.), identifies Ahab (king of the northern kingdom) as "the Israelite." "Texts from Hammurabi to the Downfall of the Assyrian Empire," translated by A. Leo Oppenheim (*ANET*, 279). With regard to biblical evidence, the eighth-century prophet Hosea occasionally refers to his northern audience as "Israel" (Hos 1:4; 5:1). Especially telling is the appearance of Israel and Judah as distinct kingdoms in the same passage (Hos 2:1-3 [Eng., 1:10—2:1]). Wolff understands this passage as reflective of the period *before* the collapse of the northern kingdom. In addition, Israel appears in parallel with Ephraim as a designation of the northern kingdom (Hos 4:16-17; 5:3). Wolff, *Hosea*, 17-19, 27-29, 91, 97, 113, 164; Mays, *Hosea*, 30-33, 77-78, 83. Similarly, the eighth-century prophet Amos also addressed the northern kingdom as "Israel" (Amos 2:6; 3:12; 5:1-7; 7:9). Mays, *Amos*, 7, 43, 84-85, 88, 133. Amos 5:6 appears to place "Israel" in parallel with the "house of Joseph" as a designation of the northern kingdom (cf. v. 4). See McKeating, *Amos, Hosea and Micah*, 40. This evidence suggests that the designation "Israel" referred to the northern kingdom, distinct from Judah, at least as early as the second half of the eighth century, when Assyrian domination was impacting the north.

The second key passage implying a northern provenience is found at Gen 48:3–5. This passage relates the final handing down of the Abrahamic covenant and its promises in the text of P^{N}. This final transmission of the covenant is communicated to Joseph, and the sons of Joseph (Ephraim and Manasseh) are explicitly named as the possession of Israel in the context of this covenant heritage. Dillmann has clarified Gen 48:3–5 as P's need to explain the recognition of Ephraim and Manasseh as two legitimate tribes, that is, a double voice for Joseph (cf. Num 1:10, 32–35; Josh 14:4; 17:14–18).[2] Westermann argues along similar lines, and observes that the beginning of Gen 48:5 with the word ועתה ("and now," "therefore") is striking. He states that this term always introduces a consequence in relation to what precedes. The consequence in vv. 5–6 serves as an expression of legitimation by P (i.e., P^{N}) on behalf of the tribes of Ephraim and Manasseh. Until this point, P had lacked any legitimation of the two sons of Joseph who were born in Egypt to an Egyptian mother. In P's view, Jacob was the only one who could legitimate the two sons of Joseph. This was because Jacob had received a direct revelation from God of the Abrahamic covenant (Gen 48:3–4), which justified him alone as the one who could "therefore" (ועתה) legitimate the two sons of Joseph by declaring them his own sons (Gen 48:5–6).[3]

Such an emphasis on Joseph and his sons reveals historical setting and intent in relation to P^{N}. P^{N} seeks to impress upon its readers the elevation of the tribe of Joseph by depicting the tribe with a double portion and by culminating the transmission of the Abrahamic covenant with the adoption of Ephraim and Manasseh (the sons of Joseph) as heirs to that covenant. This emphasis on Joseph is amplified by the blessing upon Joseph which immediately follows in the account of P^{N} (Gen 49:22–26) and which concludes P^{N}, just before the final death notice related in the document.

This climactic focus in P^{N}, on naming "Israel" (the name by which the northern kingdom is known) and "Ephraim" and "Manasseh" (both prominent northern tribes) as the final recipients of the covenant and its promises, suggests a provenience within the northern kingdom. In addition, the blessing upon Joseph (Gen 49:22, 25–26) closes the

---

2. Dillmann, *Genesis*, II:435–36.
3. Westermann, *Genesis 37–50*, 185.

document with an added emphasis on the northern patriarch and his tribal descendants.[4]

Names Used for God

A northern provenience for P[N] is further supported by its particular use of divine references. P[N] is characterized by the use of אלהים and אל שדי, as opposed to יהוה. The use of אלהים has already been traditionally associated with the northern kingdom by means of the so-called "Elohist" source, which prefers the word אלהים for God, and is considered as Ephraimitic or north-Israelite in origin.[5] Accordingly, P[N]'s use of אלהים may reflect a similar connection to northern origins.

Early Use of El Shaddai in the Bible

David Biale clarifies that the appearance of the compound אל שדי (as opposed to simply שדי) in the Bible does not necessarily indicate a late text. He demonstrates this by pointing to its occurrence in clearly early material, namely, the Testament of Jacob (Gen 49:25). In addition, שדי appears in parallel with אל in the Balaam oracles (Num 24:4, 16). Accordingly, the use of אל שדי may point to an early text.[6]

Cross recognizes a gap in the distribution of שדי in the Bible, and summarizes it as follows: "After use in the 'ēl names of Genesis and early Exodus, both Šadday and 'Ēl are found frequently in archaic poetry. There is then a gap in usage of Šadday until the sixth century when it is taken up again by Ezekiel and, above all, by the author of the dialogues of Job."[7] In Ezekiel, Cross observes that the voice of שדי is to be associated with thunder (Ezek 1:24–25; 10:5), and should be understood against the background of the theophany of the storm god. Cross explains that in early Israel the language of the storm theophany was applied to יהוה in conjunction with the role of divine warrior. Later, in the sixth

---

4. That the ascendancy of Joseph over his brothers in this blessing (v. 26) suggests a date corresponding to the period of the existence of the northern kingdom was previously recognized by Kuenen, *Hexateuch*, 240.

5. Driver, *Introduction*, xxvii, 122–23; Fohrer, *Introduction*, 152, 158.

6. The term אל שדי appears in Gen 49:25 according to a few medieval manuscripts, the Samaritan Pentateuch, the Septuagint, and the Syriac translation. In addition, Biale points out that the Masoretic ואת is less convincing contextually than ואל. Biale, "El Shaddai in the Bible," 244 n. 14, 243–45; see also Dillmann, *Genesis*, II: 477–78.

7. Cross, *Canaanite Myth*, 59.

century, the symbols of the storm theophany were resurrected by Ezekiel, Job, and Second Isaiah in descriptions of יהוה and in war songs. Thus, שדי may have received the storm god traits in Ezekiel through assimilation to יהוה.[8]

Building on Cross' observations, Biale adds that the occurrence of שדי in Isa 13:6 (which Biale attributes to second Isaiah), and in similar form in Joel 1:15, depicts שדי as a warrior god in the midst of military imagery. The association of שדי with storm and war imagery is strengthened by the numerous occurrences of שדי in Job where such descriptions of the deity are common.[9] Biale concludes: "I am in agreement with Cross's argument, that the meaning given to Shaddai in the sixth century was of a storm and war god and that this meaning was part and parcel of the image of Yahweh in the exilic and postexilic period."[10] Biale states that this view of שדי corresponds to the common translation for the term, that is, "Almighty."[11] He further observes that this view of שדי may derive from earlier sources such as the Balaam oracles (Num 24) or Ps 68, both of which reflect military imagery. Despite this possibility, the view of שדי as a warrior god is mainly a late tradition in the Scriptures.[12]

A second tradition appears attached to שדי in the Bible, distinct from that associated with storm or military imagery. This second tradition appears exclusively in relation to the compound אל שדי. We have already observed that the occurrences of אל שדי in Genesis appear in conjunction with the theme of abundance (all within P[N]). Koch has affirmed this phenomenon in pointing out that every occurrence of

---

8. Ibid., 58.

9. Biale, "*El Shaddai* in the Bible," 245. Cross mentions a second background for the imagery of god as "divine warrior," in relation to the war god who establishes the order of the cosmos, associated with creation imagery (with its setting in the cosmogonic myth in which the storm god overcomes chaos). Cross, *Canaanite Myth*, 58–59. Accordingly, as creation imagery is associated with שדי in Job (e.g., 33:4; 34:10–15), its application to שדי there may derive from the same revival of old "divine warrior" imagery. However, we must note that the term שדי never explicitly appears in the creation accounts in Genesis, but the term only appears beginning at Gen 17 in association with fertility blessings (not divine warrior imagery).

10. Biale, "*El Shaddai* in the Bible," 245.

11. Biale reviews that the King James translation of "Almighty God" was based on the tradition apparent in the LXX and the Vulgate which took the term to mean "omnipotent," while the rabbis suggested the translation "self-sufficiency" (ibid., 240).

12. Ibid., 246–47.

אל שדי in Genesis appears in conjunction with the verbs פרו ורבו ("be fruitful and multiply").[13] In light of the same evidence, Biale understands these passages as fertility blessings (Gen 17:1b–6; 28:3; 35:11; 48:3–4). The only passage in P[N] containing אל שדי which does not explicitly appear as this type of fertility blessing is Gen 43:14a. Nevertheless, in relation to this verse, Biale points out the possibility that the writer may have sensed "the association between *raḥamim* (mercy) and *reḥem* (womb)."[14]

The key to understanding this tradition regarding אל שדי appears in the Joseph blessing of the Testament of Jacob. Genesis 49:25 not only associates אל שדי with a fertility blessing by attributing "blessings of breasts and womb" to אל שדי, but also associates the term שַׁדַּי by means of wordplay to the term שָׁדַיִם (breasts). This wordplay may reveal the meaning according to which the author of the blessing, and the previous fertility blessings in Genesis, understood אל שדי, that is, "El with breasts."[15]

At this point, the argument is supported with ancient cognates.[16] After reviewing the evidence, W. F. Albright concluded that שדי is most likely derived from the Akkadian *šadû*, a word meaning "mountain," yet a word for which the most probable etymology leads to the original meaning of "breast." Words for breast often develop the alternate meanings of "elevation," "mound," "hill," or "mountain," due to associations in shape. Albright, however, had difficulty identifying the Semitic cognates meaning breast as direct antecedents from which שדי was derived, due

---

13. Koch, "*Šaddaj*," 323, 325.
14. Biale, "*El Shaddai* in the Bible," 247.
15. Ibid., 248.
16. Biale acknowledges the debate regarding the origin of שדי as deriving either from the Akkadian cognate meaning, "mountain," or the Canaanite cognate meaning, "plain." He is not concerned at the outset with settling this debate, and argues that the biblical authors did not necessarily know about Near Eastern cultures and languages as modern philologians do. Rather, the biblical author likely inherited words that had lost their original meanings, and often sought to impose his own meanings on such words. Thus, as briefly outlined above, Biale seeks to understand the biblical author's point of view before applying arguments regarding cognates. Thus, after concluding that one of the biblical uses of שדי appears related to fertility blessings and the meaning "breast," Biale returns to the Akkadian cognate which reflects a similar meaning, ibid., 240–42.

to the phonetic disjunction caused by the suffix.[17] Biale counters, however, that the concern here is not philological equivalence, but simply phonetic association. Furthermore, he points to another cognate which eliminates the problem by providing equivalence with the Hebrew, even in regard to the suffix: the Egyptian word *shdi*, which means "to suckle." Whether the derivation of שדי is taken from the Akkadian or Egyptian cognate, the result ("El with breasts," or "El who suckles") matches well with the fertility contexts surrounding the appearances of אל שדי in P^N.[18]

Some evidence suggests that the fertility blessings reflected in Genesis derive from Canaanite fertility traditions. Significant among this evidence is the description of the Canaanite fertility goddess. Asherah was depicted with prominent breasts, and the Ugaritic record contains references to "the divine breasts, the breasts of Asherah and Raḥam, a phrase noticeably similar to the biblical 'blessings of breasts and womb (רָחַם)'" (Gen 49:25).[19] Accordingly, Biale concludes: "Hence, there is abundant evidence that the fertility tradition of El Shaddai may have originated with the Israelite interest in the figure of Asherah, the fertility goddess represented by breasts."[20]

In accordance with this discussion, Biale observes that the blessing which Jacob recounts before Ephraim and Manasseh (Gen 48:3–5) and Joseph's blessing within the Testament of Jacob (Gen 49:22–26) prompt the speculation that they represent traditions reflecting a bias for the northern tribes. A northern tradition attached to fertility imagery is further reflected in the fertility images of the Ephraimite prophet Hosea (Hos 9:14).[21]

In conclusion, it appears that P^N reflects a community that is centered around the worship of אל שדי as revealed first to the patriarch Abraham (Gen 17:1b). This community understood אל שדי in association with fertility blessings. P^N initially identifies the deity of the community by the term אלהים until the revelation to Abraham at which

---

17. Albright, "*Shaddai* and *Abram*," 182–84. For a fuller discussion of the search for cognates related to שדי, see: idem, "*Shaddai* and *Abram*," 181–87; Cross, *Canaanite Myth*, 52–58; Biale, "El Shaddai in the Bible," 240–42, 248–49.

18. Biale, "El Shaddai in the Bible," 248–49, 248 n. 23.

19. Ibid., 253–54.

20. Ibid., 254.

21. Ibid., 250, 253.

time the epithet שדי appears. Nevertheless, the association of this deity with fertility blessings appears from the beginning (Gen 1:22, 28; 8:15–17; 9:1, 7). The fertility blessings appear to reflect the influence of Canaanite fertility traditions. Thus, P^N represents a community, initially centered around the fertility blessings of *El Shaddai*, which eventually found expression from within the setting of the northern kingdom.

The Catalyst of Assyrian Domination

The promises and proclamations in P^N are best understood in the context of historical crisis. The emphasis on the fertility blessings (fruitfulness and multiplication) found throughout P^N is most appropriate to a situation of homelessness and alienation. The everlasting promises in the covenants to Noah and Abraham which express the assurance that God will never allow total destruction, and which pledge land and divine oversight, present a message of hope and the promise of wellbeing. Such a focus derived from the priestly narrative in Genesis has normally been applied to the crisis of the destruction of the southern kingdom of Judah at the hands of Babylon and the resultant period of exile.[22] However, given the indications of a northern provenience, the message of P^N should be considered in relation to the devastating crisis experienced by the northern kingdom of Israel at the hands of Assyria.

The Assyrian crisis of war and devastation resulted in, not only the deportation of citizens to foreign places, but also a general uprooting of people from their land. Many would have fled as refugees seeking sanctuary in the south.[23] This period of crisis, no less than that of the Babylonian exile, would have prompted the need for a message of hope and promise such as that implied by the covenants and blessings reflected in P^N. Thus, given the northern interests reflected in P^N, the Assyrian crisis likely served as the catalyst which prompted the composition of the traditions presented in P^N.

Furthermore, as will be discussed below, P^N appears to include a polemic against the idea of Judah as the exclusive heir to the promises of God. Accordingly, P^N could not be applicable to the exilic situation experienced by Judah. For, how could a polemic against the idea of Judah

---

22. See Brueggemann and Wolff, *Vitality*, 104–7, 109; Boorer, "Kerygmatic Intention," 12; Klein, "Message of P," 60–63; Campbell, *Study Companion*, 70–73.

23. See Broshi, "Expansion of Jerusalem," 21–26.

as the exclusive heir to the promises of God possibly convey a message of hope to the exiles from Judah? Such a message could only bear significance for the northern audience. The crisis of Assyrian domination in the north would have prompted not only a need for a message of hope for the refugees, but an assurance that they were still considered among the descendants of Abraham and recipients of the covenant promises. In light of Israel's fall, and Judah's continued survival, it would be easy for refugees to imagine that God had abandoned them. In response to this fear, P^N provides a brief patriarchal history which affirms the covenant heritage of the northern tribes. This prompts the conclusion that P^N came from Ephraimite circles during the period surrounding the fall of Samaria.

A History of Origins

The theological intent of P^N begins with a concern for narrating significant origins. An evaluation of the content of P^N reveals that the document presents four major movements in its brief historical narrative. These movements are as follows: 1) the creation of humanity, 2) the sin of humanity and the flood, 3) the covenant with Abraham and his seed, and 4) the transmission of the covenant blessing. Three of these can be seen as origin traditions, and the fourth is simply an extension of the third.

Norbert Lohfink tentatively suggests that the genre of the priestly narrative may be regarded as a "history of origins."[24] This actually constitutes an appropriate designation for P^N. The creation story is certainly a narrative of origins in relation to humanity and the created order. The second major thematic element of P^N can also be considered a story of origins, that is, the origin of sin and God's original response to sin.

The creation story of P^N is left with the positive affirmation that all which God had made was very good (Gen 1:31). Following the genealogy in Gen 5, the flood story is told. However, before God responds to sin on the earth by destroying it, the existence of sin must be established. This is done by contrasting the righteous character of Noah with the corrupt character of the rest of creation (Gen 6:9, 11–13). This introduces sin on earth as the violence of humanity.[25] The sins described in

---

24. Lohfink, *Theology of the Pentateuch*, 105.

25. Lohfink contends that the word "violence" (חמס; Gen 6:11) was carefully chosen as part of a formula for P's doctrine of sin. It reflects prophetic rhetoric of accusation.

Gen 6:11–13 are presumed to be the same sins, which later in the narrative, Abraham is instructed to avoid in fulfilling God's command to be blameless (תמים, Gen 17:1).[26] This demand on Abraham corresponds to the righteousness of Noah, who was described as already being תמים (Gen 6:9), and whose character of תמים is contrasted by the corruption of others (Gen 6:11–13).

The third major component of the P[N] narrative (the Abrahamic Covenant) can also be considered an origin account, that is, the origin of God's covenant promising land and descendants to the children of Israel. This blessing begins with Abraham (Gen 17), and is transmitted to Jacob in the context of his receiving the new name, "Israel" (Gen 35:10–12).

Thus, P[N] appears initially as a brief document that narrates the origins of creation, sin and its aftermath, and God's covenant with Israel promising land and divine oversight. This narrative is tied together with genealogies, and related matters including lists of descendants, and birth and death notices. Within this document of origins, the theme of God's covenant with Israel takes on additional significance as a central concern of the writing.

Ezekiel is cited as a prime example (7:23; 8:17; 12:19; 28:16). Lohfink holds that P is exilic, and argues that the exiles upon reading the priestly flood story would recognize that they had been justly accused by their prophets. The flood story demonstrates that "violence" leads to God's wrath and destruction. Thus, the "violence" which their prophets accused them of, led to Judah's destruction and exile (ibid., 106–7, 110). Lohfink's contention does not necessarily limit the application of the flood story to exilic times. An example of the same type of prophetic rhetoric is found in prophetic address regarding the fall of Samaria (Amos 3:10, 11–12). Thus, Lohfink's argument could equally be applied to the situation surrounding the fall of the northern kingdom. The dependence of Ezekiel upon P (and not the other way around) has already been discussed. For discussion of Ezekiel's dependence on the priestly literature including a specific reference to Gen 6:11, see Kaufmann, *Religion of Israel*, 433.

26. Lohfink, *Theology of the Pentateuch*, 109–10. Lohfink discusses two other accounts which he regards as types of original sin: the spy narrative of Num 13–14, and the water miracle in the desert of Num 20. He notes the absence of sin in stories throughout P with the exception of these three accounts. Thus, these appear as an intentional system of original sin stories in P. Idem, *Theology of the Pentateuch*, 104–6, 110–14. Lohfink, however, does not convincingly demonstrate that the three accounts are necessarily related. The second and third accounts show signs of H, rather than P. The connection of the spy story to H is discussed later in this work. In regard to Num 20, Lohfink himself notes its connection to the "holiness code" (ibid., 113–14; see also Knohl, *Sanctuary*, 94–96).

Covenant and Blessing

The blessing regarding fruitfulness and multiplication appears as a thematic thread throughout P^N, and links the covenants with Noah and Abraham. This blessing first appears in the creation account (Gen 1:28; cf. 1:22), is then repeated just before the covenant with Noah (Gen 9:7; cf. 8:17), and appears again in the midst of the Abrahamic covenant (Gen 17:6).[27]

Brueggemann and Wolff see this same blessing of fruitfulness and multiplication as the kerygmatic focus of the priestly writer. They explain that P expresses a confession of faith which is shaped by the particular crisis of its time. The five verbs (be fruitful, multiply, fill, subdue, have dominion) found in the blessing of Gen 1:28 are central to the faith of the priestly circle.[28] Brueggemann and Wolff argue that this faith proclamation is specifically addressed to the situation of the exile. "This proclamation is strikingly appropriate to a people of exile who are homeless and rootless, alienated from land and traditions, an affirmation that their God is still in charge and therefore that their destiny is still well-being and dominance."[29] We have already demonstrated in relation to a northern bias represented in P^N that this very same message should be considered as addressed to the northern refugees of the Assyrian crisis. Brueggemann and Wolff highlight that the faith proclamation is repeated in the flood story (Gen 8:17; 9:1,7), in the blessing concerning Ishmael (Gen 17:20), in Isaac's blessing upon Jacob (Gen 28:1–4), in God's blessing upon Jacob (Gen 35:11), regarding prosperity in Egypt (Gen 47:27), at the end of the patriarchal narratives (Gen 48:3–4), and finally as an introduction to the Exodus material (Exod 1:1–5,7).[30] This listing clearly follows the parameters of P^N as described earlier and is therefore consistent with the proposition that P^N seeks to proclaim such a message of hope to the northern refugees.[31]

---

27. Cross, *Canaanite Myth*, 296. Cross also includes a connection to the Sinai covenant by means of the same blessing as it appears in Lev 26:9. The weakness of the argument connecting all three covenants has already been addressed earlier in this work.

28. Brueggemann and Wolff, *Vitality*, 37–38, 103.

29. Ibid., 104.

30. Ibid., 104–7.

31. Recall that Exod 1:1–7 constitutes part of the redactional transition between P^N and P. This will be elaborated further in relation to the discussion of H later in this work.

P^N composed the covenant theme in a manner which promotes the people of the northern kingdom of Israel as rightful heirs to the Abrahamic covenant and its adjoining promises from God. It appears to constitute a polemic against the idea of Judah as the exclusive heir to the promises of God. The first covenant, with Noah, is a universal covenant in which God promises never again to destroy the earth. This serves to establish God's concern for humanity as a whole, beyond the tribes of the south exclusively. This universal concern does not specify any particular people as uniquely invited to participate in a relationship with God. That only becomes evident in relation to the more exclusive Abrahamic covenant.

The second covenant is limited to Abraham and his descendants (Gen 17). Here the promise from God includes multiplying Abraham's descendants, "being God" to Abraham and his descendants, and giving to Abraham and his descendants the land of Canaan. This covenant theme in P^N is developed with subtle suspense and draws the reader with anticipation to the conclusion revealing who is the final heir of these promises from God. As previously discussed, the Abrahamic covenant of Gen 17 is a central feature of P^N. This covenant contains the promises from God regarding the prosperity of Abraham and his descendants. The possession and blessing of this covenant are of primary importance to P^N. The transmission of the covenant from generation to generation becomes critical for the well-being of the future heirs of the promises of God expressed in the covenant. Thus, after Abraham initially receives the covenant, the reader is drawn to follow its transmission to the following generations.

The structure of P^N heightens the question of who will be the direct heir of the Abrahamic covenant. The covenant itself (Gen 17) is directly enveloped, in the content of P^N, by the births of the two children of Abraham (Ishmael at Gen 16:1a, 3, 15–16; and Isaac at Gen 21:2–5). Ishmael is the first born to Abraham, and he alone is alive at the time of the initial revelation of the covenant itself. Despite God's insistence that Sarah shall bear Isaac, and the covenant will pass to him (Gen 17:19), Abraham's plea is for Ishmael to find favor before God (Gen 17:18). Furthermore, God does extend a blessing to Ishmael which reflects the terminology of the covenant promises (fruitfulness and multiplication; Gen 17:20). Thus, the story in P^N leaves the reader with some uncertainty in regard to the exact heir of the covenant at this point (with possible emphasis on Ishmael, the first born).

This uncertainty is subtly increased as the structure of P^N first treats the section introduced by the *toledoth* formula designating Ishmael (Gen 25:12–17), before the section designating Isaac (beginning at Gen 25:19). Within the material addressing the life of Isaac, one expects to find a direct revelation of the covenant from God to Isaac (as occurs with Abraham before, and Jacob later in the text). However, no such revelation occurs. In fact, the covenant is never even recited to Isaac through human communication. Thus, the covenant is not explicitly handed to Isaac through divine or human announcement. Furthermore, immediately following the introduction of the Isaac section (by means of the *toledoth* formula designating Isaac; Gen 25:19), attention shifts to the twin sons of Isaac (Gen 25:20, 24–26). Now the heritage of the covenant is confused even further. According to P^N, the first born of Isaac is Esau, and Jacob is soon sent away to choose a wife outside of Canaan. However, when Isaac sends Jacob away, Isaac wishes upon Jacob God's blessing using the terminology of the covenant (fruitfulness and multiplication, etc.; Gen 28:1–5). The reader is left wondering if Isaac ever directly received the covenant himself, and whether the first born to Isaac (Esau) would be heir to the covenant, or if Jacob who is sent away with a covenant-type blessing from his father will inherit the promises of God.

The reader's confusion is finally addressed when God appears to deliver a direct revelation of the covenant to Jacob (Gen 35:9–13). This signals a key moment in the narrative. As with Abram, God changes Jacob's name and delivers the promises of the covenant. Significantly, Jacob's name is changed at the outset of the revelation, so that it is "Israel" (for whom the northern kingdom is named) who receives the covenant promises. Thus, out of the previous confusion and anticipation regarding the exact identity of the heir to the covenant, the answer is clearly established upon the name of "Israel!"

The covenant promises are repeated once more in P^N, at Gen 48:3–6. This passage describes Jacob repeating the covenant promises to Joseph. A climactic moment is reached in P^N as the sons of Joseph (Ephraim and Manasseh) are explicitly named and designated as the possession of Israel (and thus heirs of the covenant promises).

Accordingly, the covenant promises are passed on specifically to Jacob in the context of the changing of his name to Israel (Gen 35:10–12). In addition, the promises are repeated in the context of specifically identifying the patriarchs of two prominent northern tribes (Ephraim and Manasseh) as possessions of Israel. Thus P^N serves to establish the people of the northern kingdom as recipients of God's promises by means of being children of Abraham. Furthermore, to assure this heritage for the north, particular Abrahamic descendants who are identified with northern tribes are specifically named as among those included in God's covenant promises. The document closes with a concluding blessing upon Joseph (Gen 49:22–26), and the death notice of the last patriarch, who serves as the namesake of the northern kingdom (Jacob/Israel; Gen 49:33b). Thereby, P^N communicates that the people of the southern kingdom are not the exclusive heirs of God's promises.

Central to this covenant identification, and expressed throughout P^N, is the adjoining theme of abundance (fruitfulness and multiplication). This theme serves to communicate to P^N's audience that the northern kingdom is designated, not only to possess their portion in the land of Canaan, but to prosper in it. For the northern refugees, this implied that their land, currently held by Assyria, is still subject to God's sovereignty and God will return it to them as their proper inheritance.

A seemingly glaring gap in this description of P^N is the lack of fulfillment regarding the promise of land which accompanies the Abrahamic covenant (Gen 17:8). P^N concludes with the communication of blessing in the hearing of Ephraim and Manasseh, a final blessing upon Joseph, and the death notice regarding Jacob. After this, no explicit sign of P^N is found in the Pentateuch. As will be detailed in later discussion, echoes of P^N in the rest of the priestly literature all bear signs of the redactor H. This observation leads to the conclusion that P^N is a document of hope and promise; but at the same time, it is a document which reflects the reality of the situation of its community. In the context of the Assyrian crisis, P^N was composed during a time of homelessness and devastation. The author of P^N held an inspired and hopeful outlook based on the promises of God, while portraying a realistic image of the current situation. For P^N, the fulfillment of the land promise was still in the future for the refugees who had lost everything, and must now submit themselves to a new administration in the south.[32]

---

32. An alternative explanation can be considered in relation to H's redaction of the priestly literature. If P^{N} did culminate with some account illustrating the fulfillment of God's promises in relation to northern tribes, H may have removed it in the process of attaching P^{N} to P. If so, H may have been motivated by the concern to help the northern refugees integrate into their new southern surroundings, apart from their homeland in the north. We shall now turn to H's significant work.

PART THREE

The H Redaction of the Priestly Literature

5

The Composition of H

THIS DISCUSSION OF H IS INTENTIONALLY FOCUSED ON THE INTEGRAtion of P^N into the larger work of the priestly literature. All of the references outside of Genesis that reflect the terminology of, or content specific to, P^N share some common ground besides association to P^N. Consideration of the redaction of the priestly literature at the hands of the "Holiness School" brings that common ground to light. In every case, the passages within the priestly literature which reflect P^N outside of Genesis demonstrate characteristics of the Holiness School. This suggests that H is the redactor who attached P^N to P, and extended some of its themes within the priestly literature.[1]

As is commonly accepted, I understand Leviticus 17–26 (the Holiness Code) to be the central corpus of the work of H.[2] Milgrom and Knohl have demonstrated that H is not a separate collection of laws within P, but rather, represents an independent redactor, in fact, the redactor of P itself.[3] The hand of H in the priestly literature, outside

---

1. This insight was prompted by the work of Israel Knohl (*Sanctuary*; and "Priestly Torah: Sabbath"). The Holiness School (HS) is Knohl's preferred designation for his understanding of H. Idem, *Sanctuary*, 6. Clearly Knohl did not write with P^N in mind. Rather, after investigating Knohl's work, the connection between H and the references in the Pentateuch which show affinities to P^N outside of Genesis became apparent.

2. Klostermann seems to have been the one to have coined the phrase "das Heiligkeitsgesetz" which is often translated "The Holiness Code." Klostermann, *Der Pentateuch*, 368–85 (especially p. 385). H is traditionally understood as an independent law collection that was incorporated into P (Fohrer, *Introduction*, 144–45). For further description of the Holiness Code, see idem, *Introduction*, 137–42; Kuenen, *Hexateuch*, 87–91, 275–87; Driver, *Introduction*, 47–59.

3. I embrace Knohl's thesis claiming H as the redactor of P—a conclusion that was reached independently by Milgrom and subsequently discussed between the two of them (Milgrom, *Leviticus 1–16*, 13).

of the traditional parameters of the Holiness Code, can be identified by themes and terminology characteristic of the Holiness School.[4] Recognizing these characteristics, especially in relation to texts that reflect P^N outside of Genesis, clarifies the greater picture of the composition of the priestly literature.

Significant Characteristics of H

Thematic Call to Holiness

The "Holiness Code" derives its name from its thematic emphasis, which reflects a call to holiness addressed to the people of Israel in general (Lev 19:2; 20:7–8, 26; 21:8; 22:32).[5] This call to holiness is expressed mainly through two clauses: 1) והייתם קדשים ("you shall be holy"; or alternatively, קדשים תהיו "holy you shall be"—Lev 19:2; 20:7, 26), and 2) אני יהוה מקדשכם ("I am the Lord who makes you holy/consecrates you"—Lev 20:8; 21:8; 22:32). Outside of the Holiness Code, these expressions are found at Exod 31:13; Lev 11:44–45; and Num 15:40. Corroborating evidence demonstrates that each of these passages reflect the hand of H, outside of the Holiness Code itself.[6] These clauses which reflect the thematic emphasis of H appear nowhere else in the Hebrew Bible.

Characteristic Formulas

Knohl describes the formula, אני יהוה אלהיכם ("I am the Lord your God"), as "the characteristic signature of HS," and its shortened version, אני יהוה ("I am the Lord") as "the distinguishing concluding formula of HS."[7] It appears that both of these clauses are used to conclude di-

---

4. Knohl, *Sanctuary*, 1–2 n. 3. Knohl is not the first to have recognized terminology characteristic of the Holiness Code, or to recognize elements of the Holiness Code outside of Lev 17–26. See Driver, *Introduction*, 49–50, 59; Klostermann, *Der Pentateuch*, 377.

5. Knohl, *Sanctuary*, 1–2; see also, Fohrer, *Introduction*, 137.

6. Knohl, *Sanctuary*, 15–16, 53, 69, 90. The H provenience of these passages has been recognized for some time. Klostermann includes them within the list that he describes as easily recognizable passages stemming from the same source as the Holiness Code. Klostermann, *Der Pentateuch*, 377; see also, Driver, *Introduction*, 59, 151.

7. Knohl, *Sanctuary*, 38, 16; also 9, 54; see also Kuenen, *Hexateuch*, 89; Driver, *Introduction*, 49.

vine legal pronouncements. The distinctive use of these clauses as a concluding formula occurs forty-five times within the priestly material. Of these, thirty-seven instances appear in the Holiness Code itself.[8] The remaining eight occurrences of the concluding formula are found in Exod 6:8; 12:12; 29:46; Num 3:13, 41, 45; 10:10; 15:41.[9] These two clauses appear thirty additional times in the priestly material in contexts which do not necessarily imply their employment as a concluding formula. Of these additional occurrences, thirteen instances appear within the Holiness Code.[10] The remaining seventeen occurrences are Exod 6:2, 6, 7, 29; 7:5, 17; 8:18 (Eng., v. 22); 10:2; 14:4, 18; 15:26; 16:12; 31:13; Lev 11:44, 45; Num 14:35; 35:34.

Another characteristic concluding formula of H is the phrase חקת עולם לדרתיכם ("a permanent statute for your generations"). Knohl cites the following fifteen occurrences of this formula within the priestly material, and convincingly demonstrates that each instance reveals the hand of H: Exod 12:14, 17; 27:21; Lev 3:17; 7:36; 10:9; 17:7; 23:14, 21, 31, 41; 24:3; Num 10:8; 15:15; 18:23.[11] The phrase appears in only two other instances in the Hebrew Bible: Exod 30:21; Lev 6:11 (Eng., v. 18).[12]

Punishment by כרת ("Cutting Off")

The כרת formula as a threat or warning against individuals appears twenty-nine times in the priestly literature.[13] Knohl observes that H

---

8. Lev 18:4, 5, 6, 21, 30; 19:3, 4, 10, 12, 14, 16, 18, 25, 28, 30, 31, 32, 34, 36, 37; 20:8, 24; 21:12; 22:2, 3, 8, 9, 30, 31, 32, 33; 23:22, 43; 25:38, 55; 26:2, 45.

9. At Exod 29:46 the concluding formula appears as אני יהוה אלהיהם ("I am the Lord their God"). See Knohl, *Sanctuary*, 17–18 n. 24.

10. Lev 18:2; 19:2; 20:7, 26; 21:8, 15, 23; 22:16; 24:22; 25:17; 26:1, 13, 44. In the last reference listed here, the clause appears as אני יהוה אלהיהם ("I am the Lord their God").

11. Knohl, *Sanctuary*, excursus 1 (pp. 46–55); see also pp. 12–13, 20.

12. Knohl argues that the formula חקת עולם לדרתיכם ("a permanent statute for your generations") is composed of the juxtaposition of two phrases (חקת עולם and לדרתיכם). These phrases appear independently in P, while the conflation of the two phrases is distinctive of H. Exodus 30:21 may represent a transitional stage between P and H by virtue of the fact that these two phrases appear together in this verse, though they are not directly juxtaposed. Knohl, *Sanctuary*, 54–55 n. 27. Knohl argues that Lev 6:10–11 demonstrates late editorial activity representative of H. Idem, *Sanctuary*, 126 n. 7.

13. Gen 17:14; Exod 12:15, 19; 30:33, 38; 31:14; Lev 7:20, 21, 25, 27; 17:4, 9, 10, 14; 18:29; 19:8; 20:3, 5, 6, 17, 18; 22:3; 23:29, 30; Num 9:13; 15:30, 31; 19:13, 20. Leviticus 23:30 does not use the word כרת, but uniquely substitutes the hiphil form of the word אבד ("to destroy") instead (והאבדתי את־הנפש ההוא מקרב עמה). Nevertheless, this verse

uses the כרת formula in a personal manner by indicating God in first person speech as the one who directly punishes.¹⁴ This is illustrated in the following passage:

ושמתי אני את־פני באיש ההוא ובמשפחתו והכרתי אתו ואת

כל־הזנים אחריו לזנות אחרי המלך מקרב עמם: והנפש אשר

תפנה אל־האבת ואל־הידענים לזנות אחריהם ונתתי את־פני

בנפש ההוא והכרתי אתו מקרב עמו:

> And I myself will set my face against that man and against his clan; and I will cut off him and all those playing the harlot with him, by playing the harlot with Molech, from among their people. And the person who turns to the mediums and to the spirits to play the harlot with them, I will place my face against that person and I will cut off him from among his people. (Lev 20:5–6)

H's use of the כרת formula often includes מקרב ("from among") in the wording of the formula, as illustrated in the passage just cited (see also Lev 17:4, 10; 18:29; 20:3, 5, 6, 18).¹⁵

Knohl contrasts this uniquely H application of the formula with the common way in which the formula is normally found in the priestly literature, that is, as impersonal in expression (Exod 30:33, 38; Lev 7:20, 21).¹⁶ This manner of expression is illustrated in the following passage:

איש אשר ירקח כמהו ואשר יתן ממנו על־זר ונכרת מעמיו:

> Anyone who mixes (it) like this and who places it upon a stranger shall be cut off from his people. (Exod 30:33)

---

corresponds with Knohl's argument that H uses the כרת formula in the first person of the agent directing the punishment, and includes H's unique use of the word מקרב (see below).

14. Knohl, *Sanctuary*, 1–2 n. 3, 13. See also Kuenen, *Hexateuch*, 89; Driver, *Introduction*, 49, 49 n. §.

15. Knohl, *Sanctuary*, 53. To this list of distinctively H applications of the formula, including מקרב, can be added: Exod 31:14; Lev 23:30; Num 15:30.

16. Knohl, *Sanctuary*, 1–2 n. 3. See also Driver, *Introduction*, 49 n. §, 130–33.

This form of the formula is indirect (third person passive speech) with respect to the agent of cutting off, and does not include מקרב ("from among") in the wording of the formula.

According to Knohl's analysis, the כרת formula appears in only five verses within P itself, from which this common use of the formula in the priestly literature must be derived, namely, Gen 17:14; Exod 30:33, 38; Lev 7:20, 21. That is, all other occurrences of the כרת formula appear either in the distinctive form applied by H (with a personal agent doing the "cutting off", and/or use of the term מקרב), or represent the common use of the formula appearing within a passage which is already assigned to H, based on other evidence.[17]

In discussing the occurrence of the כרת formula in Gen 17:14, Knohl observes that there is a lack of gender agreement between the sinner and the recipient of the punishment. He explains that such lack of agreement is common in H's use of the כרת formula. Thus, he concludes that Gen 17:14 may also reflect the hand of H.[18] According to this same reasoning, Lev 7:20–21 should be assigned to H. Though Knohl cites Lev 7:20 as an example of gender agreement in the common form of the כרת formula, it actually demonstrates lack of agreement, as shown in the following translation:

והנפש אשר־תאכל בשר מזבח השלמים אשר ליהוה וטמאתו

עליו ונכרתה הנפש ההוא מעמיה:

> And the person (fem.) who eats (fem.) flesh from the sacrifice of the peace offerings which are to the Lord, and his (masc.) uncleanness is upon him (masc.), that person (fem.) shall be cut off (fem.) from "her" (fem.) people. (Lev 7:20)

The same can be shown with regard to Lev 7:21, that is, it shows lack of gender agreement within the application of the כרת formula, and thus should be attributed to H.

Consequently, we are left with only Exod 30:33, 38 as models of the common form of the כרת formula in the priestly literature. With these verses as our only models, the common use of the formula can be characterized by the simple impersonal phrase ונכרת מעמיו ("and he

---

17. See Knohl, *Sanctuary*, 104–6.
18. Knohl, *Sanctuary*, 102 n. 145.

shall be cut off from his people") with איש as the subject identified earlier in each verse (Exod 30:33, 38). In contrast, the formula appears in Lev 7:20–21 (demonstrating the hand of H due to lack of gender agreement in these verses) as ונכרתה הנפש ההוא מעמיה ("And that person shall be cut off from her people") with the feminine נפש as the subject designated within the formula. This insight prompts a new distinction in relation to the characteristics of H. Among H's unique markers in relation to the use of the כרת formula is the designation הנפש ההוא ("that person"). This particular designation occurs only sixteen times in the Hebrew Bible. In each case, it appears in a pericope which Knohl otherwise assigns to H. Furthermore, in all but one of the occurrences of this designation (הנפש ההוא), it is used as part of the כרת formula.[19] Thus, we should add the use of the designation הנפש ההוא to Knohl's identifying characteristics of H's use of the כרת formula.

Leviticus 17:4, 9 stand out among the H pericopes which employ the כרת formula. Leviticus 17:4 reveals the hand of H by the characteristic use of מקרב ("from among") in the wording of the formula. Leviticus 17:4, 9 stand out, however, because they contain the unique designation of האיש ההוא as the subject of the כרת formula (thus, ונכרת האיש ההוא מעמיו; "that man shall be cut off from his people"). These two verses constitute the only occurrence of the designation האיש ההוא within the כרת formula.[20] It mimics the thirteen occurrences of the formula in H which normally use הנפש ההוא מ־ (ונכרתה הנפש ההוא מ־).[21] The apparent difference is simply the substitution of איש for נפש.

The explanation for this unique alteration may be revealed through a closer examination of the use of the term נפש in Lev 17. The word נפש appears nine times in Lev 17, all within vv. 10–15, as shown here:

---

19. The designation הנפש ההוא appears at Gen 17:14; Exod 12:15, 19; 31:14; Lev 7:20, 21, 27; 19:8; 22:3; 23:30; Num 5:6; 9:13; 15:30, 31; 19:13, 20. For Knohl's inclusion of these passages in H, see Knohl, *Sanctuary*, 104–6. The only exception is Lev 7:20–21, which should also be assigned to H in accordance with Knohl's own criteria (as demonstrated above). Numbers 5:6 is the only occurrence of this phrase which is not used in conjunction with the כרת formula. It should also be clarified that the phrase does not appear in every instance of H's use of the כרת formula, though when it does appear, it is a marker of the hand of H.

20. That is, as the passive subject immediately following the verb, as opposed to an object following an active verb; cf. Lev 20:3, 5.

21. Gen 17:14; Exod 12:15, 19; 31:14; Lev 7:20, 21, 27; 19:8; 22:3; Num 9:13; 15:30; 19:13, 20; cf. Lev 23:30; Num 15:31.

10 ואיש איש מבית ישראל ומן־הגר הגר בתוכם אשר יאכל כל־דם ונתתי פני בנפש האכלת את־הדם והכרתי אתה מקרב עמה: 11 כי נפש הבשר בדם הוא ואני נתתיו לכם על־המזבח לכפר על־נפשתיכם כי־הדם הוא בנפש יכפר: 12 על־כן אמרתי לבני ישראל כל־נפש מכם לא־תאכל דם והגר הגר בתוככם לא־יאכל דם: 13 ואיש איש מבני ישראל ומן־הגר הגר בתוכם אשר יצוד ציד חיה או־עוף אשר יאכל ושפך את־דמו וכסהו בעפר: 14 כי־נפש כל־בשר דמו בנפשו הוא ואמר לבני ישראל דם כל־בשר לא תאכלו כי נפש כל־בשר דמו הוא כל־אכליו יכרת: 15 וכל־נפש אשר האכל נבלה וטרפה באזרח ובגר וכבס בגדיו ורחץ במים וטמא עד־הערב וטהר:

> 10) "And any man from the house of Israel or from the sojourner who sojourns in their midst, who eats any blood, I will set my face against the *person* who eats the blood, and I will cut off her from among her people.
>
> 11) For the *life* of the flesh, it is in the blood, and I have given it to you upon the altar to atone your *persons*, for it is the blood, with the *life*, that atones."
>
> 12) Therefore, I said to the children of Israel, "No *person* among you shall eat blood and the sojourner who sojourns in your midst shall not eat blood."
>
> 13) And any man from the children of Israel or from the sojourner who sojourns in their midst who hunts a game animal or bird which shall be eaten, he shall pour out its blood and cover it with dirt.
>
> 14) For the *life* of all flesh, its blood, it is with its *life*, and I said to the children of Israel, "The blood of any flesh you shall not eat, for the *life* of all flesh, it is its blood, any who eat it shall be cut off.
>
> 15) And any *person* who eats a carcass or torn-animal, among the native or among the sojourner, shall wash his garments and bathe in the water and be unclean until evening, and then be clean."

Five times the term נפש is used as a reference to the "life" in the flesh of an animal, which is equated with blood and which atones (Lev 17:11, 14).[22] The other four appearances of the word are used with the

---

22. For a discussion of the exegesis of this passage, see Milgrom, "Prolegomenon to Leviticus 17:11," 150–51, 154–56.

meaning "person" (Lev 17:10–12, 15). In three of these instances, נֶפֶשׁ is used in reference to a "person" eating the flesh of an animal (vv. 10, 12, 15). The fourth use of נֶפֶשׁ in reference to persons appears as the object of atonement ("your persons/selves," v. 11). The passage seems to present a word play in relation to the term נֶפֶשׁ. It is the נֶפֶשׁ in the blood of the animal which must not be eaten and which atones (v. 11, 14). To eat the blood of the animal, which contains its נֶפֶשׁ, will result in being "cut off" (v. 10, 14, cf. v. 12). Thus, the prohibition forbids any נֶפֶשׁ (person) from eating נֶפֶשׁ (which is in the blood) in order to preserve נֶפֶשׁ (life in the blood) which serves to atone נֶפֶשׁ (persons).

It appears that the word נֶפֶשׁ was reserved for this particular passage (Lev 17:10–15) within the legislation contained in Lev 17. This may have been done in order to highlight the play on words contained therein. Thus, the rest of the legislation regarding sacrifices in this particular context (chapter 17) is addressed to persons using the word אִישׁ instead of נֶפֶשׁ. Therefore, Lev 17:4, 9 represent a change in the characteristic H designation of the subject within the כרת formula from הַנֶּפֶשׁ הַהִוא to הָאִישׁ הַהוּא. Though הַנֶּפֶשׁ הַהִוא is the preferred designation for H in the midst of the כרת formula, it is, nevertheless, interchangeable with הָאִישׁ הַהוּא for the general designation of a person, as evidenced by the juxtaposition of the two phrases in Lev 20:5–6, and Num 9:13.

The above discussion suggests that the use of the כרת formula in priestly literature signals the hand of H in all but two instances, which model the common use of the formula in the priestly literature and are attributed to P (Exod 30:33, 38).

Divine Address

There appears to be some confusion in the discussion regarding the characteristic of direct divine address in the priestly literature. Milgrom states that, "there can be no doubt that Knohl is correct in contrasting the impersonal, indirect address of God in P with the first-person address in H."[23] However, Milgrom then proceeds to question Knohl's application of this contrast. He describes Knohl's observation as one that recognizes that after Exod 6, P no longer depicts God addressing

---

23. Milgrom, *Leviticus 1–16*, 17. Kuenen and Driver include terms with first person suffixes referring to God, and phrases referring to God in the first person, as characteristic of H. Kuenen, *Hexateuch*, 89; Driver, *Introduction*, 49–50.

humanity in the first person, not even Moses.²⁴ Milgrom objects to this, and points out that P does portray God addressing Moses (and even Aaron) with direct address. For examples, he points to Lev 11:1–20, and 15:1–2a (passages which Knohl does not include in his listing of H passages).²⁵ It seems that Milgrom's objection rests on lack of clarity in Knohl's expression. Knohl's understanding of the use of divine direct discourse in P after Exod 6 appears to be as follows:

1. "the use of אני in God's speech disappears completely (even from God's speech to Moses) . . ."
2. "only in speaking to Moses does God employ the first person singular . . ."²⁶

Knohl opens the door to confusion with the statement: "In PT, the first person pronoun is used in the divine speech exclusively when God's words are addressed to Moses alone."²⁷ It appears that this statement parallels #2 above, while it flatly contradicts #1. Consequently, there is a need for clarification. Knohl lists 14 examples in P which illustrate his statement that the first person pronoun is used in divine speech addressed to Moses alone.²⁸ Not one of these examples contains the independent personal pronoun, first person, singular, אני. What Knohl must actually mean is that P never employs the independent personal pronoun, first person, singular, אני, in reference to God in divine speech. However, for P, when God speaks only to Moses, the Divine may speak in first person speech (but, without the use of the personal pronoun אני). In regard to addressing the people of Israel, Knohl sees the divine speech in P as even more limited. That is, in addressing the people, not only is the use of אני absent from divine speech, but "God never employs the first person in referring to himself" at all.²⁹ Conversely, in

---

24. Milgrom, *Leviticus 1–16*, 15.
25. Ibid.,17; Knohl, *Sanctuary*, 104–6.
26. Knohl, *Sanctuary*, 107, 95 nn. 119, 120; cf. 86.
27. Ibid., 95.
28. Ibid., 95 n. 120: Exod 25:21, 22, 30; 28:1, 3, 4, 41; 29:1; 30:6, 30, 36; Lev 6:10; 10:3; 16:2. Leviticus 6:10 is unique in that it appears in a passage in which Aaron and his sons are addressed by God through Moses. Consequently, Knohl later argues for the H provenance of Lev 6:10 (ibid., 105; 126 n. 7).
29. Ibid., 107; see also 1–2 n. 3, 91 n. 104. Definitively P material consistently refers to the children of Israel with impersonal third person references when addressed by God through Moses (e.g., Lev 1:3—2:2; 3:1–16; 4:1—5:19; 15:1–30). For recognition

addressing the people of Israel, H does employ first person divine speech, use of the personal pronoun אני in reference to God, and second person references to the people of Israel.[30] With regard to divine address directed to Moses and Aaron together, it appears that Knohl would claim that P may portray such discussion with a second person reference to Moses and Aaron, but would never include a first person reference to God. In divine speech to Moses and Aaron, only H reveals first person speech in reference to God.[31] Knohl's arguments regarding divine direct address can be charted as follows:

Divine Speech addressed to:	P	H
Moses	-No use of אני -1st person ref. to God -2nd person ref. to Moses	-Use of אני -1st person ref. to God -2nd person ref. to Moses
Moses and Aaron	-No use of אני -No 1st person ref. to God -2nd person ref. to Moses and Aaron	-Use of אני -1st person ref. to God -2nd person ref. to Moses and Aaron
People of Israel	-No use of אני -No 1st person ref. to God -No 2nd person ref. to people	-Use of אני -1st person ref. to God -2nd person ref. to people

of this particular diversity within the priestly literature, see Begrich, "Die priesterliche Tora," 82.

30. Knohl, *Sanctuary*, 1–2 n. 3, 15, 63–64 n. 11, 64 n. 14, 86 n. 78, 91, 107. See Begrich, "Die priesterliche Tora," 73–74, cf. 82; and Cholewinski, *Heiligkeitsgesetz*, 137. It should be noted that God does not address the people directly, but rather through Moses, who is instructed by God regarding what to say to the people. Knohl notes the following examples of H's use of first person divine speech directed to the people of Israel, outside of the Holiness Code: Exod 6:6–8; 12:12–13; 16:12; 29:42; 31:13; Lev 7:34. He also cites passages illustrating H's use of the personal pronoun אני in reference to God, within the Holiness Code (Lev 17:11; 18:3, 24; 20:3, 23, 24; 23:10; 25:2; 26:16, 24, 28, 32, 41), and outside of the Holiness Code (Exod 6:6–8; 10:2; 12:12; 16:12; 29:46; 31:13; Num 3:12, 13, 41, 45; 10:10; 18:6, 8, 20). Some of these citations include divine speeches to Moses alone (Knohl lists Num 3:11, but the first person personal pronoun does not occur until v. 12).

31. Knohl, *Sanctuary*, 94–95, 95 n. 119. Knohl notes the following passages which illustrate H's use of first person for divine speech addressed to Moses and Aaron together: Lev 14:33–34; 15:31; Num 14:26–27; 16:20–21; 20:12. Accordingly, Exod 7:8–9; 9:8 (P) comprise divine direct addresses to Moses and Aaron which include second person references to Moses and Aaron, but no first person references to God.

In light of the above clarification of Knohl's presentation, Milgrom's objection no longer holds. Leviticus 15:1–2a (P) does not contradict the above system; for this passage actually falls into the category of address directed to the people of Israel, in relation to whom there is no direct address. To say that Moses and Aaron are being directly addressed by virtue of the second person imperative ("speak" to the children of Israel), still fits Knohl's system; for Moses and Aaron are referred to in the second person, but no first person reference is applied to God.

Milgrom is correct in raising Lev 11:1–20 as an objection; not, however, because it constitutes divine direct address to Moses and Aaron, but because it comprises divine direct address to the people of Israel (Lev 11:2–13, 20–24, 26–29, 31, 33, 35, 38–39, 42–45). Consequently, in keeping with Knohl's system, I conclude that the presence of second person plural references to the people suggests the hand of H in Lev 11:1–20.[32] The presence of H is already attested within this passage regarding the dietary laws in vv. 43–44, evident not only by the presence of divine direct address, but also by "the characteristic signature of HS," אני יהוה אלהיכם ("I am the Lord your God").[33]

---

32. The H provenience of Lev 11:1–20 has already been suggested by others. Kuenen, *Hexateuch*, 278; Driver, *Introduction*, 59; see also Elliott-Binns, "Some Problems of the Holiness Code," 27.

33. Milgrom argues that Lev 11:43–44 does represent H, but that it contradicts the previous verses, which must be P. He contends that the terms שקץ and טמא within Lev 11 are applied to distinct categories and bear distinct meanings: that which is טמא transmits impurity by touch, while that which is שקץ may not be eaten (though it does not defile). A key to the distinction between the terms is that the person who touches the carcass of that which is טמא must be purified by bathing, washing clothes, and waiting until evening; while the one who eats that which is שקץ need do nothing. Accordingly, animals which are שקץ are "pure" and do not defile. This is contradicted by Lev 11:43–44 which implies that eating land swarmers (which are שקץ; vv. 41–42) does defile. Milgrom states that the difference between the two terms is consistent throughout P. Milgrom, "Two Biblical Hebrew Priestly Terms," 107–9, 114; idem, *Leviticus 1–16*, 684. In rebuttal, consistency throughout P is difficult to demonstrate since the term שקץ (and its related verb) does not occur anywhere else in the priestly literature except at Lev 7:21, and in the Holiness Code at Lev 20:25. Milgrom eliminates Lev 7:21 by arguing that its occurrence here should be read as šereṣ and not šeqeṣ. Thus, outside of Lev 11, the term only appears in H within the priestly materials. The alternative distinction between the two terms is one of degree: animals that are טמא defile by touch (and surely even more by ingestion), while animals which are שקץ defile only by ingestion. Consequently, Lev 11:43–44 does not contradict the previous verses, but rather clarifies their implications. Rashi affirmed that the defilement discussed in these verses stems from ingestion: "YE SHALL NOT MAKE [YOUR SOULS] ABOMINABLE, by eating

Outside of the Holiness Code, most priestly passages which include second person plural references addressed to the children of Israel are attributed by Knohl to H based on corroborating evidence. However, Knohl does not press this particular characteristic when it appears independently as a sign of the hand of H. Consequently, particular verses in three passages (Lev 1:2; 11; Num 28–29) which include second person plural references stand out as unattributed to H according to Knohl's work.[34] However, if the presence of second person plural references in divine address to the children of Israel is to be considered a characteristic of H, as Knohl's scheme implies, then these verses must also be attributed to H. We have already included the verses in Lev 11 as noted above. The verse immediately preceding Lev 1:2 appears to be secondary and has previously been attributed to H.[35] The use of the second person plural in Lev 1:2 suggests that it too is secondary due to the fact that the rest of the chapter is expressed in third person impersonal terminology. Consequently, like verse 1, this verse should also be attributed to H. The numerous second person plural references in Num 28–29 suggest that H felt it necessary to rework that entire passage. This contention is supported by the recognition that a number of verses in Num 28–29 appear to be later insertions.[36] With the fingerprint of H already so evident in Num 28–29, it seems reasonable to also attribute

---

these: *this must be the meaning*, because you see it is written '[ye shall not make] your souls [abominable]' and no soiling of the soul arises from touching *these creatures*. And similarly the words (v. 44) 'neither shall you defile [your souls]' *mean*: by eating them." Silbermann, *Leviticus*, 49a.

34. Lev 1:2; 11:2-13, 20-24, 26-29, 31, 33, 35, 38-39, 42; Num 28:3a, 11a, 18b, 19a, 20b, 24a, 25, 26, 27a; 29:1, 2a, 7, 8a, 12, 13a, 35, 36a, 39.

Leviticus 2:4-15 stands out inexplicably in the priestly literature as apparently addressed to the children of Israel with the unusual use of second person *singular* references (our discussion has centered on second person *plural* references as characteristic of H). Within this passage vv. 11-12 are in the plural. These two verses need not be considered divine direct address to the children of Israel, as Milgrom explains that these verses are likely addressed to the priests. Milgrom, *Leviticus 1-16*, 188.

35. Kuenen, *Hexateuch*, 84; Knohl, *Sanctuary*, 194 n. 68.

36. Noth, *Numbers*, 219-20. Though Knohl does not press the occurrence of second person plural references as evidence of the hand of H, based on other evidence he sees the hand of H throughout Num 28–29 (i.e., 28:2b, 6, 22-23, 30-31a; 29:5-6, 11, 16, 19, 22, 25, 28, 31, 34, 38). Knohl, *Sanctuary*, 30-32, 106. Knohl implies that H may have felt the need to rework Num 28–29 in such a drastic fashion out of concern for bringing the priestly calendar into conformance with its own ideology.

the occurrences of second person plural references to H's reworking of this pericope.

Milgrom further questions first person references to God as a distinctive mark of H, based on Lev 6:10-11 (Eng. vv. 17-18). He contends that these verses demonstrate that P may have occasionally used the first person in reference to God's speech when addressing Moses and Aaron (and Aaron's sons; Lev 6:1-2; Eng. vv. 8-9).[37] However, the edited character of the entire passage on the grain offering (6:7-11; Eng. vv. 14-18), suggests that first person references to God in this passage remain a sign of the hand of H. The first sign of editing appears in relation to the explicit references to Aaron and his sons. The text of Lev 6-7 begins with an introduction which designates Aaron and his sons (אהרן ואת־בניו; 6:2) as the objects of the following instructions. The rest of the text in these two chapters normally refers to Aaron and his sons as "the priest(s)" (הכהן or הכהנים; 6:3, 5, 19, 22; 7:5, 6, 7, 8, 9, 14, 31, 32) or simply employs the third person singular to refer to the priest (6:8; 7:2, 3, 12). The only instances in which Aaron and his sons are specifically named (with the proper name Aaron), aside from the introduction in 6:2, are in the introductions enveloping the H inserted section of chapter six,[38] or when a distinction must be made between the officiating priest and the sons of Aaron as a whole (7:10, 31, 33).[39] The only exceptions to this pattern occur in the passage of Lev 6:7-11, and at Lev 7:34-35. Instead of using the title "priest(s)" in this section (or simply a third person singular reference), these verses specifically name Aaron and his sons (vv. 7, 9, 11; Eng. vv. 14, 16, 18), and use the third person *plural* to refer to them (vv. 9, 10; Eng. vv. 16, 17). This distinction is especially evident in v. 11 by means of the phrase כל־זכר בבני אהרן יאכלנה ("every male among the sons of Aaron shall eat it") which imitates the

---

37. Milgrom contends that if H had reworked v. 10 (as Knohl claims), then why did H not rework v. 11. Milgrom concludes that these verses were not reworked, and that P may have condoned God's speaking in the first person after all. Milgrom, *Leviticus 1-16*, 17, 394; see also Knohl, *Sanctuary*, 126 n. 7. Despite this conclusion, Milgrom continues to cite the presence of God's first person speech as evidence of the hand of H. Milgrom, *Leviticus 1-16*, 866 (regarding Lev 14:34), 946-47 (regarding Lev 15:31).

38. Lev 6:13, 18a (Eng. vv. 20, 25a). Milgrom already views Lev 6:12-18a as inserted by H. Milgrom, *Leviticus 1-16*, 396, 426.

39. See, Milgrom, *Leviticus 1-16*, 411-12 (see comments on vv. 9-10), 431.

usual phrase of the text, כל־זכר בכהנים יאכל אתה ("every male among the priests shall eat it"; 6:22 [Eng. v. 29]; 7:6).⁴⁰

In addition to the unique reference to Aaron and his sons, the edited character of Lev 6:7–11 is evident by the presence of the unusual phrase in v. 11: חק־עולם לדרתיכם ("a permanent due for your generations"). This particular phrase appears nowhere else in the Hebrew Bible. It mimics the characteristic formula often used by H to conclude passages, חקת עולם לדרתיכם ("a permanent statute for your generations"). At the same time, the phrase in Lev 6:11 appears related to the shorter phrase חק־עולם ("a permanent due") which appears elsewhere in this text (Lev 6:15 [Eng. v. 22]; 7:34). Milgrom concludes, based on the unusual appearance in this context of the second-person plural suffix (לדרתיכם), that the phrase in Lev 6:11 must be an imitation of חקת עולם לדרתיכם ("a permanent statute for your generations").⁴¹ However, since this phrase (חקת עולם לדרתיכם) is characteristic of H, and H is a redaction of P, it cannot be an unconscious imitation on the part of P, but rather, must be an insert by H. Such indicators of editing suggest that the passage on the grain offering (Lev 6:7–11; Eng. vv. 14–18) was completely reworked by H.

Like Lev 6:7–11, the passage of Lev 7:34–36 stands out from the rest of Lev 6–7.⁴² It too contains divine first person speech (in this case, directed to the people of Israel), references to the priests specifically as Aaron and his sons (as opposed to merely "priests"), and the unique use of the phrase חקת עולם לדרתם ("a permanent statute for their generations") which imitates the characteristic H phrase, חקת עולם לדרתיכם ("a permanent statute for your generations").⁴³ In addition, Lev 7:34 appears to contradict the preceding vv. 31–33. In vv. 31–33, it is stated that the breast is due to Aaron and his sons, while the right thigh is due to the officiating priest. In contrast, v. 34 states that the breast *and* the thigh are given to Aaron and his sons (entire priesthood). In accordance with Milgrom's explanation for changes with regard to the priestly dues,

---

40. Cf. Noth, *Leviticus*, 55.

41. Milgrom, *Leviticus 1–16*, 395. The third person is expected here, in reference to the priests.

42. Knohl sees these verses as part of an addition made by H (Lev 7:28–36). Knohl, *Sanctuary*, 51.

43. This particular form of the phrase (with third person plural suffix) appears only here and Exod 27:21.

it appears that H, like preceding strands of P, reflects the historical need to support a growing body of priests. Thus, H accommodates changes based on the growing number of priests serving in the temple.[44]

In summation, divine address, which conforms to the stipulations outlined in the chart above, identifies passages which should be attributed to H.

Inclusion of the Stranger

Knohl points to the equality between the stranger and the citizen in Israel as another characteristic element of H.[45] This theme is grounded in the words found in the Holiness Code at Lev 19:34: "The stranger who sojourns with you shall be to you as a native among you, and you shall love him as yourself, for you were strangers in the land of Egypt, I am the Lord your God." The application of this theme is reflected in the attribution of the rights and especially the responsibilities of the people of God to the stranger, as well as the native in Israel. "There shall be for you one ordinance, it shall be for the stranger and for the native, for I am the Lord your God" (Lev 24:22). Such application is evident throughout the Holiness Code (Lev 17:8, 10, 12–13, 15; 18:26; 20:2; 22:18; 24:16). Outside of the Holiness Code, the statement that there be one law for stranger and citizen alike is found in three passages. This call for equality between stranger and citizen with regard to the law concludes two Passover texts which consequently can be attributed to H (Exod 12:49; Num 9:14).[46] Similarly, the presence of this statement in Num 15 adds

44. Milgrom does not interpret Lev. 7:34–36 in this way, but makes a parallel argument in relation to earlier priestly strands. He contends that Lev 2:10 and Lev 7:9 represent diverse assignments of the priestly dues which reflect the changing traditions from the local sanctuary to the temple. Milgrom points to three historical situations which prompt such a need: 1) beginning with the temple in Solomon's time, the need to add to the dues of the priests would have grown as the priestly members grew; 2) under Hezekiah the situation would have become critical as Levitic priests from the north emigrated to Judah; and 3) under Josiah as reforms led to the unemployment of the priests of the high places, and Josiah sought to integrate all the priests into Jerusalem. Milgrom, *Leviticus 1–16*, 33, 480–81. Accordingly, assigning H to the time of Hezekiah suggests that the H insertion at Lev 7:34 may reflect the need to add to the priestly dues in response to the influx of priests from the northern kingdom.

45. Knohl, *Sanctuary*, 21, 52.

46. Knohl, *Sanctuary*, 21–22. Exodus 12:19 can be added to these two passages regarding the Passover. It too reflects the inclusion of the stranger. Knohl argues that 12:18–20 constitutes an editorial addition to the more ancient passage of 12:1–17. Both strata, however, are assigned by Knohl to H.

to the evidence for the H provenience of that chapter (Num 15:14–16, 26, 29–30).[47] Passages in the priestly literature which communicate the related theme of inclusiveness with regard to the stranger occur at Lev 16:29, Num 19:10b, and 35:15. These texts can also be considered among those reflecting the hand of H.[48]

Extension of P^N Themes

The redaction carried out by H is further characterized by the extension of themes which have been drawn from P^N and are reflected in the rest of the priestly literature. This becomes evident as the characteristics of H (as delineated above) are traced in correspondence with passages which demonstrate affinities to P^N.

The Creation Account

Ziony Zevit points to a priestly tradent (identified as P^r) in Exod 7:14—12:36 who compiled the traditions in JE and P and redacted them into a final form which expresses the tradent's own theological interpretation of the material.[49] Zevit's P^r draws heavily on material from the creation narrative in Gen 1. Zevit concludes his argument with these words:

> P^r's image of Egypt at the conclusion of his plague-exodus narratives is of a land with no people, no animals, no vegetation (cf. Gen 1:1-2; 2:4-5). A land in which creation was undone. This is the scene which P^r supposed the Israelites to have seen after the waters stilled. It demonstrated to Israel that Yahweh was the creator and precipitated their response in faith.[50]

In light of the characteristic markers of H, it appears that the priestly tradent who edited the plague narratives should be identified as H. Zevit states that the original sources of the plague narrative, left to themselves, reflect the motif of forcing the Egyptians to acknowledge the Lord based on a localized demonstration of God's power.[51] He

---

47. Knohl, *Sanctuary*, 21–22, 53.

48. Knohl demonstrates that each of these passages reveal the hand of H. Knohl, *Sanctuary*, 27–28 (Lev 16:29), 93–94, 93 n. 111 (Num 19:10b), 99 (Num 35:15).

49. Zevit, "Priestly Redaction," 193–97.

50. Ibid., 210.

51. Ibid., 197; cf. Noth, *Exodus*, 67–68, cf. 80.

concludes, however, that with the completed work of the redactor, the theme becomes dominant for the narrative and is extended "beyond the geo-historical boundaries of the story (cf. Ex 6:6; 7:3–5; 12:12, 'all the gods of Egypt'; 14:4, 18 [P]; 10:2; 14:31 [JE])."⁵² Each of these passages, cited by Zevit as illustrative of the redactor's theological intention, can be linked to H. The only exception is the JE passage of Exod 14:31, which nevertheless, according to Zevit, is placed within the redactor's compilation in order to convey the redactor's intent. The other passages reflect characteristics of H as follows: divine direct address (6:6; 7:3; 12:12), and the formula אני יהוה ("I am the Lord"; 6:6; 7:5; 10:2; 12:12; 14:4, 18).⁵³ The hand of H can be seen elsewhere in the final compilation of the plague narrative as follows: the formula אני יהוה (7:17; 8:18 [Eng. v. 22]), the phrase חקת עולם לדרתיכם ("a permanent statute for your generations"; 12:14, 17),⁵⁴ punishment by כרת (12:15, 19), and inclusion of the stranger (12:19). Accordingly, the echoes of the creation account found in the plague narrative, demonstrate how H extended concepts from P^N (in this case, the creation account) beyond Exod 6.

The dietary laws of Lev 11 also reflect terminology taken from the creation account in P^N. Leviticus 11:10 refers to sea creatures as שרץ המים ("the swarming things of the waters"), and as נפש החיה אשר במים ("the living creatures which are in the waters"). This reflects similar terminology taken from Gen 1:20, which describes the creation of sea creatures with the clause: ישרצו המים שרץ נפש חיה ("Let the waters swarm with swarms of living creatures"). Similarly, Lev 11:44 refers to השרץ הרמש על־הארץ ("the swarming things which creep upon the earth"). This reflects the terminology from Gen 1:21, הרמשת אשר שרצו המים ("the creeping things with which the waters swarm"). In addition, the repeated use of the prepositional phrase למינה ("after its kind") to indicate the various categories of creatures (as well as plants) is found throughout the creation account (Gen 1:11, 12, 21, 24, 25). This same pattern of indicating various types of creatures through the use of this prepositional phrase is used to identify animals in the account of the dietary laws (Lev 11:14, 15, 16, 19, 22, 29).

---

52. Zevit, "Priestly Redaction," 197.

53. The H origin of Exod 12:12 was recognized by Klostermann, *Der Pentateuch*, 377.

54. The phrase is inverted in these verses; see Knohl, *Sanctuary*, 52.

The hand of H can be seen in Lev 11 as follows: divine direct address (vv. 2–13, 20–24, 26–29, 31, 33, 35, 38–39, 42–45), the characteristic phrase—אני יהוה אלהיכם ("I am the Lord your God"; v. 44, cf. 45), and the thematic call to holiness—והייתם קדשים ("you shall be holy"; vv. 44, 45).[55] Consequently, the reflection of terminology taken from the creation account suggests the extension of P^N concepts into these dietary laws, by the hand of H.

God of the Covenant

The formula which reflects the characteristic signature of H (אני יהוה אלהיכם—"I am the Lord your God") constitutes the fulfillment of a promise which is first communicated at Gen 17:8, in the context of the Abrahamic covenant in P^N. At that point the Lord promised to be God to Abraham's descendants by means of the phrase, והייתי להם לאלהים ("I shall be their God"). H identifies the divine subject in Gen 17 as יהוה by inserting the divine name into the introduction of the covenant account (Gen 17:1), constituting the only instance in all of P^N in which this divine name is used. The Abrahamic covenant of Gen 17 is explicitly linked to Exod 6 by the direct reference to the covenant in Exod 6:3–4 (cf. Gen 17:1–8). At this important transitional link between P^N and the rest of the priestly literature, the promise to be God is repeated, only this time with the more personal 2nd person pronoun: והייתי לכם לאלהים ("I shall be *your* God"; Exod 6:7). It is precisely at this point that H first introduces its "characteristic signature," אני יהוה אלהיכם ("I am the Lord your God"; Exod 6:7) which then appears throughout H.[56] Thereby, H

---

55. The H provenience of much of Lev 11 has already been suggested by others. See Kuenen, *Hexateuch*, 278 (re.: Lev 11:1–23, 41–47); Driver, *Introduction*, 59 (re.: Lev 11:43–45); Klostermann, *Der Pentateuch*, 377 (re.: Lev 11:43–45); see also Elliott-Binns, "Some Problems of the Holiness Code," 27.

56. The phrases והייתי להם לאלהים ("I shall be their God"), and והייתי לכם לאלהים ("I shall be your God") each appear in only one other instance: Exod 29:45 and Lev 26:12 respectively. The Leviticus reference is within the Holiness Code itself. For the H provenience of Exod 29:45–46, see Kuenen, *Hexateuch*, 278; Milgrom, *Leviticus 1–16*, 686; and Knohl, *Sanctuary*, 102 n. 145. A related phrase, "to be your God" (להית לכם לאלהים) appears in the Holiness Code at Lev 22:33; 25:38; 26:45. The last reference contains the phrase with the 3rd person pronoun; thus, להית להם לאלהים. Outside of the Holiness Code this phrase appears at Lev 11:45 and Num 15:41. These verses contain the following additional characteristics of H: the phrase אני יהוה ("I am the Lord"; Lev 11:45); the phrase אני יהוה אלהיכם ("I am the Lord your God"; Num 15:41); the thematic call to holiness, והייתם קדשים ("you shall be holy"; Lev 11:45); and divine direct address (Lev

expresses a type of fulfillment for the promise of the covenant (i.e., the promise that the Lord will be God to the descendants of Abraham; Gen 17:7) by means of the transition in terminology from והייתי להם לאלהים ("I shall be their God"; Gen. 17:8), to the more personal phrase והייתי לכם לאלהים ("I shall be your God"; Exod 6:7), and finally, throughout H, the fulfillment phrase אני יהוה אלהיכם ("I am the Lord your God"; beginning at Exod 6:7). Given that this series of phrases appears to be an intentional development by the hand of H, the phrase והייתי להם לאלהים ("I shall be their God") at Gen 17:8 must be an insertion by H.[57]

The text of Exod 6 is identified with H by the presence of the phrase אני יהוה אלהיכם ("I am the Lord your God," v. 7) and its shortened version אני יהוה ("I am the Lord," vv. 2, 6, 8, 29), and by the presence of divine direct address (vv. 5–8, 29).[58] Thus, H extends the theme of God's promise to be God to the descendants of Abraham as originally stated in P^N (Gen 17:7).

The Toledoth Formula

Another example of H borrowing from P^N can be seen in the appearance of the *toledoth* formula within H material. The formula appears only once, outside of P^N, at Num 3:1. P^N organized its document by introducing each section with the *toledoth* formula designating the main character discussed in the corresponding section. Using the same formula, H designated the two main characters in P, that is, Moses and Aaron. The placement of the *toledoth* formula in H appears near the end of the Sinai account (ending at Num 10:10), at the beginning of a section which describes the numbering of the Levites and their work in relation to the tabernacle. This numbering of tabernacle workers is significant to the core of the priestly literature which focuses on the tabernacle and its surrounding cult. Thus, the numbering of those who officiate in the cult (priests) and those who do the labor regarding the tabernacle and its furnishings (Levites), appropriately appears after the construction of

---

11:45; Num 15:41).

57. I am grateful to Jeffrey Kuan who suggested this possibility to me by observing that this phrase contains the only 3rd m.pl. suffix in the entire text of Gen 17 (cf. the usual reference to the descendants of Abraham in this text [זרעך אחריך—"your seed after you"]; vv. 7, 8, 9, 10).

58. For more on the H provenience of Exod 6, see Knohl, *Sanctuary*, 17 n. 24; 61; Driver, *Introduction*, 151; Kuenen, *Hexateuch*, 278; Klostermann, *Der Pentateuch*, 377.

the tabernacle (Exod 35–40), and following the instructions regarding offerings and sacrifices (Lev 1–7). Accordingly, the priests serving at the time (Eleazar and Ithamar) are listed initially (Num 3:2-4), followed by the numbering of the Levites (Num 3:5-39). H subsumes the two lists under the general *toledoth* heading designating Moses and Aaron (Num 3:1).[59]

The presence of the hand of H is revealed in this passage by the signature phrase, אני יהוה ("I am the Lord") at Num 3:13, 41, 45. In addition, divine direct address characteristic of H is revealed as God is identified by the first person personal pronoun, אני, in speaking to Moses (Num 3:12).[60] Thus, it appears that H has borrowed a phrase common to P^N (the *toledoth* formula), and used it within its redaction of the priestly literature.

Theme of Abundance

The theme of abundance is reflected in H at Lev 26:9 by means of the terminology common to P^N (fruitfulness and multiplication). This reflection of P^N at Lev 26:9 appears in the context of a passage which refers back to the covenant of Gen 17 (P^N). The covenant is reflected in Lev 26:12 through the repetition of the promise to "be God" to the children of Israel (cf. Gen 17:7-8). Leviticus 26:12 also echoes the unique description found in P^N of faithful people "walking about" with God (cf. Gen 5:22, 24; 6:9; 17:1).[61] These reflections of P^N clearly appear within the core of the Holiness Code itself (Lev 17–26). These verses reflecting the terminology of P^N are immediately followed by H's characteristic signature in the phrase אני יהוה אלהיכם ("I am the Lord your God"; Lev 26:13). Thus, this material further reflects H's tendency to extend themes taken from P^N.

---

59. Cross has noted the secondary character of the *toledoth* heading in Num 3:1 (*Canaanite Myth*, 302 n. 33, 308 n. 47).

60. For more on the H origin of Num 3, see Knohl, *Sanctuary*, 54; 72–73; 116, n. 18; Klostermann, *Der Pentateuch*, 377; Kuenen, *Hexateuch*, 278.

61. The connection in each case is the use of the hithpael form of the verb הלך with regard to Divine-human relationships.

The Sabbath

The Sabbath accounts which are traditionally attributed to P are: Gen 2:2-3; Exod 16:23-30; 31:13-17; 35:2-3; Num 15:32-36; and 28:9-10. The passages in Exod 16:23-30; 31:13-17; 35:2-3, and Num. 15:32-36 all show signs of the hand of H, rather than P.[62] Exodus 16:23-30 is within a passage which includes the following signs of H: the phrase אני יהוה אלהיכם ("I am the Lord your God"; v. 12); and divine direct address (vv. 23, 28-29). Exodus 31:13-17 includes these characteristics of H: divine direct address (vv. 13, 14, 17), the phrase אני יהוה מקדשכם ("I am the Lord who makes you holy/consecrates you"; v. 13), and the כרת formula distinctive of H (v. 14).[63] The text of Exodus 35:2-3 includes direct divine address. In addition, the LXX conclusion to the Sabbath instruction in Exod 35:2-3 consists of the added phrase, ἐγὼ κύριος (אני יהוה; "I am the Lord"). This suggests the possibility that the LXX reflects an established manuscript tradition which included the phrase. Accordingly, it has been suggested that the LXX may reflect the original wording of Exod 35:3. If so, the passage reflects a second characteristic of H by means of the presence of the phrase.[64] With regard to Num 15:32-36, Knohl adds to evidence brought forth by Wellhausen and Kuenen, and assigns the entire text of Num 15 to H. The chapter includes the following signs of H: divine direct address (vv. 2, 18-22), inclusion of the stranger (vv. 14-16, 26, 29-30), the formula חקת עולם לדרתיכם ("a permanent statute for your generations"; v. 15), punishment by כרת ("cutting off"; v. 30, 31), the thematic call to holiness expressed in the phrase והייתם קדשים ("you shall be holy"; v. 40), and the concluding signature of H: אני יהוה אלהיכם ("I am the Lord your God"; v. 41).[65]

This leaves only Gen 2:2-3 and Num 28:9-10 as Sabbath pericopes within the priestly literature which are not assigned to H. Knohl contrasts the instruction in Num 28:9-10 with the work prohibitions of the

---

62. See Knohl, "The Priestly Torah: Sabbath," 73-76; idem, *Sanctuary*, 14-19.

63. For more on the H origin of Exod 31:13-17, see Driver, *Introduction*, 59; Kuenen, *Hexateuch*, 278; Klostermann, *Der Pentateuch*, 377.

64. Knohl, *Sanctuary*, 16. Dillmann alludes to the H provenience of this passage by suggesting that, based on the LXX reading, Exod 35:3 may stem from an "old lawbook" which he identifies with the Holiness Code by citing another occurrence of the phrase in Lev 18:2. Dillmann, *Exodus und Leviticus*, 398.

65. Knohl, *Sanctuary*, 18, 53; Wellhausen, *Composition des Hexateuchs*, 175; Kuenen, *Hexateuch*, 96. Also see Driver, *Introduction*, 59; Kuenen, *Hexateuch*, 278; Klostermann, *Der Pentateuch*, 377.

Sabbath passages in H by pointing out that Num 28:9–10 does not mention any forbidden labors. The lack of a work prohibition in relation to the Sabbath stands out in light of the presence of work prohibitions for the various other occasions listed in the same passage (Num 28:18, 25, 26; 29:1, 7, 12, 35). Knohl defends the conclusion that, "PT nowhere explicitly forbids labors on the Sabbath."[66] This prompts the question regarding the origin of H's strong Sabbath restrictions.

The only text remaining among the priestly associated Sabbath passages is Gen 2:2–3. Knohl contrasts this passage with those in H by pointing out that this passage never explicitly mentions the name "Sabbath," nor does it prohibit any human labor.[67] Nevertheless, the Genesis passage concerning the seventh day does communicate an elevated status for the seventh day (it is blessed, ברך and consecrated, קדש; v. 3), and characterizes the day as that in which God rested (שבת; v. 2, 3). Though the institution of the Sabbath is not declared here, the association between the verb "to rest" (שבת) and the noun "Sabbath" (שבת), and between the declaration of the seventh day as the day when the Creator rested "from all his labor" (מכל-מלאכתו) and the prohibition against work (מלאכה) on the Sabbath (Exod 31:15), suggest that Gen 2:2–3 may have been the foundation upon which H built to express its Sabbath perspective. This is reinforced by the obvious allusion to Gen 2:2–3 (P^N) in Exod 31:13–17 (H). The connection between the seventh day and the Sabbath is made clear in Exod 31:15, and the reference to the creation account is obvious in Exod 31:17. Accordingly, H appears to have expressed its Sabbath perspective based on the consecration of the seventh day as described in the creation account of P^N. The Sabbath, with its work restrictions, and elevated status, reflects H's extension of the Creator's rest on the seventh day as presented in P^N.

Finally, the Sabbath pericope in the Decalogue must be considered (Exod 20:11). Knohl argues that this verse should be added to those assigned to H because of its similarity in style to Exod 31:17. At the same time, he contrasts Exod 20:11 from Gen 2:2–3 due to the diverse style between them.[68] Yet, a relationship between all three texts is clear in that both Exodus texts (20:11; 31:17) explicitly allude to Gen 2:2–3.

---

66. Knohl, *Sanctuary*, 18–19, 19 n. 28, 163, 163 n. 155.
67. Knohl, "The Priestly Torah: Sabbath," 76; Knohl, *Sanctuary*, 18.
68. Knohl, *Sanctuary*, 67.

This is evident by the statement in each Exodus text that "for six days the Lord made the heavens and the earth, and in the seventh day, he rested." Knohl's objection to an association between the two Exodus passages and the Genesis text can be released with the recognition that Gen 2:2–3 stems from P^N, and not P.[69] This allows for the recognition that the Genesis pericope regarding the seventh day (P^N) serves as the foundation from which H extends the consecration of this day through a popular proclamation of a strict work prohibition.

Blood Prohibition

As with the Sabbath, H expresses its restrictions regarding blood based on the foundation of corresponding conceptions originating in P^N. The creation account designates only plants as a source of food, thus, restricting the shedding of animal blood (Gen 1:29–30 [P^N]). After the flood, the eating of meat is allowed, so long as the blood, which is the life of the creature, is drained and not eaten (Gen 9:3–4 [P^N]). Thereby, P^N reflects initial restrictions regarding blood. The passages within the priestly literature which explicitly reflect the concept of a blood prohibition are found within texts which can all be attributed to H (Lev 3:17; 7:26; 17:14; 19:26). The last two passages appear within the Holiness Code itself. Leviticus 3:17 appears in conjunction with H's characteristic formula, חקת עולם לדרתיכם ("a permanent statute for your generations"), and Lev 7:26 appears within a pericope including the following characteristics of H: divine direct address (Lev 7:23–24, 26), and the כרת formula characteristic of H (Lev 7:27).[70] Thus, the prohibition against eating blood is explicitly expressed only in H within the priestly literature after Exod 6, and appears to be a development based on blood restrictions stemming from P^N.

---

69. Knohl's objection is based on his contention that P does not reflect a work prohibition related to the Sabbath, while H does. Thus, by assigning Gen 2:2–3 to P, he must deny any association with a work prohibition related to Sabbath in this text, and maintain a disjunction between this text and the Exodus Sabbath accounts which are assigned to H.

70. For more on the H origin of these two texts, see Knohl, *Sanctuary*, 49–51; Milgrom, *Leviticus 1–16*, 216, 426; and Kuenen, *Hexateuch*, 278.

Popular Faith Perspective

Knohl recognizes the disjunction between priestly material before and after Exod 6, and describes it as merely two different periods of divine revelation within P itself. The first period is characterized by the use of אלהים and אל שדי in reference to God, and is labeled as "the Genesis period." The second period, characterized by the use of יהוה in reference to God, is called the "period of Moses." Knohl depicts the Genesis period as one which describes humanity as the summit of creation, depicts God in personal and anthropomorphic ways, and portrays a direct relationship between God the Creator and human beings based on principles of morality. In contrast, the Moses period describes humanity as unrelated to the divine nature, depicts God with impersonal language, and is detached from human needs or the shaping of moral order. Though the two periods are seen as complementary and not contradictory, Knohl describes a tension between H and P based on H's opposition to "the total disjunction of the two modes of divine revelation, as described in PT."[71] The tension between H and P comes from H's affinity with the Genesis period and H's contrast with the period of Moses. H depicts the God of Moses with personal descriptions reflecting a closeness to humanity, as illustrated by God's direct address to the people of Israel and such phrases as "I am the Lord *your* God." In addition, H's emphasis on the inclusion of the stranger corresponds with the more universal character of the Genesis period.[72]

The dichotomy which is evident between these two periods of P (Genesis and Moses) creates a strain which is more than can be sustained by the single document P. For example: how could P "shape a cultic system completely detached from anthropomorphic images of God—creator, supervisor, and savior" in the Moses Period material, while maintaining "the heritage of popular cultic practices which developed around the faith in God as the providential Creator who rewards the righteous" as expressed in the Genesis Period material?[73] How could P build up the popular faith in the first installment of the work, and then deny (or at least suppress) that faith in the second installment? This disjunction in relation to faith perspectives, as well as diverse

---

71. Knohl, *Sanctuary*, 173, see also 125, 146–47, 197.
72. Ibid., 173.
73. See ibid., 162–63.

terminology, is more than a unified text and intention can bear. The strain and tension in this dichotomy is released when the text comprising the Genesis period of the priestly literature is recognized as the distinct work of P[N]. Accordingly, H's opposition to the supposed dichotomy within P disappears, and is replaced with the understanding that H shares perspectives with P[N]. H's redactionary work reflects an attempt to bring together the faith community represented by P[N] with the faith community represented by P (as opposed to reflecting an attempt to reconcile diverse perspectives within a single document, P).

The H Redaction

Following is an index of the contents of the H redaction and expansion of the priestly literature as discussed above. This index is not intended to be comprehensive of every passage which may be attributed to H. Rather, this listing is the product of two avenues of investigation: 1) the identification of passages which demonstrate significant H characteristics, and 2) the demonstration that passages beyond Exod 6 which reflect affinities with P[N] consistently reveal H associations.

Genesis:

17:1 (insertion of יהוה); 8 (insertion of והייתי להם לאלהים); 14
36:8–14, 43

Exodus:

1:1–7, 13–14
2:23–25
6:2–8, 28–30
7.1–6, 17a, 19–20a, 21b–22
8:1–3, 12–14, 18 (Eng., vv. 5–7, 16–18, 22)
10:2
11:9–10
12:1–20, 49
14:1–4, 15–18
15:26
16:4–34
20:11

25:1–9
27:21
29:42, 45–46
31:1–17
35:1–19

Leviticus:

1:1–2
3:17
6:7–18a (Eng. vv. 14–25a)
7:20–29a, 34–36
10:9
11:1–24, 26–29, 31, 33, 35, 38–39, 42–45
14:33–34
15:31
16:29
17–26

Numbers:

3:1, 11–13, 40–51
5:1–4
6:22–27
9:1–14
10:1–10
13:1–2
14:5, 21, 26–35
15
16:20–24
17:16–28 (Eng. 17:1–13)
18:1–32
19:10b, 13, 20
20:12, 23–29
25:10–13
27:1–11
28:2b, 3a, 11a, 18b, 19a, 20b, 22b, 23b, 24a, 25, 26, 27a, 30b, 31
29:1, 2a, 5b, 7, 8a, 12, 13a, 35, 36a, 39
32:8–13

33:50–56
34:1–18
35:1–15, 29, 31–34
36:1–12

Deuteronomy:
32:48–52
34:1–9

Joshua:
11:15–20
14:1–5
21:1–8

6

The Provenience and Intent of H

Association with the Period of Hezekiah

THE REFORMS OF HEZEKIAH AND JOSIAH HAVE ATTRACTED ATTENTION as likely points of origin in relation to dating certain components of the priestly literature. The correspondence between passages in P and Deuteronomy led Friedman to conclude that P was composed concurrently with D, and therefore P originated from the time of the Josianic reform. He suggests that Dtr[1] and the preexilic compositions of P are derived from two separate priestly families of the Josianic period.[1] Haran, however sees P as deriving from the earlier period of reform in Israel, that is, the period of Hezekiah. He argues that P's tabernacle represents the Jerusalem temple at a time when the vessels of the inner sanctum (cherubim and ark) were still present. Since Manasseh's violent measures resulted in the loss of the vessels of the inner sanctum, P must stem from a period before that loss. The period of Hezekiah represents an appropriate time, prior to Manasseh, which reflects the historical crisis that may have served as the backdrop for P's composition. Haran points out that the destruction of the northern kingdom would have brought many groups of priests into Jerusalem from the north. He argues that these newcomers were not admitted into the inner circle of cultic activity. Such a background provides the explanation for the functional dichotomy between priests and Levites which is depicted in P.

> In no place other than the temple in Jerusalem, and apparently in no other period of time, could there take place that meeting of contrasts which brought priests and "Levites" under one

---

1. Friedman, *Exile and Biblical Narrative*, 70.

roof—priests who are members of the tribe boasting of their descent from Aaron (and scattered through the territories of Judah and Benjamin), who alone officiate in cultic functions, as against Levites who are all the other members of the tribe (scattered throughout the north), who were compelled to satisfy themselves with auxiliary tasks beside the cult, being offered no access to the cultic sanctity itself.[2]

Consequently, Haran suggests that while Josiah's reform was based on D, the reform of Hezekiah was based on the aspirations expressed in P.[3]

We have already discussed the origins of P in relation to the even earlier context of the tabernacle at Shiloh. However, as Haran has highlighted, the functional dichotomy between priests and Levites expressed in the priestly literature does suggest an association with the time of Hezekiah. Knohl points out that this association is not between the P strand of the priestly literature and the time of Hezekiah, but rather, this association is specifically between H and the time of Hezekiah. Knohl argues that H is responsible for the innovation of the distinction between priests and Levites in the priestly literature, and that H originates in the period of Hezekiah.[4] I agree that H originates with the period of Hezekiah, though it is not necessarily the case that H innovated the distinction between Levites and priests. H may have inherited this distinction from P, and re-emphasized it in light of the situation evident at the time of Hezekiah.[5]

---

2. Haran, "Behind the Scenes," 331.

3. Ibid., 332.

4. Knohl, *Sanctuary*, 85, 209–12.

5. Knohl attributes the innovation of the distinction between priests and Levites to H and argues that there is no mention of the distinction in P itself, outside of Numbers. As Milgrom explains, however, the absence of the mention of Levites outside of Numbers is appropriate to their role. Since Levites are restricted to the transport and protection of the sancta, they would only be mentioned in Numbers where such duties are discussed. Exodus discusses the construction of the Tabernacle, and Leviticus focuses on the sacrificial and purity laws. An appropriate exception appears in Exod 38:21 where the עבדה of the Levites is mentioned in relation to the construction of the Tabernacle (Milgrom, *Leviticus 1–16*, 1, 7). Thus, the distinction between Levites and priests is not necessarily an innovation of H. Rather, H may have inherited the distinction already present in P.

H Innovations Associated with the Period of Hezekiah

Knohl highlights a number of innovations (in comparison to P) reflected in the Holiness Code which point to the period of Hezekiah as the likely historical setting for the composition of H. They can be summarized as follows:

1. Centralization of the sacrificial cult (Lev 17:1–9)[6]
2. Prohibitions against incest and abominable sexual relations (Lev 18:6–24; 20:10–21), Molech worship (Lev 18:21; 20:2–5), and soothsaying and the conjuring of familiar spirits (Lev 19:26, 31; 20:6, 27)
3. Collection of moral and cultic commands linked to the call to "be holy" (Lev 19)
4. Blending of the "priestly" cult with "popular" festival customs (Lev 23)
5. Agrarian and social reform aimed at the rehabilitation of a social class (farmers) whose financial stability had been eroded and who had been uprooted from their land (Lev 25)
6. Blessings and curses including a warning of destruction and exile (Lev 26)[7]

H was composed in reaction to developments which would have prompted such innovations. Knohl affirms the period of the reigns of Ahaz and Hezekiah in Judea as a time reflecting such developments, for the following reasons:

1. Hezekiah, the heir of Ahaz, enacted reforms to purify and centralize the cult.

---

6. The issue of cult centralization in H remains uncertain. Milgrom stands in contrast to Knohl and argues that H innovated the ban on common slaughter, but like P, H presumes multiple sanctuaries. Milgrom, *Leviticus 17-22*, 1503-14. Knohl, on the other hand, argues that H legislates a type of centralization which recognizes only one legitimate altar for sacrifice (while possibly allowing for multiple sanctuaries whose altars have been torn down in line with Hezekiah's version of reform). Knohl, *Sanctuary*, 207-9. Baruch Schwartz complicates the matter with evidence that H not only advocates cult centralization, but that centralization of the cult is presupposed throughout the priestly literature (P itself presumed centralization). Schwartz, "'Profane' Slaughter," 15-42.

7. Knohl, *Sanctuary*, 204-5.

2. Molech worship, along with soothsaying and the conjuring of familiar spirits, were popular in Israel during the reign of Ahaz.
3. During the reigns of Ahaz and Hezekiah, Isaiah and Micah prophesied in Judea and spoke against moral, as well as social, injustice.
4. The prophecies of Isaiah and Micah reveal evidence of social polarization which led to the uprooting of many farmers from their land and their being sold into slavery.
5. During the reigns of Ahaz and Hezekiah, the northern kingdom of Israel fell to Assyria, and many people were exiled from their land.[8]

The Evidence of D's Dependence on H

The dating of H to the period of Hezekiah is further supported by the relationship in time evident between D and H. The date of H, and the attachment of P^N to P (part of H's redactionary work), is prior to the composition of D (Josianic period). We have previously discussed arguments which claim that D is dependent on P. Specifically, Deut 29:12 (Eng., 29:13) demonstrates dependence upon Gen 17:7-8; Exod 6:7; Lev 26:12, and the dietary laws in Deut 14:1-21 show dependence upon Lev 11 (which in turn echoes Gen 1, as demonstrated earlier). All of these passages have been previously linked to P^N or to the H redaction of the priestly literature (except for Lev 26:12 which is itself within the Holiness Code). This demonstrates that D refers, not only to P, but to the redaction by H, with its extension of P^N material. Therefore, H and the attachment of P^N to P should be dated prior to D.

H and the Program of Hezekiah

The fall of the northern kingdom, with the resultant influx of refugees into the southern kingdom, represents a central concern in relation to the intent of H. Evidence of this concern in H further demonstrates the related period of Hezekiah as the likely date for the composition of H.

The account of the second Passover in Num 9:1-14 demonstrates the hand of H by the inclusion of the stranger among those who are permitted to observe the ordinance (v. 14).[9] It has been suggested

---

8. Ibid., 205-6. In relation to item #4, see Mays, *Micah*, 63-64.
9. For further evidence attributing the second Passover account to H, see Knohl, "The Priestly Torah: Sabbath," 79-80.

that the historical background to the second Passover legislation was Hezekiah's celebration of the Passover in the second month (2 Chr 30).[10] Milgrom points out that, besides the regulation in Num 9, there are no recorded instances of a second month Passover in the Bible, except that of 2 Chr 30. Furthermore, the Chronicles account shows dependence on the legislation in Numbers by the fact that the reason given for the postponement of the Passover in Chronicles corresponds to the reasons given for delaying the celebration according to the legislation in Numbers (i.e., impurity of the priests, and distance for the people to journey [2 Chr 30:3; Num 9:10]).[11]

The historical circumstances for Hezekiah's actions may be detected within Hezekiah's appeal to northern refugees to come and join the observance in Jerusalem (2 Chr 30:1, 5–9). Hezekiah sought to reconcile the northern population and gain their allegiance in hopes of reuniting the northern tribes with his kingdom.[12] Accordingly, the reason for moving the Passover to the second month was to accommodate northerners who were already accustomed to celebrating the Passover in the second month.[13]

Talmon explains that the experience of the north had been fixed earlier by Jeroboam. In Jeroboam's attempt to sever ties with Judah by emphasizing northern traditions, he established an exclusive northern calendar. Jeroboam's actions were not random, but rather were in line with actual climatic and agricultural conditions prevalent in the north of Palestine. The climatic and geographical conditions of Palestine result in an earlier ripening of crops in the south than in the north. Therefore, the farmer in Judah would be finishing the harvest of his crops at the same time that the farmer in Israel would still be at the peak of harvest season. As a result, the early festal calendar, which was governed by the agricultural seasons, would bring about an earlier celebration of the festivals in the south than in the north. An illustration of this appears in 1 Kgs 12:32–33 which records that Jeroboam celebrated Tabernacles in

---

10. Regarding the historical reliability of the Chronicler's account of Hezekiah's Passover (despite its absence in Kings), see Talmon, "Divergences in Calendar-Reckoning," 61–62; and Todd, "Reforms of Hezekiah and Josiah," 290–91.

11. Milgrom, *Numbers*, 372.

12. See ibid.; Silver, "Lunar and Solar Calendars," 305; and Talmon, "Divergences in Calendar-Reckoning," 58–61.

13. Silver, "Lunar and Solar Calendars," 306.

the eighth month, in relation to the same festival celebrated in Judah in the seventh month. Talmon further explains that Jeroboam's action did not affect Tabernacles alone, but actually indicated a complete adjustment of the calendar in order to bring the seasonal festivals in line with climatic conditions in the north.[14] It can be seen, therefore, that after the destruction of the north, Hezekiah's invitation to the refugees from Israel to join in the Passover at Jerusalem would be more acceptable if it were held at the time to which the northerners were accustomed. Accordingly, Hezekiah's celebration of the Passover in the second month was a one time occurrence, and not a complete shifting of the Judean festival calendar.[15]

In light of the above context, the second Passover legislation in Num 9:1–14 can be attributed to the same motivation and historical situation as Hezekiah's second month celebration. The H redactor, like Hezekiah, sought to include the northern refugees. The concern of H, however, comes from a priestly purview. H sought to incorporate the northern populace into the proper observance of the liturgical calendar. The second Passover legislation gives the northerners legal justification for their experience of having celebrated the Passover in the second month, while maintaining that the primary and proper time to celebrate the festival is in the first month, beginning on the fourteenth day (Num 9:5). Thus, H grants validity to the northern practice, but at the same time subtly reinforces that the actual appointed time of the Lord for Passover was originally ordained to be held in the first month (Num 9:1–3).

The Inclusion of P^N and Northern Refugees

The work of H reflects a significant concern for the inclusion of northern refugees within the community and worship of Judah following the fall of the northern kingdom. A literary means of addressing this concern was to attach the document P^N (representative of a northern

---

14. Talmon, "Divergences in Calendar-Reckoning," 54–58. See also Silver, "Lunar and Solar Calendars," 305. Though Passover itself may not have been affected by the agricultural seasons, it was nevertheless tied to the agricultural cycle within the cultic calendar. Milgrom explains that "since the *omer*-rite with the first grain (barley) has to take place after the paschal sacrifice (Lev. 23:10–11), the northern tribes had no choice but to celebrate it in the second month" (Milgrom, *Numbers*, 372).

15. Talmon, "Divergences in Calendar-Reckoning," 62–63.

tradition) to the priestly literature and to redact the whole in a manner which was inclusive of the refugee community.

Merging Two Traditions

As previously observed, P^N refers to God using the terms אלהים and אל שדי, while P favors the use of יהוה. The agenda of H was to bring together the two traditions associated with these respective references for the Divine, and to promote the recognition that they represent one and the same Deity. This agenda reflects H's desire to incorporate the refugees from the north within the program of P. An initial means of accomplishing this was through the merging of the two references for God. The pivotal pericope of Exod 6:2-8 highlights the significance of the phrase והייתי לכם לאלהים ("I shall be your God") in relation to this merging. The divine referent אלהים is identified with יהוה in verse 2, and by verse 7 this same God promises to be God to the children of Israel. Thus, this pericope serves to bring those who follow אל שדי/אלהים into the same community as those who know God as יהוה. H's use of the phrase והייתי לכם לאלהים serves to remind the adherents of אל שדי/ אלהים that יהוה (as God is identified throughout the rest of P) is indeed their God. The same can be said regarding the repeated use of the H formula אני יהוה אלהיכם ("I am the Lord your God").

H's intent to merge the traditions associated with יהוה and אל שדי/ אלהים in the priestly literature is further evident in the unique phrase, וידבר אלהים אל־משה ("And God said to Moses") which appears only once in the Hebrew Bible (Exod 6:2, [H]). It mimics the 91 occurrences of וידבר יהוה אל־משה ("And the Lord said to Moses"), which appear throughout P. The placement of this unique phrase within the transitional passage of Exod 6 serves to identify the two referents for God as one and the same.

H's work of combining the two faith traditions represented by P^N and P provides a sense of the needed fulfillment missing from P^N. Recall that P^N is characterized by the covenant promises including "fruitfulness and multiplication" and the promise of land, yet concludes without explicit indication of their fulfillment. Jonathan Magonet has argued that the reference to אל שדי at Exod 6:3 carries with it, not only the name by which God was identified to the Patriarchs, but includes the promises associated with that name, that is, to be "fruitful and multiply" and "inherit the land" (Gen 17:1-2, 6-8; 28:3-4; 35:11-12; [43:14]; 48:3-4). Magonet contends that the generations associated with אל שדי did not know God as יהוה in the complete sense of being the one who will fulfill the promises connected to אל שדי.[16] Rashi initially expressed this view in his comment on Exod 6:3:

> AND I APPEARED to the patriarchs באל שדי BY THE NAME OF GOD ALMIGHTY—I made *certain* promises to them and in the case of all of these I said unto them, "I am God Almighty", ושמי ה' לא נודעתי להם BUT BY MY NAME THE LORD WAS I NOT KNOWN TO THEM—It is not written here לא הודעתי [My name the Lord] I did not make known to them, but לא נודעתי [by My name the Lord], was I not known [unto them]—i. e. I was not recognized by them in My attribute of "keeping faith", by reason of which My name is called ה', *which denotes* that I am certain to substantiate My promise, for, *indeed*, I made promises to them but did not fulfill them *during their lifetime*.[17]

Accordingly, the attachment of P^N to P through the transitional passage of Exod 6 (H) brings fulfillment to the faith of the אל שדי community by transferring it to יהוה, the name by which God will fulfill the promises attached to אל שדי.[18] Thereby, H provides the northern refugees, who were associated with the worship of אל שדי, with a hope of fulfillment regarding the promises of God by bringing completion to their representative text P^N.

Further evidence of the intent to merge these traditions appears in the rare occurrences of the hand of H within P^N itself. Containing the only occurrence of יהוה in all of P^N, Genesis 17:1 appears as an H insertion for the purpose of identifying the God revealed to the patriarchs as אל שדי (Gen 17:1; cf. Exod 6:3) with the God of the rest of the priestly literature, known as יהוה.[19] Another instance of the hand of H within P^N is revealed at Gen 36.[20] The secondary character of Gen 36:9 is

---

16. Magonet, "The Rhetoric of God," 66.

17. Silbermann, *Exodus*, 24–25.

18. Fulfillment of the promise of land is evident in P at Josh 11:15–20, a text which will be discussed below.

19. As previously discussed in relation to the redactional link of Exod 6, and H's extension of P^N themes.

20. Knohl, *Sanctuary*, 103 n. 150. Knohl argues that the form מושבתיכם only appears in H passages within the Pentateuch. Based on this, and the recognition that Gen 36 contains information that appears contradictory to information in other material

apparent due to the redundant occurrence of the *toledoth* formula regarding Esau, as well as repetitive descendants lists for Esau (Gen 36:9–14; cf. vv. 1–7).[21] This suggests that one of the lists, in conjunction with its respective *toledoth* heading, may stem from a different hand than P^N. The recognition that H inserted the second occurrence of the *toledoth* formula regarding Esau as well as the second descendants list for Esau (Gen 36:9–14) opens the door to a striking suggestion with regard to the argument that H sought to bring together the two traditions which adhered to the two respective designations for the Divine, יהוה and אל שדי/אלהים. This becomes clear in light of van der Toorn's proposal regarding the origin of YHWH worship in Israel.

As previously discussed, van der Toorn linked the origin of YHWH worship in Israel to the topographical area of Edom through biblical and extra-biblical evidence which pointed to such related designations as "Edom," "Seir," and "Teman."[22] Consequently, it is striking that the secondary Esau material in Gen 36 (vv. 9–14) contains all three of these designations. The transitional verse (v. 8), between the initial Esau list (Gen 36:1–7) and the secondary material, designates Esau as living in Seir and explicitly identifies Esau as Edom. Then, the second use of the *toledoth* formula designating Esau (v. 9) adds the descriptive phrase, "the father of Edom, in the hill country of Seir." Finally, a grandson of Esau is identified as Teman (v. 11). The association of these place names with the origin of YHWH worship as van der Toorn has suggested, prompts the contention that H inserted this seemingly redundant material into the document P^N as part of its program of integrating the respective communities associated with יהוה and אל שדי/אלהים. Why is the *toledoth* formula for Esau repeated? Why are two descendants lists given for Esau back to back? These occurrences in P^N bring about an unexplained emphasis on Esau who, otherwise, bears little importance for the document in comparison to the more significant patriarchal characters, each of whom only receive one genealogical listing (Abraham, Isaac, and Jacob). The explanation may be that H created this unusual emphasis to draw attention to Edom, associated with the

---

normally attributed to P, Knohl concludes that the final form of Gen 36 should be attributed to H.

21. Regarding the secondary character of the second *toledoth* heading for Esau (Gen 36:9), see Cross, *Canaanite Myth*, 302 n. 33, 308 n. 47.

22. Van der Toorn, "Saul and Israelite Religion," 538–39.

origin of YHWH worship. Thereby, H subtly incorporated the heritage of YHWH worship into the same genealogical heritage which defined the community of the worshipers of אל שדי/אלהים.

Ban on Alien Cults

The ban on alien cults reflects H's concern for holiness, and highlights H's response to the situation of refugees who came from the north. Knohl contends that H formulated the concept of holiness in response to the needs evident during the period of Hezekiah. "The holiness that is extended to the entire community and to the land also serves as a platform in the struggle against the infiltration of alien cults (e.g., Molech worship). This struggle is also expressed in the reform program for concentrating the cult proposed by HS, which was implemented during the reign of Hezekiah under HS inspiration."[23] Molech worship became prevalent beginning with the reign of Ahaz.[24] The practice of giving one's children to Molech is clearly condemned by H (Lev 18:21; 20:2–4). The passage in Lev 18:21 describes this rite as להעביר למלך ("to cause to pass over to Molech"). Similar terminology is reflected in apparent references to this rite in the history of certain Kings of Judah and Israel: Ahaz of Judah (2 Kgs 16:3), Hoshea of Israel (2 Kgs 17:17), and Manasseh of Judah (2 Kgs 21:6).[25] The rite described in these passages is worded as follows: העביר באש ("he caused to pass over in the fire" [2 Kgs 16:3; 21:6; cf. 17:17]). Though these texts do not mention Molech, the connection is made in 2 Kgs 23:10, in relation to Josiah's reform, where the following terminology is found: להעביר באש למלך ("to cause to pass over in the fire to Molech"). In addition, 2 Chr 28:3, the parallel passage to 2 Kgs 16:3 (regarding Ahaz), mentions that the scene of the rite was in the valley of Ben hinnom. This valley is attached to the rite, explicitly in relation to Molech, in Jer 32:35.[26]

---

23. Knohl, "Priestly Torah: Ideological Aspects," 57.

24. Knohl, *Sanctuary*, 207; Elliott-Binns, "Some Problems of the Holiness Code," 38.

25. Admittedly, 2 Kgs 17:7–18 appears as the comment of the later Deuteronomistic redactor explaining the reason for the fall of the north. Gray, *I & II Kings*, 645–46. The indictment, though it may not specifically attribute the sins described in v. 17 to the reign of Hoshea, does attach these sins to the kingdom of Israel in the north.

26. Ibid., 277.

The rite of offering children to Molech may reflect Assyrian influence. All three of the kings accused of passing their children over into the fire came under the subjugation of Assyria.[27] In addition, 2 Kgs 17:31 points to human sacrifice in honor of "Adrammelech" and "Anammelech." This appears to refer to the actions of a group of colonists whom the Assyrians imported into Samaria. The first term designating the gods being honored may represent "the lordship of Malik," while the second appears to be a syncretism of Molech and Anu.[28] The Assyrian connection with Molech worship suggests that H's condemnation of the cult is likely addressed to northern refugees, as well as to others in Judah under the influence of Ahaz' former practice.[29]

The struggle against soothsaying and sorcery constitutes a related concern of H (Lev 19:26, 31; 20:6, 27).[30] It has been understood that the practice of divination was a natural inclination in times of crisis, such as the falls of Israel and Judah respectively. Thus, forms of divination flourished during the periods when Assyria and Babylon subjugated Palestine. The prominence of such practices during these respective periods of crisis may also be attributed to the influence of Assyrian and Babylonian religion.[31] Consequently, Assyrian influence in this regard adds to the recognition that H's warnings may be addressed to the northern refugees as well as others.

H also legislates against improper sexual relations (Lev 18:6–20, 22–23; 20:10–21).[32] Such prohibitions are commonly traced to the influence of Canaanite culture and its affiliation with fertility cults.[33] As

---

27. Bright, *History of Israel*, 274–76, 311. The altar which Ahaz built according to the pattern of the one in Damascus appears to serve as a symbol of subservience to Assyria (2 Kgs 16:10–13). Gray, *I & II Kings*, 635.

28. Gray, *I & II Kings*, 277.

29. The evidence for Assyrian origins of the Molech cult is not conclusive and has been disputed. See Heider, *The Cult of Molek*, 291–96; Day, *Molech*, 44–46. Nevertheless, Day argues that the Molech cult, which he views as Canaanite in origin, experienced a sudden revival as a direct response to the Assyrian crisis. Day, *Molech*, 62–64. Despite the uncertainties, it seems evident that the cult of Molech was manifest in Israel during the reign of Ahaz and following.

30. Knohl, *Sanctuary*, 205, 205 n. 17, 207.

31. Gray, *I & II Kings*, 648.

32. Knohl, *Sanctuary*, 204; Noth, *Leviticus*, 134, 146, 149–50.

33. Noth, *Leviticus*, 135, 143. Kaufmann, *Religion of Israel*, 319. It must be noted that what was once a standard understanding regarding the existence of cult

previously discussed, Canaanite fertility cults may have influenced the community represented by P^N (a community we have associated with northern refugees). Accordingly, H's prohibitions against improper sexual relations may, in part, be addressed against the influence of Canaanite fertility cults evident within the community represented by P^N. By means of the prohibitions against improper sexual relations, H strips the fertility associations from the community associated with the worship of אל שדי. Accordingly, the referent of אל שדי is never again used by H (after Exod 6), perhaps due to fertility cult associations.

The efforts of H reflect a desire to integrate the refugees from the north into the proper cultic program of the south. The infiltration of alien northern cult traditions was abated as northerners were forced to abandon the altars in the northern kingdom, and were exhorted to follow the legislation of P as redacted by H. The work of H, however, not only addressed the situation in terms of condemning northern practices in favor of the Jerusalem cult, but also sought to express an inclusive attitude toward northern refugees and the faith tradition represented by P^N.

Fulfillment Notices

H provides a sense of fulfillment to P^N (in relation to the promise of land) by attaching it to the rest of the priestly literature. To accentuate this provision, H adds notices to the priestly literature which enhance the expression of fulfillment in regard to God's promise of land.

Deuteronomy 32:48–52 and 34:1–9 are commonly understood to represent P's notice of Moses' death.[34] This is confirmed by the final appearance in the priestly literature of P's command formula

---

prostitution in relation to fertility rites has recently been called into question. Van der Toorn argues that the term "cultic prostitution" can only be maintained in the limited sense which recognizes that money or goods secured by means of prostitution went to the temple funds. In addition to being a source of profit to the temple, van der Toorn argues that prostitution may have occurred on occasion as an individual's means of securing goods in order to fulfill a vow. As an integral part of fertility rituals, however, van der Toorn argues that such a connection lacks evidence and remains speculative. Toorn, "Cultic Prostitution," 510–513; see Goodfriend, "Prostitution," 507–9. See, in addition to Kaufmann and Noth cited above, the common understanding of cultic prostitution in relation to fertility rites, in: Pope, "Fertility Cults," 265; Baab, "Prostitution," 932–34.

34. Campbell and O'Brien, *Sources*, 260; Noth, *Pentateuchal Traditions*, 19 n. 61, 226, 276.

(וידבר יהוה אל־משה ["And the Lord spoke to Moses"]) at Deut 32:48, and the presence of P's execution formula (כאשר צוה יהוה את־משה ["according as the Lord commanded Moses"]) at Deut 34:9. In these particular texts, it appears that H has borrowed these formulas and composed the notice of Moses' death. The hand of H is apparent due to the presence of direct divine address (Deut 32:49, 52).[35] In addition, H refers to the Abrahamic covenant in P^N in the passage in Deut 34. The extension of themes from P^N has already been demonstrated to be a characteristic of H. In this case, H appeals to the promise of land reflected in the Abrahamic covenant as recorded in P^N (Gen 17:8; 35:12; 48:4; cf. Deut 34:4). Significantly, in describing the land which Moses is instructed to view, H explicitly mentions the land of Ephraim and Manasseh (Deut 34:2). This reflects an emphasis on the northern tribes in the same way that P^N expresses that emphasis at the final recitation of the covenant promise. Recall, the last repetition of the covenant promise in P^N explicitly names Ephraim and Manasseh as descendants who will inherit the covenant promise (Gen 48:5). Accordingly, H brings the fulfillment of the promise into view for the northern community represented by P^N through the particular wording of the notice of Moses' death.

The command to take the land of promise is given in Num 33:50–53. P's command formula appears at verse 50. The execution formula attached to the fulfillment of this command appears in Josh 11:15, 20. Since the hand of H is present in Num 33:50–53, it is likely that H also provided its fulfillment in Josh 11:15–20. The hand of H is evident in the former passage by the presence of direct divine address (Num 33:50–53).[36] Consequently, H provides a narrative expressing the fulfillment of the promise of land within the priestly literature.

The command to divide the land of promise is given in Num 34:1–18, with the command formula appearing at verse one. Again, the hand of H is apparent by the presence of direct divine address (Num 34:1–4, 6–10, 12–13, 17–18). The fulfillment of this command appears in Josh 14:1–5, with the execution formula appearing at verse five. Notice that the command given in Num 34 explicitly mentions the lot of the nine and a half tribes (v. 13), and that the land was to be apportioned by Eleazar, Joshua, and a leader of every tribe (vv. 17–18). Accordingly, the

---

35. Regarding the H provenience of Deut 32:48–52, see Knohl, *Sanctuary*, 95–96.

36. For more on the H provenience of Num 33:50–53, see Kuenen, *Hexateuch*, 98 n. 39; Driver, *Introduction*, 69; Knohl, *Sanctuary*, 98.

fulfillment passage in Josh 14 also explicitly mentions these details (vv. 1–2). Once again, circumstances prompt H to explicitly name Ephraim and Manasseh in the course of this notice (Josh 14:4), as was done in the notice concerning Moses' death.

Finally, the command to give cities to the Levites appears in Num 35:1–8, beginning in verse one with the command formula. The fulfillment of this appears at Josh 21:1–8, with the execution formula appearing at verse eight.[37] Direct divine address reveals the hand of H at Num 35:1–2, 4–8.[38]

These notices bring to completion the promise of land; beginning with its viewing through the eyes of Moses and finding fulfillment in the taking of the land, the division of the land, and the granting of cities to the Levites. By adding these notices to the priestly literature, H brings closure to the promise of land. Thereby, H provides the community represented by P^N with fulfillment of the promise which was left open at the end of P^N.[39]

---

37. The formula appears here as כאשר צוה יהוה ביד־משה. This minor alteration simply adds the prepositional phrase, "by the hand of." This variation stems from the only other place it appears in the Hebrew Scriptures, i.e., Josh 14:2 which is part of the description of the fulfillment of the general division of the land (see above). A nearly identical phrase (אשר צוה יהוה ביד־משה) appears at Lev 8:36; Num 36:13; and Neh 8:14. The Leviticus passage simply functions as the execution formula regarding God's commands for Aaron and his sons as described in the preceding verses. The reference in Num 36:13 is not so much an execution formula for a specific command, but is simply a final summation referring to the preceding laws. Milgrom points out that the reference could refer to all the laws since Num 22:1 or since 35:1, based on the fact that each of these references contain the same identification regarding location, i.e. "the plains of Moab." Milgrom, *Numbers*, 299. The reference in Nehemiah (8:14) is clearly a reference back to Lev 23:42 as Ezra read it in the Torah. Thus, Torah (in this case, priestly literature) is being cited in Nehemiah. Milgrom explains that the way "Tabernacles" was celebrated in Nehemiah is based on Ezra's reading of the stipulations in H's appendix to the "Tabernacles" instructions in the cultic calendar. Milgrom, *Leviticus 1–16*, 27–28.

38. See Knohl, *Sanctuary*, 99–100.

39. The attribution of these notices to H, leaves P itself originally with no picture of the fulfillment of the promise of land. However, the promise of land is not a concern of P. P does not contain the Abrahamic covenant. H must appeal to P^N when referring to the promise of land. Since God's command to Moses to take the land (Num 33:50–53) appears at the hand of H, then P itself has no related command which needs fulfilled. This affirms, as previously stated, that P is not a narrative document such as JE. P's primary concern is the codification of the legislation concerning the temple and its accompanying sacrificial cult. Thus, P itself appropriately ends with the statement:

Redaction of Southern Traditions

H further reflects an inclusive attitude toward the northern refugees though the redaction of southern traditions. An example of this is found in the spy story of Num 13–14. The conflation of texts within the spy story reveals a tight blending which has often frustrated efforts to sort out sources in the passage.[40] Milgrom observes that two inconsistencies in the text are especially revealing:

> (1) The country reconnoitered by the spies is, on the one hand, the entire land of Canaan (13:2,17) from its southern to its northern extremity (13:21), and, on the other hand, it includes only the area around Hebron in the south (13:22–24). (2) Although Caleb appears as both the lone dissenter to the spies' report (13:30) and the lone exemption from the punishment (14:24), he is also joined by Joshua in both these roles (14:6–7, 38).[41]

Typically, Num 13:22–24, 30; 14:24 which contain the first tradition (Caleb-Hebron) are attributed to J; while Num 13:2, 17, 21; 14:6–7, 38 which contain the second tradition (including Joshua and all of Canaan) are attributed to P. In addition, the list of scouts in Num 13:3–16 is attributed to P.[42]

The presence of these two traditions (Caleb-Hebron, and Joshua-all of Canaan) suggests a possible dichotomy based on southern and northern biases respectively. The scout list explicitly identifies Caleb as the representative of Judah (Num 13:6), while Joshua (Hoshea, see Num 13:16) is explicitly identified as the representative of Ephraim (Num 13:8). The original JE tradition focuses the reconnaissance mission on the area of Hebron in the south and exalts a hero from the southern tribe of Judah. By itself, this tradition appears to exclude northern-

---

אלה המצות והמשפטים אשר צוה יהוה ביד־משה אל־בני ישראל בערבת
מואב על ירדן ירחו:

> These are the commands and ordinances that the Lord commanded by the hand of Moses to the children of Israel in the Plains of Moab beside the Jordan (opposite) Jericho. (Num 36:13)

40. Kuenen, *Hexateuch*, 333–334; Knohl, *Sanctuary*, 91.

41. Milgrom, *Numbers*, 389.

42. Noth, *Pentateuchal Traditions*, 273, cf. 130–36; Campbell and O'Brien, *Sources*, 260–61.

ers from the significant history of the spying of the land. A redactor appears to have blended the second account (Joshua-all of Canaan) with the original JE account in order to expand the story to include the spying out of *all* the land of Canaan even to its northern extremity, and to include a hero from the northern tribe of Ephraim. The redactor appears to have been H. The H characteristic of direct divine address is present throughout. The first person pronoun, אני, is used for God in Num 13:2; 14:21, 28, and divine direct address is communicated to Israel in 14:28–34. In addition the characteristic formula of H, אני יהוה ("I am the Lord"), appears at 14:35. Knohl adds that certain expressions linked to H also attest to H's presence in this story, and he concludes that H was possibly responsible for the editing of the entire pericope.[43]

The redactional work of H upon the spy story provides a more inclusive account by expanding the tradition of the spying of the promised land in order to include northerners within the collective history of the total community now gathered in the south. This further reflects H's concern to include northern refugees within the community present in Judah during the period of Hezekiah.

Addressing Inheritance Rights

The concern in H for addressing the needs of northerners can also be found in the narrative containing the legislation regarding the inheritance of daughters. Numbers 27:1–11 describes the crisis of the possible exclusion of the name of Zelophehad from among his clan because he had no sons (v. 4). In the introduction of this passage, the significance of portraying this dilemma through this particular family becomes evident. The family of Zelophehad is explicitly identified as within the line of Manasseh, the son of Joseph (v 1). The crisis represents the exclusion of an Israelite family from hereditary possession among the children of Israel, specifically, the exclusion of a family identified with a prominent northern tribe. The resolution of the crisis guarantees that a family in this position should not be excluded as previously feared (v. 7–11).

A further complication of the crisis is expounded in Num 36:1–12. In this case, the brothers of Zelophehad (those in his clan) fear that if the daughters of Zelophehad marry men from another tribe, then the family inheritance will be added to that other tribe, and thus, with-

---

43. Knohl, *Sanctuary*, 91–92, 92 n. 109.

drawn from the tribal heritage of Zelophehad (v. 3–4). This extension of the crisis is not only once again identified as concerning a family in the line of Manasseh, the son of Joseph (v.1), but the situation is specifically identified as a crisis concerning the needs of "the tribe of the sons of Joseph" (v. 5). The significance of the passage regarding the crisis of the daughters of Zelophehad is found in the legislation which the narrative serves to justify.

7 ולא־תסב נחלה לבני ישראל ממטה אל־מטה כי איש בנחלת

מטה אבתיו ידבקו בני ישראל:

9 ולא־תסב נחלה ממטה למטה אחר כי־איש בנחלתו ידבקו

מטות בני ישראל:

7) An inheritance for the children of Israel shall not go around from tribe to tribe, for each of the children of Israel shall cling to the inheritance of the tribe of his fathers.

9) And an inheritance shall not go around from (one) tribe to another tribe, for each one from the tribes of the children of Israel shall cling to his inheritance. (Num 36:7, 9)

The resolution of this crisis guaranteed that no inheritance should be transferred from one tribe to another. Such legislation secured the inheritance of northern refugees during the unsettled period in which they were separated from their own land (tribal allotment) and forced to dwell among southern tribes. This presumes the idealistic notion that all of Canaan is still included in the heritage of the children of Israel (as described in the H redaction of the spying out of the land; see above). Thus, the hope remains that the northern tribes will ultimately be restored to their allotments within the promised land which are currently being held by Assyria. If such hope comes to fulfillment, and the northern territory is regained, the legislation of Num 36:7, 9 restricts other tribes from taking the spoils of victory by claiming northern property for themselves. The legislation promotes the hope that the northern refugees will regain their inherited property.

The two passages of Num 27:1–11; and 36:1–12 clearly go together and thus represent the same hand. Knohl points out that the linkage of the two is made explicit by the reference in 36:2 to the command which the Lord had given regarding the giving of the inheritance of Zelophehad to his daughters in 27:1–11. In addition, the phrase in Num 27:7 is paralleled in 36:5 as follows:

כן בנות צלפחד דברת

כן מטה בני־יוסף דברים

27:7 True are the daughters of Zelophehad in speaking

36:5 True is the tribe of the children of Joseph in speaking[44]

The hand of H is evident in these accounts based on the presence of divine direct address to the children of Israel (27:8–11). Knohl further argues the H origin of these passages based on various other terminological clues.[45] Thus, through the legislation supported by these narratives (Num 36:7, 9), H provides hope that northern refugees ultimately will not lose their inheritance.

Extension of Themes from P

The intent of H is shaped by the concern to address the situation of the refugees from the northern kingdom during the time of Hezekiah. H's concern was not only to assure the newcomers that they would worship the same God, but H was also concerned with bringing the refugees into proper alignment with the perspectives of the community of P, especially, the traditions and practices surrounding the central sanctuary in Jerusalem.

The Tabernacle and the Presence of God

The work of H demonstrates consistency with the themes of P and expands those themes in accordance with H's own theological perspective. This includes P's central concern regarding the tabernacling presence of God and the need to maintain the purity of the tabernacle. Among the primary texts which Cross cites as evidence of this theme in P are Exod 29:45–46, and Lev 26:11–13.[46] Both of these passages describe God's

---

44. Ibid., 100.
45. Ibid.
46. Cross, *Canaanite Myth*, 298–300.

promise to dwell among the children of Israel. The Leviticus passage is clearly within the parameters of the Holiness Code. The Exodus passage, likewise, reflects the hand of H. It includes divine direct address, apparent by the use of the pronoun אני in reference to God's speech, and a form of the characteristic phrase of H, אני יהוה אלהיכם ("I am the Lord your God").[47]

H's concern regarding the defiling of the tabernacle is evident from the insertion which H places at the conclusion of the impurity regulations: "And you shall keep the children of Israel separate from their uncleanness so that they shall not die in their uncleanness *because they defiled my Tabernacle* which is in their midst" (Lev 15:31).[48] This statement clarifies that impurities impact the sanctuary as well as the individual. The reason for the cleansing of the tabernacle is that God cannot abide impurity. This defines a major aim of the sacrificial cult in relation to atonement rites. Milgrom expresses the importance of this aim with these words: "If persons unremittingly polluted the sanctuary they forced God out of his sanctuary and out of their lives."[49] Thus, the purgation of the sanctuary was necessary in order to eradicate impurity and to maintain God's presence among the children of Israel. H recognized the problem of the defilement of the tabernacle, and identified its source in the impurities of the children of Israel.

H attributes the defilement of the tabernacle not only to impurities (such as listed in Lev 11–15), but also to unacceptable practices such as Molech worship: "And I shall set my face against that man, and I shall cut him off from the midst of his people because he gave from his own seed to Molech *so as to defile my sanctuary*, and to profane my holy name" (Lev 20:3 [H]). Thus, H shows consistency with the concern in P regarding the defilement of the tabernacle and the importance of its cleansing in order to maintain the presence of God among the children of Israel. H attaches this concern, not only to legislation regarding impurity, but also to a polemic against unacceptable worship practices.

---

47. See Knohl, *Sanctuary*, 17–18 n. 24.

48. The H origin of this verse is evident through divine direct address in God's speech to Moses and Aaron. Also, see Knohl, *Sanctuary*, 69–70; and Milgrom, *Leviticus 1–16*, 946–47.

49. Milgrom, *Leviticus 1–16*, 43.

Divine and Human Relationships (Call to Holiness)

The thematic concern in P for positive Divine and human relationships is also developed by H. The theme is extended in H through the call to holiness which H emphasized not only for the priests who serve God, but even for the individual who worships God. Milgrom explains that, for H, holiness extends to all Israel. This is because the land is holy, and all who dwell in it must be holy.[50] This theme constitutes the emphasis from which the Holiness Code derives its designation. It is most evident in the call to holiness that is issued therein: "Speak to all the assembly of the children of Israel, and say to them, 'You shall be holy for I the Lord your God am holy'" (Lev 19:2; cf. 20:7, 26). As the purity of the tabernacle allowed the presence of God to remain in the holy of holies, so the holiness of the people makes possible the presence of God among the children of Israel. H extends P's conception of God's presence in the tabernacle to an even more intimate depiction of God dwelling among the people. This is expressed most clearly within the Holiness Code at Lev 26:11–12: "And I shall set my dwelling place in the midst of you, and I shall not abhor you. And I shall walk about in your midst, and I shall be your God, and you shall be my people." These words not only depict God as dwelling among the people, but communicate the more intimate description of God "walking among" the children of Israel. This terminology echoes P^N who reserves such intimacy with God for those who are blameless (Gen 5:22, 24; 6:9) and those who are called to blamelessness (Gen 17:1). H now extends such a call to the whole community of Israel.

Reverence for Life

As with other major themes, H shows continuity with P by developing the concern of "reverence for life." This is illustrated by the restriction which H places on common slaughter. H requires that all slaughter for food be brought to the altar and made into a well-being offering (Lev 17:3–7). Milgrom explains that the well-being offering serves to ransom the life of the offerer for taking the life of the animal. H implies that killing an animal is considered murder unless expiation is made by means

---

50. Milgrom, "Priestly Source," 457.

of the well-being offering. This strict view against killing, even for food, clearly reinforces the theme of reverence for life.[51]

As the dietary laws (Lev 11) also reflect the hand of H, they further illustrate H's involvement in the development of the theme of reverence for life. Milgrom explains that the dietary laws form a continuum with the purity laws. As the purity laws provide a symbolic system which emphasizes the importance of choosing life by means of obedience to God's commands, likewise the dietary laws reflect a system which promotes reverence for life by means of obedience to God's commands.[52] Milgrom clarifies that the criteria used to define clean and unclean animals for food serves the rationale of holiness. The dietary restrictions limit Israel's consumption of meat to only a few animals. This enforces a discipline upon Israel which cultivates a great reverence for life. Not only do the dietary laws restrict what can be killed, but even allowable slaughter must be carried out properly (in the most humane way), and the blood appropriately drained. The result is a system that is intended to "inculcate reverence for life."[53]

The extension of themes from P within the redactionary work of H demonstrates H's sense of continuity with the theology of P. It can be seen, however, that H is not limited by P's intentions. H introduces concepts that go beyond P's legislation, such as the ban on common slaughter, and the call of holiness extended to the whole community of Israel. Nevertheless, such differences are not contradictions or reversals in relation to P's legislation. Rather, H's redaction can be seen as extending P by means of even greater demands. This reflects H's strong concern to maintain holiness in the face of threats to Israel's sanctity stemming from the situation of the times. H redacts P, and adds even stricter regulations, in response to the crisis of the influx of northern refugees. The resultant priestly literature is not only inclusive of the northern traditions, but it imposes upon them the accepted traditions reflected in P. H reflects the desire to exclude the importing of any unacceptable traditions from the north. For example, H's theology repudiates practices such as that of sacrificing one's own offspring, as was done in the worship of Molech (Lev 20:2). Thus, the intent of H can be summed

---

51. Milgrom, *Leviticus 1–16*, 49; idem, "Priestly Source," 457.

52. Milgrom, *Leviticus 1–16*, 46, 50. Milgrom limits the hand of H to vv. 43–44 of Lev 11, as previously discussed.

53. Milgrom, "Ethics and Ritual," 189–90.

up in accordance with the following concerns: 1) promote the inclusion of northern refugees within the worship community of the south, 2) provide a polemic against the possible incursion of unacceptable practices from the north, and 3) extend priestly theology in relation to a comprehensive call to holiness.

Bibliography

Albright, W. F. "The Names *Shaddai* and *Abram*." *JBL* 54 (1935) 173-204.
Anderson, Gary A. *Sacrifices and Offerings in Ancient Israel: Studies in their Social and Political Importance.* HSM 41. Atlanta: Scholars, 1987.
Baab, O. J. "Prostitution." In *IDB* 3:931-34.
Begrich, Joachim. "Die priesterliche Tora." In *Werden und Wesen des alten Testaments*, edited by Paul Volz, Friedrich Stummer and Johannes Hempel, 63-88. BZAW 66. Berlin: Töpelmann, 1936.
Biale, David. "The God with Breasts: *El Shaddai* in the Bible." *History of Religions* 20 (1982) 240-56.
Blenkinsopp, Joseph. "An Assessment of the Alleged Pre-Exilic Date of the Priestly Material in the Pentateuch." *ZAW* 108 (1996) 495-518.
———. *The Pentateuch: An Introduction to the First Five Books of the Bible.* Anchor Bible Reference Library. New York: Doubleday, 1992.
———. "The Structure of P." *CBQ* 38 (1976) 275-92.
Boorer, Sue. "Kerygmatic Intention of the Priestly Document." *Australian Biblical Review* 25 (1977) 12-20.
Bright, John. *A History of Israel.* 3rd ed. Philadelphia: Westminster, 1981.
Broshi, M. "The Expansion of Jerusalem in the Reigns of Hezekiah and Manasseh." *Israel Exploration Journal* 24 (1974) 21-26.
Brueggemann, Walter, and Hans Walter Wolff. *The Vitality of Old Testament Traditions.* 2nd ed. Atlanta: John Knox, 1982.
Buttrick, George Arthur, editor. *The Interpreter's Dictionary of the Bible.* 4 vols. New York: Abingdon, 1962.
Campbell, Antony F. *The Study Companion to Old Testament Literature: An Approach to the Writings of Pre-Exilic and Exilic Israel.* Old Testament Studies 2. Wilmington, DE: Glazier, 1989.
———, and Mark A. O'Brien. *Sources of the Pentateuch: Texts, Introductions, Annotations.* Minneapolis: Fortress, 1993.
Carmichael, Calum. *Illuminating Leviticus: A Study of Its Laws and Institutions in the Light of Biblical Narratives.* Baltimore: Johns Hopkins University Press, 2006.
Carroll, Michael P. "One More Time: Leviticus Revisited." In *Anthropological Approaches to the Old Testament*, edited by Bernhard Lang, 117-26. Issues in Religion and Theology. Philadelphia: Fortress, 1985.
Cholewinski, Alfred. *Heiligkeitsgesetz und Deuteronomium: Eine vergleichende Studie.* AnBib 66. Rome: Biblical Institute Press, 1976.
Clifford, Richard J. "The Tent of El and the Israelite Tent of Meeting." *CBQ* 33 (1971) 221-27.
Coats, George W. "The Wilderness Itinerary." *CBQ* 34 (1972) 135-52.

Cohen, Chayim. "Was the P Document Secret?" *Journal of the Ancient Near Eastern Society of Columbia University* 1.2 (1969) 39–44.

Coote, Robert B., and David Robert Ord. *In the Beginning: Creation and the Priestly History*. Minneapolis: Fortress, 1991.

Cross, Frank Moore. "The Tabernacle: A Study from an Archaeological and Historical Approach." *Biblical Archaeologist* 10 (1947) 45–68.

———. *Canaanite Myth and Hebrew Epic: Essays in the History of the Religion of Israel*. Cambridge: Harvard University Press, 1973.

Dalley, Stephanie. "Yahweh in Hamath in the 8th Century BC: Cuneiform Material and Historical Deductions." *VT* 40 (1990) 21–32.

Davies, G. I. "The Wilderness Itineraries and the Composition of the Pentateuch." *VT* 33 (1983) 1–13.

Day, John. *Molech: A God of Human Sacrifice in the Old Testament*. University of Cambridge Oriental Publications 41. Cambridge: Cambridge University Press, 1989.

Dillmann, August. *Genesis*. Translated by Wm. B. Stevenson. 2 vols. Edinburgh: T. & T. Clark, 1897.

———. *Die Bücher Exodus und Leviticus*. American Theological Library Association. Leipzig: Hirzel, 1897. Text-fiche.

Douglas, Mary. *Purity and Danger: An Analysis of Concepts of Pollution and Taboo*. New York: Praeger, 1966.

———. *Leviticus as Literature*. Oxford: Oxford University Press, 1999.

Driver, S. R. *An Introduction to the Literature of the Old Testament*. 9th ed. Edinburgh: T. & T. Clark, 1913.

Eerdmans, B. D. *Die Komposition der Genesis*. Alttestamentliche Studien 1. Giessen: Töpelmann, 1908.

Elliott-Binns, L. E. "Some Problems of the Holiness Code." *ZAW* 67 (1955): 26–40.

Emerton, John A. "New Light on Israelite Religion: The Implications of the Inscriptions from Kuntillet 'Ajrud." *ZAW* 94 (1982) 2–20.

———. "The Priestly Writer in Genesis." *Journal of Theological Studies* 39 (1988) 381–400.

Finkelstein, Israel. *The Archaeology of the Israelite Settlement*. Jerusalem: Israel Exploration Society, 1988.

———, et al. *Shiloh: The Archaeology of a Biblical Site*. Tel Aviv University, Sonia and Marco Nadler Institute of Archaeology Monograph Series 10. Tel Aviv: Institute of Archaeology, Tel Aviv University, Publications Section, 1993.

Fohrer, Georg. *Introduction to the Old Testament*. Translated by David E. Green. Nashville: Abingdon, 1968.

Freedman, David Noel, editor. *The Anchor Bible Dictionary*. 6 vols. New York: Doubleday, 1992.

Friedman, Richard Elliott. *The Exile and Biblical Narrative: The Formation of the Deuteronomistic and Priestly Works*. HSM 22. Chico, CA: Scholars, 1981.

Ginsberg, H. L. *The Legend of King Keret: A Canaanite Epic of the Bronze Age*. New Haven, CN: American Schools of Oriental Research, 1946.

Goodfriend, Elaine Adler. "Prostitution." In *ABD*, 5:505–10.

Gottwald, Norman K. *The Hebrew Bible—A Socio-Literary Introduction*. Philadelphia: Fortress, 1985.

Graf, Karl Heinrich. *Die Geschichtlichen Bücher des Alten Testaments*. Leipzig: Weigel, 1866.

Gray, John. *I & II Kings*. 2nd ed. OTL. Philadelphia: Westminster, 1970.

Haran, Menahem. "Shilo and Jerusalem: The Origin of the Priestly Tradition in the Pentateuch." *JBL* 81 (1962) 14–24.

———. *Temples and Temple-Service in Ancient Israel: An Inquiry into the Character of Cult Phenomena and the Historical Setting of the Priestly School*. Oxford: Clarendon, 1978.

———. "Behind the Scenes of History: Determining the Date of the Priestly Source." *JBL* 100 (1981) 321–33.

———. "The Character of the Priestly Source: Utopian and Exclusive Features." In *Proceedings of the Eighth World Congress of Jewish Studies (1981)*, 5:131–38. Jerusalem: World Union of Jewish Studies, 1983.

Heider, George C. *The Cult of Molek: A Reassessment*. JSOTSup 43. Sheffield: JSOT Press, 1985.

Hildebrand, David R. "A Summary of Recent Findings in Support of an Early Date for the So-called Priestly Material of the Pentateuch." *Journal of the Evangelical Theological Society* 29 (1986) 129–38.

Hurvitz, Avi. "The Evidence of Language in Dating the Priestly Code." *Revue Biblique* 81 (1974) 24–56.

———. "The Language of the Priestly Source and Its Historical Setting—The Case for an Early Date." In *Proceedings of the Eighth World Congress of Jewish Studies (1981)*, 5:83–94. Jerusalem: World Union of Jewish Studies, 1983.

———. "Dating the Priestly Source in Light of the Historical Study of Biblical Hebrew a Century After Wellhausen." *ZAW* 100, supplement (1988) 88–100.

Kaufmann, Yehezkel. *The Religion of Israel: From Its Beginnings to the Babylonian Exile*. Translated and abridged by Moshe Greenberg. Chicago: University of Chicago Press, 1960.

Klein, Ralph W. "The Message of P." In *Die Botschaft und die Boten: Festschrift für Hans Walter Wolff zum 70. Geburtstag*, edited by Jörg Jeremias and Lothar Perlitt, 57–66. Neukirchen: Neukirchener, 1981.

Klostermann, August. *Der Pentateuch: Beiträge zu seinem Verständnis und seiner Entstehungsgeschichte*. Leipzig: Deichert, 1893.

Knohl, Israel. "The Priestly Torah versus the Holiness School: Ideological Aspects." In *Proceedings of the Tenth World Congress of Jewish Studies (1989)*, edited by David Assaf, 51–57. Jerusalem: World Union of Jewish Studies, 1990.

———. "The Priestly Torah versus the Holiness School: Sabbath and the Festivals." *HUCA* 58 (1987) 65–117.

———. *The Sanctuary of Silence: The Priestly Torah and the Holiness School*. Minneapolis: Fortress, 1995.

Koch, Klaus. "P—Kein Redaktor! Erinnerung an zwei Eckdaten der Quellenscheidung." *VT* 37 (1987) 446–67.

———. "Šaddaj." *VT* 26 (1976) 299–332.

Kuenen, Abraham. *An Historico-Critical Inquiry into the Origin and Composition of the Hexateuch*. Translated by Philip H. Wicksteed. London: Macmillan, 1886.

Levine, Baruch A. "Late Language in the Priestly Source: Some Literary and Historical Observations." In *Proceedings of the Eighth World Congress of Jewish Studies (1981)*, 5:69–82. Jerusalem: World Union of Jewish Studies, 1983.

———. Review of Jacob Milgrom, *Leviticus 1–16: A New Translation with Introduction and Commentary*. Biblica 74 (1993) 280–85.

Lohfink, Norbert. *Theology of the Pentateuch*. Translated by Linda M. Maloney. Minneapolis: Fortress, 1994.

Magonet, Jonathan. "The Rhetoric of God: Exodus 6.2–8." *JSOT* 27 (1983) 56–67.

Mays, James Luther. *Amos*. OTL. Philadelphia: Westminster, 1969.

———. *Hosea*. OTL. Philadelphia: Westminster, 1969.

———. *Micah*. OTL. Philadelphia: Westminster, 1976.

McCarter, P. Kyle Jr. *II Samuel*. AB 9. Garden City, NY: Doubleday, 1984.

McEvenue, Seán. *Interpreting the Pentateuch*. Collegeville, MN: Liturgical, 1990.

———. *The Narrative Style of the Priestly Writer*. AnBib 50. Rome: Biblical Institute Press, 1971.

McKeating, Henry. *The Books of Amos, Hosea and Micah*. Cambridge Bible Commentary. Cambridge: Cambridge University Press, 1971.

Milgrom, Jacob.

———. "Ethics and Ritual: The Foundations of the Biblical Dietary Laws." In *Religion and Law: Biblical, Jewish, and Islamic Perspectives*, edited by Edwin B. Firmage et al., 159–91. Winona Lake, IN: Eisenbrauns, 1989.

———. *Leviticus 1–16*. AB 3. New York: Doubleday, 1991.

———. *Leviticus 17–22*. AB 3A. New York: Doubleday, 2000.

———. *Leviticus 23–27*. AB 3B. New York: Doubleday, 2001.

———. *Numbers*. JPS Torah Commentary. Philadelphia: Jewish Publication Society, 1990.

———. "Priestly ('P') Source." In *ABD*, 5:454–61.

———. "A Prolegomenon to Leviticus 17:11." *JBL* 90 (1971) 149–56.

———. "Response to Rolf Rendtorff." *JSOT* 60 (1993) 83–85.

———. *Studies in Cultic Theology and Terminology*. Studies in Judaism in Late Antiquity 36. Leiden: Brill, 1983.

———. "Two Biblical Hebrew Priestly Terms: ŠEQEṢ and ṬĀMÊʾ." *Maarav* 8 (1992) 107–16.

Nicholson, Ernest. *The Pentateuch in the Twentieth Century: The Legacy of Julius Wellhausen*. Oxford: Oxford University Press, 1998.

Noth, Martin. *Exodus*. OTL. Translated by J. S. Bowden. Philadelphia: Westminster, 1962.

———. *A History of Pentateuchal Traditions*. Translated by Bernhard W. Anderson. Englewood Cliffs: Prentice-Hall, 1972.

———. *Leviticus*. OTL. Translated by J. E. Anderson. Rev. ed. Philadelphia: Westminster, 1977.

———. *Numbers*. OTL. Translated by James D. Martin. Philadelphia: Westminster, 1968.

Polzin, Robert. *Late Biblical Hebrew: Toward an Historical Typology of Biblical Hebrew Prose*. HSM 12. Missoula, MT: Scholars, 1976.

Pope, Marvin H. "Fertility Cults." In *IDB*, 2:265.

Pritchard, James B., editor. *Ancient Near Eastern Texts Relating to the Old Testament.* 3rd ed. Princeton: Princeton University Press, 1969.

Rad, Gerhard von. *Genesis.* OTL. Rev. ed. Philadelphia: Westminster, 1972.

Rendsburg, Gary A. "Late Biblical Hebrew and the Date of 'P.'" *Journal of the Ancient Near Eastern Society of Columbia University* 12 (1980) 65–80.

Rendtorff, Rolf. *The Problem of the Process of Transmission in the Pentateuch.* Translated by John J. Scullion. JSOTSup 89. Sheffield: JSOT Press, 1990.

———. "Two Kinds of P? Some Reflections on the Occasion of the Publishing of Jacob Milgrom's Commentary on Leviticus 1–16." *JSOT* 60 (1993) 75–81.

Reuss, Eduard. *Die Geschichte der Heiligen Schriften Alten Testaments.* 2nd ed. Braunschweig: Schwetschke, 1890.

Schley, Donald G. *Shiloh: A Biblical City in Tradition and History.* JSOTSup 63. Sheffield: Sheffield Academic, 1989.

Schwartz, Baruch J. "'Profane' Slaughter and the Integrity of the Priestly Code." *HUCA* 67 (1996) 15–42.

Silbermann, Dr. A. M., editor. *Genesis, Exodus.* Pentateuch with Rashi's Commentary 1. Translated by Rev. M. Rosenbaum and Dr. A. M. Silbermann. London: Shapiro, Vallentine & Co., 1946.

———. *Leviticus, Numbers, Deuteronomy.* Pentateuch with Rashi's Commentary 2. Translated by Rev. M. Rosenbaum and Dr. A. M. Silbermann. London: Shapiro, Vallentine & Co., 1946.

Silver, Abba Hillel. "The Lunar and Solar Calendars in Ancient Israel." In *Essays in Honor of Solomon B. Freehof,* edited by Walter Jacob, Frederick C. Schwartz, and Vigdor W. Kavaler, 300–309. Pittsburgh: Rodef Shalom Congregation, 1964.

Snaith, Norman H. "Sacrifices in the Old Testament." *VT* 7 (1957) 308–17.

Soler, Jean. "The Dietary Prohibitions of the Hebrews." *The New York Review of Books* (June 14, 1979) 24–30.

Talmon, S. "Divergences in Calendar-Reckoning in Ephraim and Judah." *VT* 8 (1958) 48–74.

Todd, E. W. "The Reforms of Hezekiah and Josiah." *Scottish Journal of Theology* 9 (1956) 288–93.

Toorn, Karel van der. "Prostitution (Cultic)." In *ABD,* 5:510–13.

———. "Saul and the Rise of Israelite State Religion." *VT* 43 (1993) 519–42.

Vaux, Roland de. *Studies in Old Testament Sacrifice.* Cardiff: University of Wales Press, 1964.

Vervenne, Marc. "The 'P' Tradition in the Pentateuch: Document and/or Redaction?" In *Pentateuchal and Deuteronomistic Studies: Papers Read at the XIIIth IOSOT Congress, Leuven 1989,* edited by C. Brekelmans and J. Lust, 67–90. Bibliotheca Ephemeridum theologicarum Lovaniensium 94. Leuven: Peeters, 1990.

Vink, J. G. "The Date and Origin of the Priestly Code in the Old Testament." In *The Priestly Code and Seven Other Studies.* Oudtestamentische Studiën 15. Leiden: Brill, 1969.

Walsh, Jerome T. "From Egypt to Moab: A Source Critical Analysis of the Wilderness Itinerary." *CBQ* 39 (1977) 20–33.

Watts, James W. *Reading Law: The Rhetorical Shaping of the Pentateuch.* Biblical Seminar 59. Sheffield: Sheffield Academic, 1999.

Wellhausen, Julius. *Die Composition des Hexateuchs und der historischen Bücher des Alten Testaments*. 4th ed. Berlin: de Gruyter, 1963.

———. *Prolegomena to the History of Israel*. Translated by J. Sutherland Black and Allan Menzies. Edinburgh: A. & C. Black, 1885.

Wenham, Gordon J. *The Book of Leviticus*. New International Commentary on the Old Testament. Grand Rapids: Eerdmans, 1979.

———. "Pentateuchal Studies Today." *Themelios* 22 (1996) 3–13.

———. "Pondering the Pentateuch: The Search for a New Paradigm." In *The Face of Old Testament Studies: A Survey of Contemporary Approaches*, edited by David W. Baker and Bill T. Arnold, 116–44. Grand Rapids: Baker, 1999.

———. "The Priority of P." *VT* 49 (1999) 240–58.

Westermann, Claus. *Genesis 1–11*. Translated by John J. Scullion. Continental Commentaries. Minneapolis: Augsburg, 1984.

———. *Genesis 37–50*. Translated by John J. Scullion. Continental Commentaries. Minneapolis: Augsburg, 1986.

Wette, Wilhelm Martin Leberecht de. *Kritischer Versuch über die Glaubwürdigkeit der Bücher der Chronik mit Hinsicht auf die Geschichte der Mosaischen Bücher und Gesetzgebung*. Vol. 1 of *Beiträge zur Einleitung in das Alte Testament*. 1806. Reprinted, Hildesheim: Olms, 1971.

———. *Kritik der Israelitischen Geschichte*. Vol. 2 of *Beiträge zur Einleitung in das Alte Testament*. 1807. Reprinted, Hildesheim: Olms, 1971.

Whybray, R. N. *The Making of the Pentateuch: A Methodological Study*. JSOTSup 53. Sheffield: JSOT Press, 1987.

Wolff, Hans Walter. *Hosea*. Translated by Gary Stansell. Hermeneia. Philadelphia: Fortress, 1974.

Zevit, Ziony. "Converging Lines of Evidence Bearing on the Date of P." *ZAW* 94 (1982) 481–511.

———. "The Priestly Redaction and Interpretation of the Plague Narrative in Exodus." *Jewish Quarterly Review* 66 (1976) 193–211.

———. "Timber for the Tabernacle: Text, Tradition, and Realia." *Eretz-Israel* 23 (1992) 136–43.